# Community-Based
# Qualitative Research

# Community-Based Qualitative Research

## Approaches for Education and the Social Sciences

Laura Ruth Johnson
*Northern Illinois University*

Los Angeles | London | New Delhi
Singapore | Washington DC | Melbourne

FOR INFORMATION:

SAGE Publications, Inc.
2455 Teller Road
Thousand Oaks, California 91320
E-mail: order@sagepub.com

SAGE Publications Ltd.
1 Oliver's Yard
55 City Road
London EC1Y 1SP
United Kingdom

SAGE Publications India Pvt. Ltd.
B 1/I 1 Mohan Cooperative Industrial Area
Mathura Road, New Delhi 110 044
India

SAGE Publications Asia-Pacific Pte. Ltd.
3 Church Street
#10-04 Samsung Hub
Singapore 049483

Acquisitions Editor:   Helen Salmon
Editorial Assistant:   Anna Villarruel
Production Editor:   Veronica Stapleton Hooper
Copy Editor:   Sheree Van Vreede
Typesetter:   C&M Digitals (P) Ltd.
Proofreader:   Wendy Jo Dymond
Indexer:   Sheila Bodell
Cover Designer:   Anupama Krishnan
Marketing Manager:   Susannah Goldes

Printed in the United States of America

*Library of Congress Cataloging-in-Publication Data*

Names: Johnson, Laura Ruth, author.

Title: Community-based qualitative research : approaches for education and the social sciences / Laura Ruth Johnson.

Description: Thousand Oaks, California: SAGE, [2017] | Includes bibliographical references and index.

Identifiers: LCCN 2015039149 | ISBN 978-1-4833-5168-1 (pbk. : alk. paper)

Subjects: LCSH: Communities—Research. | Qualitative research. | Social sciences—Methodology.

Classification: LCC HM756 .J637 2017 | DDC 001.4/2—dc23
LC record available at http://lccn
.loc.gov/2015039149

This book is printed on acid-free paper.

16 17 18 19 20 10 9 8 7 6 5 4 3 2 1

# • Brief Contents •

# • Detailed Contents •

# • Preface: Repaying the Sea •

It is the year 2003, the eve before May 1, and I am in Puerto Rico, more specifically the town of Fajardo, about to board a *lancha*, or ferry, to the tiny island of Vieques. The occasion for this trip is the U.S. Navy's removal from the island after a nearly 50-year presence. I am here with around 30 *compañeros* and *compañeras* from Chicago, some that I have known for more than 10 years, others that I have just met but will get to know more intimately in the years that follow. The ferry ride is a bumpy one and marked by a palpable sense of anticipation regarding the weekend's events, which were achieved through a hard-fought struggle by *Viequenses*, as well as by those living on the larger island and stateside. As we make our way to Vieques, the sun is beginning to set and a large group begins to sing popular protest songs, accompanied by traditional instruments. We are fortunate to have with us on the ferry a famous Puerto Rican musician and vocalist who leads the group of nearly 50 crowding the outside lower deck in dozens of traditional songs. During the weekend, we participate in marches, rallies, and concerts, and we explore the many beautiful features of the island, including a bioluminescent bay and a beach unused for years because of the naval occupation. In the water, I collect a large conch shell, which I decide to take home as a memento of the occasion. Many of the others on the trip have also gathered shells as souvenirs, and a Puerto Rican friend, an older woman, reminds us that for every item we take from the sea, we must drop a coin in the water as a way of repaying Yemayá, the Taíno goddess of the sea, for these treasures. Although I am mindful of her exhortation, and have the best intentions to "repay the sea," I forget my friend's advice until I have arrived home in Chicago and am horrified at my oversight. I am a staunch believer in karma, as well as a spiritual person, and feel somehow that my failure to compensate the natural elements will anger the gods and cause me to incur their wrath in some way. Moreover, I am sensitive to the notion of excavation and expropriation involved in our collecting of natural artifacts from the island and have started to feel that I took something that was not mine to take, that did not belong to me, and even worse, that I have not paid my way to do so.

Afterward, the incident and my ensuing feelings of guilt and regret spilled into my role as a researcher and caused me to reflect on my 12-year relationship with the Puerto Rican Cultural Center and the many community activists who work there. At that time, I was conducting my dissertation research, which examined the familial and community experiences of young Latina mothers who were attending a family literacy program in Chicago's Puerto Rican community. Although at this point I had not begun the writing process, I was particularly thoughtful regarding how I would represent the women who were participating in my study and how, once finished, it would be received by the women at the program and community members, as well as within the academic field. Would the women "see themselves" in the finished work? Would they view it as an accurate and respectful portrayal of their experiences and beliefs? Or would I be accused of taking something that "isn't mine," of exploiting the community for my own benefit and purposes? These issues are important ones to be cognizant of within the field of qualitative and ethnographic research, especially so when the researcher in question—as I am—is a White woman from a middle-class suburban background conducting research in an urban community of color. I was fearful of providing what writer Michelle Tea (2003) described as a "decidedly creepy experience," when working class women of color read about their lives as portrayed by middle-class researchers and are made to feel "invisible" (p. xiv).

The notion of invisibility and exclusion on the part of historically marginalized groups within educational research continues to be a problematic area. During my decades of work as a researcher within Chicago's Puerto Rican community, I have heard testimony from a variety of constituencies—alternative educators, young Latina mothers, community youth and activists, and other residents—regarding how they often feel excluded from and marginalized within public debates and academic scholarship and routinely ignored by policy makers related to issues of importance to the community and their lives. Although there has been much research bent on understanding issues of concern to marginalized communities and populations, such as high-school dropout rates, achievement gaps, adolescent motherhood, gang violence, and food deserts, less of this research has provided the opportunity for individuals and groups impacted by such issues to provide their perspectives and experiences. Even research that has taken a richer, more qualitative approach, and has attempted to "give voice" to marginalized and underrepresented groups, has predominately spoken *about* or *for* these groups, rather than *with* them (Kelly, 2000).

After I completed my dissertation research and obtained an academic position at a local university, I continued to return to the notion of "repaying the sea" in relation to my role as a researcher and reflected on how I might maintain some of my earlier relationships with community programs and institutions while fulfilling the expectations to receive tenure. In particular, I was interested in building more reciprocal research relationships with some of the programs that I had previously worked with and in developing university–community partnerships that could bring university resources to help support the community's work and success, as well as initiatives that would provide space within the academy for community knowledge to be disseminated and discussed. To be frank, despite my best intentions and my desire to "repay the sea," during the first few years as an assistant professor, I was unable to do much partly because of the demands of a new job but also because of limited institutional support. Although I was involved in the community as an activist, most of my research just followed up on my dissertation work. I was inspired by other scholars who were working in the Paseo Boricua community, in particular, Drs. Ann Peterson Kemp and C. Bertram Bruce, then faculty at the University of Illinois, who were involved as professors in the Graduate School of Library & Information Science (GSLIS) in work in the area of community informatics, and Dr. Howard Rosing and the Steans Center for Community-based Service Learning at DePaul University. These individuals were offering course work for students enrolled in their programs, as well as working with programs at the Puerto Rican Cultural Center and Dr. Pedro Albizu Campos High School to help support and highlight their work. One particular initiative that GSLIS was instrumental in developing and implementing was the Community as Intellectual Space (CIS) Symposium, which brought together university scholars and students and community leaders, activists, educators, and youth to exchange and discuss relevant issues and concepts; the event, which took place annually for 6 years, included neighborhood tours, panel discussions, live performances by arts groups and community youth, and special exhibitions. For several years of the symposium, I was involved as a member of the coordinating committee as well as a presenter. The event was unique in its acknowledgment of the ways that communities serve as significant sites and sources of intellectual thought and inquiry and in the way it brought together researchers and community members to engage in meaningful dialogue. An important aspect of this work was the collaborative and collective relationship between community leaders and university scholars throughout the planning, implementation, and evaluation process.

My involvement in CIS helped inform the development of my efforts to build university–community partnerships. After my second year at my institution, I was able to offer a research methods course for graduate students at the Puerto Rican Cultural Center. The course was offered in the summer, and the first session took place as part of the CIS conference; students attended the conference and participated in the community Puerto Rican parade. Subsequent sessions were held on Saturdays and involved students in conducting fieldwork at different community sites and programs—a café, a community newspaper, an Afro-Caribbean music group, and a health education initiative. Students were assigned readings that provided them with background on the community and offered a context for their experiences. Course discussions and reflective assignments focused on their reaction to what they were experiencing in the community and their reflections on their roles as researchers. This group presented at CIS the following year, which enabled discussion and dialogue with community members and scholars regarding research within the community, as well as provided some connection between subsequent years of the program as a new group of students enrolled in the course were attending the conference.

Although I acknowledge the import of providing graduate students with community engagement experiences, over the 6 years of offering the course, I, along with many enrolled students, felt that we were not doing enough to "give back" to the community for the opportunity that it furnished us to conduct research projects; we wanted the opportunity to collaboratively research *with* the community rather than just conduct research within the community. Students were certainly walking away with expanded notions of the community and often acted as ambassadors of the community within their educational and professional contexts. But the projects were more about them learning about the community rather than more directly helping to support community institutions and programs or collaborating with community organizations.

In light of this concern, in 2012, I redesigned the course to more explicitly focus on participatory action research (PAR) and youth participatory action research (YPAR). These approaches grew out of a desire on the part of social activist and advocacy-oriented researchers to design and implement studies and projects that would involve the creation of participatory and reciprocal research relationships and conduct research *in concert with* communities rather than without them, or despite them—or even worse using one's research against them. These strands of research have also maintained a commitment to using research to devise solutions to persistent educational and social problems and issues, to not just write and speak "for," "about," and/or "with" but also "to do," or in the words of Puerto Rican poetess Julia De Burgos, to "go in their midst with the torch in [your] . . . hand" (Santiago, 1995, p. 144).

Another issue that has been problematic within the area of community-based research is the need for continuity and projects and initiatives that can be sustained and developed over time. This continuity contrasts with projects that determine an end date at the outset, as well as research relationships that terminate once data collection is concluded. Well-meaning researchers may make promises to research participants to return for visits, or hint at continuing to work with the program as a volunteer, but the exigencies of their lives and other research projects often take precedence. Some researchers might make good on these intentions, and often continue relationships with participants, but these are largely personal in nature and do not involve ongoing research. The danger in this case, where the project or book is "closed" and finished at end of data collection, is that the research setting and participants serve as a means to an end, and for the researcher, it remains merely "the field," an "other place," rather than a dynamic, ever-changing setting within which the researcher still participates in meaningful ways. Furthermore, in these sorts of projects, rarely are findings shared and discussed with participants, and those who participated in the research are often not afforded the opportunity to "talk back" to the researcher and provide their commentary, insight, or critique of the research methods and findings. The type of research that I describe in this text advocates for projects that take place over a sustained period of time and urges for community-based studies—taking place in one community or a network of communities—that build on one another to promote meaningful and collaborative dialogue and discussion of findings among researchers, community members, and other research participants and stakeholders.

For me, the maintenance of my personal, professional, and research relationships with the Puerto Rican Cultural Center and many of the community residents who have participated in my previous research has been one of the more powerful aspects of my life, as well as one of the things of which I am most proud and grateful. In addition to the personal benefits I have gained, I believe it has enhanced my skill and perspective as a researcher and has allowed me to continually reflect on research findings and how they can be used to inform program practices and public policies. In this regard, I am inspired by Rosaldo's (1993) notion of the "'double vision' that oscillates between the viewpoint of a social analyst" and those of research participants. He acknowledges that "each viewpoint is arguably incomplete—a mix of insight and blindness, reach and limitations, impartiality and bias—and taken together they achieve neither omniscience nor a unified master narrative but complex understandings of ever-changing, multifaceted social realities" (Rosaldo, 1993, pp. 127–128). It is hoped that the development of these complex understandings, achieved through a collaborative and reciprocal research process, can begin to "repay the sea," to fulfill the large debt that many researchers owe to communities and their members for allowing them to learn from them. It is my belief that this sort of research can also help us move from research that merely focuses on what researchers can learn *about* certain communities to projects that seek to learn *with* communities and their residents.

This book is divided into three parts. Part 1 provides an introduction to community-based qualitative research, reviewing related models and discussing relevant theories and concepts. Part 2 focuses on the design and implementation of community-based qualitative research and includes chapters that delve into the particulars of various data collection techniques, such as participant observation and interviewing; this section also discusses the process of data analysis within such projects. Part 3 explores how the results or findings of community-based qualitative research projects might be disseminated in various arenas, as well as how they might be used to inform public policy and practice. This section also includes examples and case studies of community-based qualitative research initiatives and projects.

# • Acknowledgments •

As anyone who has written a book is well aware, it is rarely an individual endeavor. Although I am listed as the sole author of this text, there were numerous other individuals who provided their expertise and support toward the creation of this book. I am greatly indebted to Helen Salmon, my editor at SAGE, for approaching me in the first place to encourage me to prepare a book proposal on community-based qualitative research (CBQR). Her thoughtful comments and feedback on the proposal and chapter drafts were invaluable, and her belief in this project helped keep me from getting discouraged during the long process of writing a book. Thanks also to her tireless assistant, Anna Villarruel, whose consistent attention to detail helped me keep track of all of the "moving parts" entailed in completing a text. The reviewers and copyeditors at SAGE were instrumental in helping me through the revision and production process.

My interest in conducting CBQR was inspired by my experiences working and living in Chicago's Humboldt Park community, and it was facilitated by the support of a number of organizations in the community and the willingness of numerous individuals to allow me, and many students enrolled in classes I instruct, to research and learn within various community contexts. Many of the examples included in this text are culled directly from my experiences instructing this course and conducting research within the community for the last 13 years. Over the years of offering the course, the Puerto Rican Cultural Center and Dr. Pedro Albizu Campos High School have generously offered facilities and staff members have been welcoming to students and gracious in offering their time and expertise to them as they developed and implemented projects. In particular, José Elías López the executive director of the Puerto Rican Cultural Center, was extremely supportive of the course and regularly took time out of his busy schedule to make presentations to students, provide them with tours of the community, and participate in interviews, furnishing students with invaluable background on the community.

In addition, the following institutions, programs, and businesses provided support and assistance to students and their projects: AfriCaribe, Association House, Batey Urbano, Block by Block, Café Colao, Chicago Public Library, Ciclo Urbano/West Town Bikes, Humboldt Park No Se Vende, La Voz de Paseo Boricua newspaper, Lolita Lebrón Family Learning Center, Muévete!, National Museum of Puerto Rican Arts & Culture, and Vida/SIDA. The following individuals were extremely helpful to students as they conducted research: Juanita García Avilés, Xavier Luis Burgos, Leonilda Calderón, Diana Castillo, Carlos DeJesus, Brenda Torres Figueroa, Jessie Fuentes, Elizabeth Hoffman, Ricardo Jiménez, Matthew McCanna, Alejandro Luis Molina, Diamond Montana, Michael Rodríguez Muñiz, Lisa Ortiz, Judith Díaz Rodríguez, Matthew Rodríguez, Elaine Vázquez, and Alyssa Villegas, as well as Dr. Pedro Albizu

Campos High School students/graduates Jashlee Turbe, Graciela Arellano, and Tashira Vélez. Furthermore, I offer a heartfelt thanks to Elías Carmona Rivera, whose photographs of community life, events, and activities greatly enliven this text.

I would also like to acknowledge Drs. Ann Peterson-Kemp and Bertram Chip Bruce, both professors emeriti at the University of Illinois, Urbana–Champaign. Their tireless and incisive work and scholarship within the area of community informatics and inquiry inspired my efforts to engage in community-based qualitative research. This type of research is often viewed as ancillary within the academy, as "service" rather as rigorous research, and the exemplars of and support from other scholars have been an essential part of my journey and development in the area of CBQR. Support and resources from my academic institution, Northern Illinois University, were essential in enabling the course and allowing me to initiate and participate in a number of community-based research projects and initiatives. Thanks in particular to Drs. Lara Leutkehans and Wei-Chen Hung, both chairs of the Department of Educational Technology, Research and Assessment, for their recognition of the importance and value of my work and teaching within community contexts.

Since initially offering a community-based research course in 2008, a number of enthusiastic graduate students have been drawn to community-based research and have joined me as part of the Paseo Boricua Research Group (PBRG), a collaborative group that convenes regularly to reflect on the experiences of the group members conducting research in the community. PBRG has also presented at conferences and prepared manuscripts for publication. Thanks to PBRG members Anne Almburg, Amy Brodeur, Chia-Pao Hsu, Antoinette Jones, Kathy Preissner, Nicole Rivera, and Colleen Stribling for their willingness to sometimes step out of their comfort zones to learn about and with a community and its institutions and residents. I am appreciative of the myriad ways that they shared their experiences as community-based researchers with community members, students, and scholars, as well as for allowing me to include many of their experiences and reflections in this text.

A community-based research project that is most near and dear to my heart is one that I undertook with the Lolita Lebrón Family Learning Center and Danette Sokacich, the director of the program and now the principal of Dr. Pedro Albizu Campos High School. The Proyecto Atabey mentorship program provides intergenerational mentoring services to young mothers and has given me the opportunity to work and collaborate with a dynamic and inspirational group of mothers, as well as to employ some of the work and research I have been engaged in for over a decade toward the establishment of innovative and transformational programming. Thanks to Danette for her hard work to realize our vision, as well as for her persistence and relentlessness in advocating for the needs and experiences of young parents in school. Many thanks to mentors Roxanne Medina Padilla, Cynthia Brito, Teneisha Robles, Tilsa Fernandez, Elizabeth Ruth Alaniz, Angela Escobar, and Jacqueline Allamandolla for devoting their time and energies and for sharing their experiences to support young mothers, as well as to Dr. Pedro Albizu Campos High School students/young mothers Desiree Aponte, Tanairis Torres, and Natasha Hampton for being active participants in our communal process of teaching and learning.

Throughout this process, the support and advice of my research *comadres* Dr. Enid Rosario-Ramos and Dr. Jessica Zacher-Pandya helped me keep from getting discouraged and overwhelmed in the face of looming deadlines. Thanks especially to my family for keeping me grounded and for being so patient and flexible when research and writing took over my time, attention, and energies. My daughter, Olivia Johnson-Ellis, has been a somewhat compliant and often good-natured companion to many a community meeting, event, or weekend class, and her father, Ken Ellis, and my sister, Ann Elizabeth Johnson, have often stepped in to cover childcare duties so that I could participate in community-based research and work.

And, finally, I would like to dedicate this text to the memories of Dr. Steve Whitman, Irma Romero, and Josefina Rodríguez, stellar and passionate exemplars of how to use one's intellect, experiences, and knowledge to collectively struggle against racism and injustice, improve our communities, and make the world a better place for all.

## Reviewer Acknowledgments

SAGE wishes to acknowledge the valuable contributions of the following reviewers.

Karen I. Case, University of Hartford

Deborah, Gioia, University of Maryland, Baltimore

Cynthia R. Jasper, University of Wisconsin–Madison

Christian Winterbottom, The Ohio State University at Mansfield

Wendy Griswold, University of Memphis

Doris L. Watson, University of Nevada–Las Vegas

# • About the Author •

---

**Laura Ruth Johnson** is an associate professor in the Department of Educational Technology, Research and Assessment in the College of Education at Northern Illinois University, DeKalb. She teaches classes in qualitative research methods, including courses in ethnographic research, interview methods, and community-based and participatory action research. Her research focuses on civic engagement and community involvement among Latino/a and African American youth, with a focus on young mothers. In her research, she collaborates with staff and students at an alternative high school in Chicago's Humboldt Park community to help strengthen services and develop initiatives that focus on youth activism and intergenerational mentorship for young parents. Her teaching and research also focus on the creation of community–university partnerships and on the engagement of graduate students in community-based research projects.

# Introduction and Background to Community-Based Research

# PART 1

# Theoretical and Conceptual Background

## Introduction

To improve our understanding of community-based qualitative research (CBQR), it is important to review some related models and approaches, as well as to examine the views of learning and teaching that inform it. Several models, such as participatory action research (PAR), youth participatory action research (YPAR), and service learning and community-based action research (CBAR), share much in common with CBQR. In addition, particular ethnographic designs, such as collaborative ethnography (Lassiter, 2005) and reciprocal ethnography (Lawless, 2000), are instructive in their focus on a sharing authority with participants during the research process. This chapter will also identify and discuss key theoretical concepts and frameworks related to learning and teaching within community contexts that inform CBQR, such as funds of knowledge theories (González, Moll, & Amanti, 2005), experiential learning (Kolb, 1984), communities of practice (Lave & Wenger, 1991), and counter-storytelling (Solórzano & Bernal, 2001; Yosso, 2005).

## Learning Goals

After reading this chapter, students will be able to:

1. Identify and describe research approaches related to community-based qualitative research (CBQR).

2. Describe community-based research models related to CBQR.

3. Discuss the strengths and challenges associated with research methods and models that use participatory and/or collaborative approaches.

4. Discuss views of teaching and learning that inform participatory and collaborative models of research, and explain how these function within CBQR projects.

## Introduction to Related Models

The models and designs associated with community-based qualitative research (CBQR) are generally part of the interpretive family of approaches within research in education and the social sciences (Erickson, 1986). In opposition to positivist research, which attempts to determine a single "truth" or answer to a research "problem," interpretive approaches recognize that there are multiple perspectives on a particular issue or phenomenon and seek to identify the local meanings and particulars of a given phenomenon, be it reading instruction, health literacy, or civic engagement. CBQR designs also draw heavily from critical and activist research paradigms in that the intent is not just to reveal or uncover multiple and divergent community perspectives but also to produce some solutions and responses that are meaningful to the community, as well as often to involve community organizations and members in the design and implementation of research projects.

Although the positivist tradition is most associated with quantitative methods, and interpretive with qualitative approaches, many of the participatory and action research designs described in this section also use quantitative methods, and quantitative data do have a place within community-based qualitative studies. For example, surveys and other demographic data can provide useful background and context, as well as offer an overview of trends and patterns related to community attitudes and behaviors that can be probed and examined more richly through qualitative data collection, such as in-depth interviews and detailed and sustained observation and participation in various community settings. The models reviewed in this section include participatory action research (PAR), youth participatory action research (YPAR), service learning courses, community-based action research (CBAR), and collaborative and reciprocal ethnography. In addition to providing an overview of key characteristics and approaches for specific designs, each section also highlights some exemplary studies and projects related to each approach.

## Participatory Action Research/Youth
## Participatory Action Research

PAR is a research approach that challenges more traditional, positivist paradigms, which view research as objective and value neutral (Hall, 1992; Lather, 1986). PAR approaches are theoretically grounded in the work of Paulo Freire (1970), particularly in the way that they focus on action and transformation as central to research, and in the ways in which they seek to raise critical consciousness among research group members. Antonio Gramsci's (1971) work has also been influential to PAR, particularly his notion of "organic intellectuals," whereby intellectuals are created within the working class (p. 5). His view of education as a dialectic process, and exhortation to develop a "praxis of present" (in Lather, 1986), has helped shape the theory and practice of PAR. Other models that have inspired and informed PAR include popular education, a movement begun in Latin America and affiliated with Freire's work. In the United States, a prominent popular educator was Myles Horton who founded the Highlander School in the 1930s in Appalachia, which involved community residents in educational efforts and activism on behalf of their communities and their concerns (Horton & Freire, 1990). PAR projects usually have a critical, social-justice orientation, paying special attention to race, gender, ethnicity, class, and sexual orientation, and the ways in which these might function to marginalize certain groups (Hall 1992; Lather, 1986). Researchers such as Michelle Fine and her colleagues have spent decades developing PAR and YPAR approaches "to generate evidence that can be used in specific state and local policy debates and in local organizing campaigns on a wide range of educational justice concerns" (Fine, Ayala, & Zaal, 2012, p. 686). As part of their work with the Public Science Project, they have used them to investigate a variety of issues, such as mass incarceration, the education of immigrant youth, and sexuality education (Fine et al., 2012).

PAR researchers acknowledge the inherent subjectivity in all research endeavors and take an activist stance within the research studies they undertake. What particularly sets PAR apart from other forms of research—within both the positivist and interpretive traditions—is that research purpose statements, hypotheses, and questions are not designed ***a priori***, or before entering a research setting. Rather, PAR researchers work with community organizations and members to identify salient and germane issues and topics, and they collaboratively design and implement the research study. Even more significant is PAR's focus on action and transformation, of research participants, as well as the conditions and contexts that impact their daily lives. Therefore, a PAR study would be interested in not just exploring gender stereotypes and oppression that impact women of color within a specific community, but also they would connect this oppression with larger social structures and shifts, such as gentrification and community displacement, and speak back and challenge the stereotypes, as did the PAR group the Fed Up Honeys when they created stereotype stickers and wrote a report titled *Makes me Mad* (Cahill, Rios-Moore, & Threatts, 2008). Another example of PAR is the work of Andrea Dyrness (2012) with immigrant mothers. In this study, she did not merely investigate the inception and implementation of a small school but instead worked collaboratively with immigrant mothers instrumental in founding the school, forming a research group called Las Madres Unidas (Mothers United). The group worked together to conduct interviews and focus groups to gather various perspectives on the implementation of the school. Their identification of ways in which parents' voices were silenced and ignored facilitated advocacy efforts on the part of the women, and ultimately, it led to the establishment of a parent education center at the school.

Central to PAR is the notion of **praxis** or the "dialectical tension, the interactive, reciprocal shaping of theory and practice" (Lather, 1986, p. 258). PAR aims to build reciprocal research relationships with individuals and communities toward the development of emancipatory knowledge:

> For praxis to be possible, not only must theory illuminate the lived experience of progressive social groups; it must also be illuminated by their struggles. Theory adequate to the task of changing the world must be open-ended, nondogmatic, informing, and grounded in the circumstances of everyday life; and, moreover, it must be premised on a deep respect for the intellectual and political capacities of the dispossessed. (Lather, 1986, p. 262)

Thus, within PAR, research and theory must be grounded in and generated by the everyday realities and struggles of participants, as well as rooted in respectful and reciprocal processes and research relationships.

In PAR studies, community members are not viewed as "research subjects" or even as "primary informants" or "research participants," but serve as co-researchers and partners in the research process. For example, In the work by Dyrness (2012), mothers developed research questions, led focus groups, and presented research findings at class assemblies and conferences. Similarly, the Fed Up Honeys were engaged in the collective analysis of research findings that were used to design the sticker campaign and a website (Cahill et al., 2008). These aforementioned activities point to the pedagogical aspects of PAR, wherein research is viewed as an opportunity to impart research skills to individuals and communities who have often been marginalized or left out of the research process. Therefore, within PAR studies, a university researcher might be involved in teaching workshops on various aspects of data collection, facilitating practice interviews and focus groups, and leading data analysis sessions. This collaborative process requires that university researchers—who are typically used to being "in charge" of a project—part with control and authority at all stages of the research process and that they empower co-researchers to implement and lead the project. Similarly, community members and co-researchers will be looked at to share their knowledge and expertise, about the community and relevant issues, with community researchers (McIntyre, 2008). This shared authority may also mean co-authoring research articles and book chapters (Irizarry, 2011) and presenting as a group at conferences (McIntyre, 2008).

The role of the researcher, then, can be "complicated" within PAR projects because researchers are often positioned as researchers and as activists and concerned community members, as both insiders and outsiders, and as inhabiting political and social spaces in ways that are "unsettling" within more traditional research paradigms that urge neutrality and distance (Stovall, 2006, p. 98). Often, within PAR projects, university researchers become advocates for co-researchers and their issues and concerns. They can also be seen as "crossing the line" as researchers when they engage in advocacy efforts and align themselves with marginalized groups. For example, Dyrness (2012) was at times "disciplined" or "chastised" by the administration at the school she was working with because she was considered too closely affiliated with the mothers who, through their research, were challenging the process of inclusion at the school (p. 216).

In PAR, the products of the research are not limited to research reports and articles, but they might also include curricula, public service announcements, action plans, advocacy efforts, and/or media campaigns. Research findings are also often used to design new programs or to refashion existing community services to meet local needs better. For example, a youth group that Alice McIntyre (2008) worked with developed a community clean-up group, which entailed creating a logo and T-shirts. Given that PAR is interested in "individual and collective well-being" (McIntyre, 2008, p. 40), the purpose of the research is not just to generate products, or to contribute to "generalizable knowledge," but also to lead to the enrichment and betterment of group members and the larger community and societal context. Research dissemination takes more public forms, such as on websites and within community meetings. The research is meant to engage diverse audiences, beyond academic scholars, including youth, community residents, practitioners, policy makers, and the broader public.

Although PAR can be an effective means for conducting transformative research and enacting change, several researchers have spotlighted the "messiness" of PAR and urge that researchers allow themselves "enough space to withstand the bumps and bruises that characterize humanizing experiences of reflection, action, and change" (McIntyre, 2008, p. 37). Despite researchers' best intentions, and the enthusiasm and commitment of co-researchers, sometimes the projects do not affect the change sought at the outset of the project. And although PAR is premised on building reciprocal relationships between academic researchers and co-researchers, and emphasizes "equal" roles of power within the research project, in some cases, academics can reproduce the unequal power hierarchies that they are trying to disrupt through the process of PAR (Nygreen, 2013). For example, Kysa Nygreen (2013) reflected on the ways that she initially glossed over her role in silencing youth voices and privileging her own agenda in her youth research group. She concedes that her candid discussion of some of the ways her project was unsuccessful, and her reflection on her tacit role in propagating deficit discourses about youth in her study, might provide fodder to the detractors of PAR, yet she avers that PAR can be "strengthened by our willingness to write honestly and self-reflexively about the ethical, political, and intellectual dilemmas of the method" (Nygreen, 2013, p. 16). Others have also acknowledged and grappled with the inherent "speed bumps" entailed in conducting such research and exhort researchers to be mindful of obstacles and dilemmas at all stages of the research (Weis & Fine, 2000). Some of the aforementioned difficulties that researchers face in PAR projects stem from the fact that the research is situated within a larger societal context that privileges certain racial, gender, class, and educational categories over others. These hierarchies and hegemonic relationships can certainly be replicated within PAR projects if researchers do not constantly interrogate and critique their positionality and practices.

Emerging from the tradition of PAR is YPAR, which as the name indicates focuses specifically on youth as research partners (Cammarota & Fine, 2008). Many of the researchers mentioned conducted projects with youth, but they did not explicitly refer to their study as YPAR, which is a more recent term. Because of its pedagogical aspect, PAR seems especially appropriate for work and research with youth. Ernest Morrell (2004, 2006) has referred to his work as "youth-initiated research," whereby youth become critical researchers through their exploration of issues pertinent to their lives, which are also topics of their choosing. Other notable examples include the work of Shawn Ginwright and Julio Cammarota (2007), who have examined the role that praxis-based community organizations can play in engaging youth. Jason Irizarry (2011) employed YPAR to engage "Latino youth in urban schools in meaning-ful, co-constructed research while enhancing their academic skills" (p. 6). To do this, he taught a course in a public high school, where students were involved in research-ing their experiences within schools, and used this to challenge deficit discourses that position low-income youth of color as "problems." His findings were intended to inform the knowledge and practices of teachers and schools, as well as to be part of professional development efforts, and they were published in a book where each chapter was coauthored (Irizarry, 2011). Many who use YPAR view it as both an ide-ology and a methodology (Irizarry, 2011), where youth are positioned as producers of knowledge and research is viewed as a means of resisting the status quo.

## Community-Based Participatory Research

By building on PAR design and approaches, community-based participatory research (CBPR) uses a collaborative, partnership approach toward conducting research, and it "recognizes the community as a social and cultural entity" that involves community partners in all aspects of the research and "in the process of creating knowledge and change" (Israel, Schulz, Parker, & Becker, 2001, p. 184). CBPR acknowledges commu-nity strengths and resources and uses these as the foundation for a research study; as in PAR, co-learning and capacity building among researchers, and community partners are integral components of the act of conducting research. Mostly employed within community health research, CBPR aims to develop "effective translational practice" (Hacker, 2013, p. 2), which involves forging and strengthening equitable relationships between academic researchers and community members. Interventions that are developed through CBPR are intended to be relevant and responsive to com-munity concerns, as well as part of iterative and cyclical processes of data collection and systems development (Hacker, 2013).

CBPR uses a variety of nonexperimental methods, including qualitative and quan-titative approaches, as well as approaches associated with evaluation research. CBPR has been used to examine issues such as the impact of immigration enforcement on immigrant health in Everett, Massachusetts (Hacker et al., 2011), health-care disparities (Wallerstein & Duran, 2010), and the relationship between teen suicide and drug use (Hacker et al., 2008). As with other participatory models, some challenges included the time required to form and develop partnerships and relationships with community members, as well as the potential lack of respect for and value placed on such research within the academic arena.

## Collaborative and Reciprocal Ethnography

Ethnography, or the study of cultural phenomena and human societies and behavior, usually involves intense observation and participation—also referred to as "fieldwork"—on the part of the researcher in particular settings, which are often localized communities (Geertz, 1973). However, very early anthropological work often did not include this sort of immersion, and it was critiqued for being inauthentic and produced by "armchair ethnographers," who had limited participation in the contexts and with the groups they depicted in their writings (Heath & Street, 2008; Malinowski, 1922/1961). As fieldwork has become an integral component of ethnography, others have been critical of "the myth of the lone ethnographer," wherein research is viewed as a solitary endeavor and the sole purview of the researcher, when in fact, they assert, ethnographic research is always a collaborative process involving dialogue with participants (Brown, Collins, & Duguid, 1989; Lassiter, 2005). Increasingly, ethnographic researchers have called for increased participation and involvement within the settings and communities where they conduct their research, as well as self-reflexivity regarding their own positionality in relation to participants (Abu-Lughod, 1993; Behar, 1996).

Some ethnographers have exhorted researchers to move beyond mere participation and self-reflexivity for the sake of the researcher only to more explicit and deliberate collaboration, where collaboration is part of the research design rather than just an incidental outgrowth of immersive participation and fieldwork that is a feature of most ethnographic work (Lassiter, 2005; Lawless, 2000). These researchers seek to upend traditional researcher/subject power hierarchies, urging instead for collaborative ethnography, which involves a shared process and dialogue among ethnographers and community members and research participants (Lassiter, 2005). Under this model—much like PAR and YPAR described earlier—those often referred to as "subjects" or "informants" are viewed, and treated, as consultants and co-intellectuals, who possess mutual authority and vision with the academic researcher. These researchers critique most ethnographic work as inauthentic and irrelevant as it produces "academically-positioned narratives" rather than "community-positioned" ones (Lassiter, 2005, p. 4). They call for work that involves an ongoing conversation with community members and cultural groups, where dialogue plays a central and primary role, not just during fieldwork but also during "all phases of the research process," from design to write-up (Schensul & Schensul, 1992, p. 162).

Some researchers have described this type of ethnographic research as "reciprocal" ethnography:

"Reciprocal ethnography" will occur when and if they (researcher and participants) are able to cross paths and engage in dialogue and discussion openly about the subject matter they are each writing and thinking about, recognizing and embracing the potential to take their conversations beyond their current perceptions. (Lawless, 2000, p. 200)

Lawless (2000) differentiates her notion of "reciprocal" from "reciprocity" in that it involves not just an exchange of goods, such as presents or material resources, given to research participants as a token of thanks for their time. Rather, true reciprocal ethnography is premised on an "exchange of ideas and meaning" and includes "emergent dialogue in field research that is then carried into scholarly writing" (Lawless, 2000, p. 199).

In collaborative and reciprocal ethnography, consultants are involved in co-processes of co-interpretation and reciprocal analysis, collaborative writing and editing, and serve as readers and editors, members and facilitators of focus groups, participants in community forums, and authors of co-authored texts (Lassiter, 2005). The finished products of research projects are written to be accessible, as well as publically and locally available. In this way, the research process also serves to "cultivat[e] co-citizenships" and enable

wider possibilities for collaborative engagements in the very specific context of cooperatively conceived community–university research partnerships: that is, between and among community- and university-situated constituencies, where students, faculty, and members of local communities have opportunities to research, learn, work, and act together in the framework of care and responsibility for the communities they collectively inhabit. (Campbell & Lassiter, 2010, p. 378)

The type of democratic civic engagement entailed in these projects is not just related to activity and place—for example, that the research takes place within a particular community setting—but also to purpose and process, that the research is intended to address multiple audiences and contribute to social equity, and that the process involves a "reorder[ing]" of the conventional hierarchical and unidirectional relationship between "the researcher and the researched" (Campbell & Lassiter, 2010; Schensul & Schensul, 1992, p. 166)

Some examples of collaborative or reciprocal ethnography include Elizabeth Campbell and Luke Lassiter's (2010) work in Muncie, Indiana, where students and ethnographers worked with teams of community advisors to remediate a former community study that ignored the African American residents; "The Other Side of Middletown" brought together students, researchers, and various community constituencies to engage in important conversations about race and difference (Campbell & Lassiter, 2010). Elaine Lawless (1993) created co-produced texts with women in the clergy by participating in intimate discussions with them about their daily lives and work, as well as about their families and personal lives, including successes and challenges. Through these discussions, they "worked through and toward an understanding of their own experience(s)" that helped her "envision" her final work (Lawless, 1993, p. 59). As part of the research, Lawless attended the clergy women's existing lunch discussions, collected life stories from the women, and established "book work" groups that allowed for discussions and explorations of the women's stories and experiences. The goal in all these collaborative projects is to embrace multiple voices and integrate "community and consultant commentary into an ethnographic text" (Lassiter, 2005, p. 136). In the eyes of some researchers, this sort of process "moves beyond mere bureaucratic rubber stamping and toward an increasingly difficult engagement with differing visions, agendas, and expectations" (Lassiter, 2005, pp. 136–137).

However, as in the case of PAR/YPAR, this sort of ethnographic work is often marginalized in the field as not serious or rigorous research and viewed as siding with participants instead of maintaining the objective stance many associate with research. Some view the projects as social work rather than as academic research; for this reason, engaging in collaborative ethnography can often be "unprestigious" and "professionally risky" (Lassiter, 2005, p. 151).

## Course-Based Models

Much of the community-based research currently taking place is connected with specific course work and campus-wide initiatives aimed at increasing community and civic engagement on the part of students and the broader institution, and it is designed to build community–university partnerships. Many of these initiatives were developed in response to critiques of academic institutions as ignorant of—or even worse, insensitive to—community needs and concerns, as well as separated from the "real world" in an "ivory tower." Many universities and colleges were viewed as mining and exploiting surrounding communities for research opportunities but not sharing or purveying adequate resources to compensate communities for their time and efforts. Increasingly, higher education institutions have been charged with providing real-world and engaged learning experiences to students to prepare them better for their professional lives after college in a variety of contexts.

**Service Learning.** Service learning can be integrated into courses as part of a volunteer requirement or a class project that involves engagement in a community setting; sometimes these projects are aligned with course objectives (Vogel, Seifer, & Gelmon, 2010). Increasingly, service learning has been integrated into the mission of schools, particularly those with a religious affiliation and an explicit social-service mission. Research has found that at institutions with high levels of service learning, faculty are often provided release time to enable the planning and implementation of service-learning projects (Vogel et al., 2010). Several institutions, such as DePaul University, have institutional service-learning requirements for students, as well as designated service-learning courses. Other service-learning opportunities might be provided through alternative spring breaks, where students take trips to be involved in direct service volunteer projects in high-need areas, for example, to build houses in New Orleans post–Hurricane Katrina. For these sorts of service-learning initiatives to be successful, and to institutionalize efforts, colleges and universities develop infrastructure and dedicate resources for service learning, such as a center that coordinates initiatives and course work and provides professional development and support for faculty (Vogel et al., 2010). Nationwide, the Campus Compact, an organization founded in 1985 by a group of university presidents and now a national coalition of 1,100 college and university presidents, helps support institutions in developing community partnerships and service-learning initiatives (www.compact .org). Service-learning projects are intended to be more than volunteerism or community service, as well as aligned with learning objectives, but they are not necessarily focused on collaborative research.

**Community-Based Action Research (CBAR).** CBAR is a term developed by Howard Rosing and Nila Hofman (2007) that "encompasses a variety of community-focused research, including community-based research (CBR), community-focused experiential learning (EL), and participatory action research (PAR)" (p. vii). According to Rosing and Hofman, these approaches share "an underlying commitment to engaging undergraduates, faculty, and local community partners in building intercommunity ties through the goal of improving the lives of members of marginalized communities" (p. vii). In these courses, the emphasis is on advocacy and conducting research "for and with" community partners rather than just on student-centered research or civic engagement projects that merely generate descriptions of community settings or that only benefit student learning (Rosing & Hofman, 2007). The intent is to provide college students with authentic experiences within communities, while building university–community partnerships, and developing something of use to community stakeholders. CBAR shares much in common with aforementioned service-learning and community-service initiatives as part of required course work, yet what sets CBAR apart from many service-learning projects is that it emphasizes a critical perspective on the larger societal conditions within which projects are situated, thus, enabling "students to critically evaluate their sociopolitical surroundings" (Rosing & Hofman, 2007, p. viii). Whereas many volunteer and service-learning initiatives involve students in community service as part of a one-day project, CBAR entails sustained participation and engagement in community settings and sites, and it is anchored in specific course work. Furthermore, it aims to empower community entities and stakeholders toward the achievement of positive social change and betterment of the local community.

An example of a CBAR project includes a course focused on access to food within a low-income neighborhood on the west side of Chicago, which involved students in conducting research at local corner stores (Rosing, 2007). Another CBAR project took an asset-based approach to challenge deficit-oriented and stereotypical views of low-income communities and youth of color by bringing together teenage boys from Bedford-Stuyvesant in Brooklyn, New York, and premed students from Cornell University to document healthy places in the community (Beck, 2007). One research group used urban geography and mapping approaches to address gentrification within a particular community (Curran, Hague, & Gill, 2007).

Although CBAR has proven to be a successful model for enacting change through course work, nevertheless some challenges are associated with CBAR. Some researchers have pointed to the essential need for sufficient preparation for students prior to beginning projects and to be wary of how, if not implemented properly, projects might reinforce or reproduce the negative stereotypes that they are attempting to challenge (Hofman, 2007). Furthermore, to be successful, adequate preplanning and preparation on the part of faculty members is necessary; this additional preparation requires more support from institutions in terms of funding and release time (Hofman, 2007).

## Community-Based Learning and Research (CBLR/CBR)

A model that is strongly associated with service-learning is community-based learning and research (CBLR) or community-based research (CBR) (Dallimore, Rochefort, & Simonelli, 2010; Stoeker, 2013; Strand, Marullo, Cutworth, Stoeker, & Donohue, 2003). According to Elise Dallimore, David Rochefort, and Kristen Simonelli (2010), "CBLR focuses on engaging faculty, community-based organizations, and students in partnerships to actively meet academic-learning and community goals" (p. 15). It arose out of similar concerns that motivated service learning, a desire to build and formalize academy–community partnerships and engage in research for the public good, as well as a belief that the university was "largely failing in its efforts to prepare students for lives of social responsibility and civic and public engagement" (Strand et al., 2003, p. 2). Key elements of CBLR are "community engagement, learning by doing, and guided reflection" (Dallimore et al., 2010, p. 17).

CBLR and CBR involve outreach to organizations and communities, as well as learning and research with groups that are "disadvantaged" and "disenfranchised" (Strand et al., 2003). The model is rooted in some of the aforementioned research and learning models, such as popular education (Freire, 1970; Horton & Freire, 1990), action research (Lewin, 1951), and participatory action research (Fals Borda, 2006). It employs an "active learning and problem-centered pedagogy" (Strand et al., 2003, p. 10), which validates local knowledge. Dallimore and colleagues (2010) also identify three models of CBLR. In the direct service-learning model, students provide regular direct service to a community-based organization or nonprofit, for example, tutoring or mentoring. Throughout the project, students are expected to engage in ongoing guided reflection. In the second model, project-based service learning, advanced students are involved in consulting with a community partner to lend their expertise (usually aligned with course content) to help partners develop solutions to an identified problem that they might not have time or resources to address. For example, at Northeastern University, in a "consultation skills" course, students "assess organizational needs, conduct benchmarking data, and then provide recommendations for organizational change" (Dallimore et al., 2010, p. 18). To sustain projects, work from previous students is built on by students in subsequent classes. The CBR model involves more collaboration with the community partner, where much of the work on a project would be conducted in collaboration with the partner, and the emphasis is on capacity building so that partners can continue work and initiatives after the CBR project has ended.

In sum, although much attention has been paid to civic engagement within academic institutions, many have pointed out the need for more research on engaged scholarship, as well as the context and conditions that support engagement on the part of academic scholars (O'Meara, Sandmann, Saltmarsh, & Giles, 2010). Researchers have also called for clearer definitions of the "scholarship of engagement" and have highlighted the need for redefining promotion and tenure policies to allow for this sort of community engagement and collaborative research to expand "what counts" as scholarly research (Israel et al., 2001; Saltmarsh, Giles, Ward, & Buglione, 2009).

In sharing these various models related to CBQR, it should also be pointed out that these are not meant to be an exhaustive list of community-based approaches in the area of research, teaching, and learning. Furthermore, there is much overlap among aspects of these models, and they are certainly not exclusive or singular examples of the ways in which civic and community engagement have been integrated into scholarly research and university course work and initiatives. Although some features might be particular to the specific models mentioned, many shared concepts and terms exist.

## Views of Teaching and Learning

In addition to the aforementioned models, some particular concepts and views of teaching and learning provide a theoretical and philosophical foundation for CBQR. These notions challenge traditional views of where knowledge resides and how individuals gain skills and expertise. These views of teaching and learning can help academic scholars reconceptualize their research and teaching, as well as offer an essential grounding for the design and implementation for CBQR projects.

### Funds of Knowledge

By drawing on Vygotskian and sociocultural theories of learning and development, a group of educational researchers developed the concept of funds of knowledge to describe the everyday practices of households and families (González, Moll, & Amanti, 2005). It initially emerged from a project—"The Tucson Project"—which involved extensive ethnographic interviews with working and middle-class Mexican American households in Tucson, Arizona (Vélez-Ibáñez, 1983), and documented the important resources, networks, knowledge, and support that were exchanged among households. This study inspired researchers to explore further "the transformative effect of knowing the community in all its breadth and depth" and provided the foundation for the Funds of Knowledge Project (González, Moll, & Amanti, 2005, p. 3). This project aimed to develop collaborative relationships between researchers and teachers with the goal of documenting and describing knowledge and practices employed in the families and households of students in their classrooms, as well as with the goal of using these to transform classroom instruction. To gather data, teachers visited households and communities and used ethnographic methods, such as participant observation, in-depth interviews, life history narratives, and reflective writings.

The funds of knowledge concept asserts that families and communities are repositories of significant resources and knowledge, as well as sites for the development of important skills and practices for individuals, including adults and children. In particular, the project sought to identify such sources of knowledge and practices among low-income and minority households, which traditionally have been viewed through a deficit-perspective focused on weaknesses rather than on strengths. Underlying the concept of funds of knowledge is "a critical assumption . . . that educational institutions have stripped away the view of working class minority students as emerging from households rich in social and intellectual resources" (González, Moll, Tenery, et al., 2005, p. 90).

The notion of funds of knowledge provides an important antidote to deficit-oriented perspectives that focus on what certain families and communities lack, and labels that classify entire communities as "impoverished" and "disadvantaged," as well as those who reside in these communities as "at risk." A funds of knowledge perspective also assists researchers and practitioners in moving away from "cycles of poverty" rhetoric that has characterized some research and policy aimed at low-income, minority families (Moynihan, 1965) and that has pathologized communities and families as sites of numerous social problems that are transmitted intergenerationally. In contrast, a funds of knowledge approach views families and communities as repositories and purveyors of valuable resources, skills, and knowledge. Such a concept is an important one for those interested in conducting CBQR as it helps orient researchers toward community strengths and assets and in viewing communities as contexts for teaching, learning, and development.

## Experiential Learning

Another important concept involves views on how individuals learn. Some researchers and theorists have highlighted the role of everyday experiences within the learning process and have called attention to the way individuals' experiences provide the context for gaining new knowledge and skills (Kolb, 1994; Lewin, 1951). David Kolb (1984) draws on the work of John Dewey (1958), Kurt Lewin (1951), Jean Piaget (1952), and others to describe "how learning transforms the impulses, feelings, and desires of concrete experience into higher-order purposeful action" (Kolb, 1984, p. 22). Experiential learning views education as a lifelong process that is not confined to the realm of classroom instruction, acknowledging the "critical linkages that can be developed between the classroom and the 'real world'" (Kolb, 1984, p. 4).

According to experiential learning theorists, this sort of learning should be conceived as a process rather than viewed in terms of outcomes; a central assumption of experiential learning is that ideas are not "fixed and immutable elements of thought but are formed and re-formed through experience" (Kolb, 1984, p. 26). Experiential learning is a continuous process, rooted in one's experiences, and it involves an interplay between expectation and experience and the resolving of tensions between divergent ways of viewing the world. In this view, learning requires adaptation and relearning rather than the simple intake of facts and information. Experiential learning entails a transactional relationship between learner and environment, objective and subjective experiences, and social and personal knowledge. Finally, reflective observation on one's experiences is a key component of experiential learning (Kolb, 1984).

Experiential learning notions are integral to CBQR as this type of research is premised on an interest in the ways that individuals' distinct experiences can serve as contexts and foundations for learning. The central tenets of experiential learning, related to the role that experience plays within the learning process, also help researchers structure the research process to be grounded in the everyday realities of participants and co-researchers. Furthermore, experiential learning's premise that thought and ideas are dynamic and flexible can help researchers question their *a priori* assumptions and take-for-granted theoretical frameworks and view knowledge as malleable and open to change.

## Situated Learning/Communities of Practice

Situated learning theory posits that learning occurs through individuals' participation in communities of practice (CoP)—or a group of practitioners who share an area of expertise or profession—and through "legitimate peripheral participation" in that CoP (Lave & Wenger, 1991; Wenger, 1998). These communities can exist in the workplace, in a larger community setting, or in virtual space. Early work in CoP examined Yucatán midwives, Liberian tailors, navy quartermasters, butchers, members of Alcoholics Anonymous, and dieters in Weight Watchers (Brown et al., 1989; Lave & Wenger, 1991). A primary component of situated learning is *in situ* learning or "learning by doing." Learning is viewed as "an integral part of a generative social practice in the lived-in world" (Lave & Wenger, 1991, p. 35). Thus, learning occurs in authentic activities, or the everyday activities and social practices, of individuals engaged in a CoP. As part of legitimate peripheral participation, "a person's intentions to learn are engaged and the meaning of learning is configured through the process of becoming a full participant in sociocultural practice" (Lave & Wenger, 1991, p. 29).

This body of work is also interested in the ways in which meaning, practice, community, and identity intersect to inform processes of knowledge acquisition. Within this model, meaning refers to "a way of talking about (changing) ability—individually and collectively—to experience our life and the world as meaningful" (Wenger, 1998, p. 5). Practices involve shared historical and social frameworks that "can sustain mutual engagement in action," whereas the concepts of community and identity provide a means of "belonging" and "becoming" within the learning process (Wenger, 1998, p. 5). This work also highlights the difference between explicit and tacit knowledge, or those practices and behaviors that are declared and known and others that might be more taken for granted or implicit.

Situated learning theory can help those interested in conducting CBQR pay attention to the ways in which particular settings and contexts are teeming with practices that reflect particular sociocultural histories and experiences. A focus on *in situ* learning also helps researchers identify learning that takes place outside of formal classroom settings, as well as the ways that individuals acquire knowledge and skills in everyday activities. Finally, as John Seely Brown, Allan Collins, and Paul Duguid (1989) point out, "because tools and the way they are used reflect the particular accumulated insights of communities, it is not possible to use a tool appropriately without understanding the community or culture in which it is used" (p. 33). Thus, a CoP perspective assists researchers in exploring how conceptual tools, such as learning strategies, are influenced and shaped by such "accumulated insights," as well as a respect for and interest in a larger community setting.

## Critical Pedagogy and Problem-Posing Education

The critical, liberatory pedagogy articulated by Brazilian educator and theorist Paulo Freire (1970) has been extremely influential in shaping critical perspectives on teaching and learning, particularly in the area of adult education. Freire's theory faulted traditional "banking" educational approaches—where information is deposited into students and the emphasis is on rote learning—as creating passive objects and instead urged for a problem-posing education that uses education to help students identify and reflect on the generative themes and issues in their lives, with the ultimate goal of taking action to transform the world around them. This process of identification, reflection, and action also requires that teachers not replicate hegemonic and dominating colonial practices, where they are the ultimate authority within the classroom. Instead, under a problem-posing approach, teachers serve as facilitators, and they assist in the "constant unveiling of reality" (Freire, 1970, p. 68). Instead of merely acting as information "depositors," who assume that students know nothing, critical educators engage in a dialogic process with students where they are jointly educated, in which students become teachers and vice versa.

Freirian notions of critical pedagogy are particularly relevant to the research process necessary for conducting CBQR. In particular, the dialogue and collaboration that are integral to problem-posing education are also essential components of CBQR. Moreover, Freire's (1970) emphasis on education as a process of transformation provides a model for how to reconceptualize research projects to enact changes that can benefit communities and research participants.

## Counterstorytelling and Counterspaces

Critical race theory (CRT) and LatCrit draw from critical theory "to examine the multiple ways that African Americans, Native Americans, Asian Americans,

Pacific Islanders, Chicanas/os, and Latinas/os continue to experience, respond to, and resist racism and other forms of oppression" (Ladson-Billings & Tate, 1995; Solórzano & Bernal, 2001; Yosso, Smith, Ceja, & Solórzano, 2009, p. 662). In addition, CRT and LatCrit are interested in the intersectionality of various forms of oppression; LatCrit, in particular, addresses issues often not tackled by CRT, such as language, immigration, ethnicity, culture, identity, phenotype, and sexuality (Solórzano & Bernal, 2001). Both use a methodology called counterstorytelling, which is

> both a technique of telling the story of those experiences that are not often told (i.e., those on the margins of society) and a tool for analyzing and challenging the stories of those in power and whose story is a natural part of the dominant discourse—the majoritarian story. (Yosso et al., 2009, p. 662)

Related to the technique of counterstorytelling is the notion of counterspaces. These are safe places for minoritized individuals to build community and "cultivate . . . students' sense of home and family" (Yosso et al., 2009, p. 677) and often serve as sites for nurturance and restoration from oppression, as well as settings that promote resilience, resistance, and transformation (Haymes, 1995; Solórzano & Bernal, 2001).

Examples of such counterspaces have included social groups and activities that Latinos/as might construct in college where they can speak Spanish, or celebrate certain cultural symbols, and position their cultural knowledge as valuable (Yosso, 2005; Yosso et al., 2009). The concept is similar to bell hooks's (1990) notion of "homeplace," which was articulated to describe African American women's domestic spaces, where women could find solace and recuperate from the injustices of racism exacted by the outside world: "one's homeplace was the one site where one could freely confront the issue of humanization, where one could resist" (p. 42). Others have also spotlighted the emancipatory potential of counterstorytelling and counterspaces (Fernández, 2002).

The notions of counterstorytelling and counterspaces are relevant for community-based qualitative researchers because of their emphasis on privileging the narratives of marginalized groups and individuals. Furthermore, CRT and LatCrit's analysis of the power and hegemony functioning within public, majoritarian spaces and narratives and how counterstories and counterspaces represent acts of survival and resistance are instructive for those interested in conducting research that can challenge mainstream ways of knowing. Research has examined how communities and institutions can serve as counterstorytelling contexts and counterspaces (Johnson & Rosario-Ramos, 2012), and it has examined the specific ways that those from marginalized communities serve as "holders and creators of knowledge" (Bernal, 2002). These sorts of studies provide exemplars of how researchers can seek to uncover what Yosso and García (2007) have referred to as "community cultural wealth" (Yosso et al., 2009, p. 677).

## Chapter Summary

This chapter reviewed theories and models related to CBQR. In particular, this chapter discussed participatory research approaches, such as PAR, YPAR, and reciprocal ethnography, as well as models that are often anchored in college course work, such as service-learning models and CBAR. These approaches and models share many commonalities with CBQR, most notably, their commitment to collaborative inquiry with particular communities and community-based groups and constituencies. Although these participatory and course-based based models offer many benefits to researchers and students interested in community engagement and collaborative research, they also pose some challenges related to implementation, as they often require significant time, resources, and coordination to be successful. CBQR has also been informed by various views of teaching and learning, including experiential learning theories and critical pedagogical approaches. Other related concepts we learned about involve views of communities that are asset-based and that regard communities as repositories of knowledge and rich sites for the acquisition of skills.

## Key Terms

A priori   4                          Praxis   5

## ● Activities for Reflection and Discussion

1) Examine informal learning: With a partner, share something that you have learned outside of a formal educational context, such as school or a training/workshop. What did you learn? How did you learn it? How was the process different than learning in a classroom setting?

2) Discuss some of the research models discussed in this chapter: PAR/YPAR, collaborative and reciprocal ethnography, and community-based models. What do they all have in common? What makes each model unique? What are the advantages of each model? What are the challenges associated with each model? Use Handout 1 to organize information.

3) Identify a community–university partnership or initiative on an institutional website or through a program that you are involved in. What sorts of models did they follow? How do they address or integrate the views of teaching and learning articulated in this chapter?

# HANDOUT 1
## Comparing Research Models

| Research Model | Characteristics | Key Concepts | Advantages | Challenges |
|---|---|---|---|---|
| PAR | | | | |
| YPAR | | | | |
| Reciprocal Ethnography | | | | |
| Service Learning | | | | |
| Community-Based Action Research | | | | |

# What Is Community-Based Qualitative Research?

## Introduction

As Chapter 1 discussed, many different models of research entail conducting research within community settings and/or building collaborative relationships with community members. CBQR builds on many of the aforementioned models and designs and employs many of the approaches discussed in Chapter 1. To provide some clarity, this chapter delineates key elements of the CBQR model, as well as offers examples of course work that incorporates the model and projects that use this approach to conduct research.

## Learning Goals

After reading this chapter, students will be able to:

1. Identify core concepts underlying the community-based qualitative research (CBQR) model and be familiar with their theoretical/philosophical origins.

2. Apply core concepts to aspects of the design and implementation of CBQR projects.

3. Discuss important elements of CBQR, and explain how these can be integrated into specific components and processes of the project.

4. Describe particular projects and initiatives that have used a CBQR design or related model, and explain how they are collaborative, critical, and transformative.

# Core Concepts

This section introduces central concepts at the heart of community-based qualitative research (CBQR) and discusses some of the theoretical underpinnings of these concepts. In addition, examples of what these core concepts "look like" in the practice of conducting research within communities is provided. Knowledge of these core concepts can help researchers employing this approach better understand how to design projects that integrate key attributes.

### Praxis

The concept of *praxis* has its roots in Aristotelian philosophy. Aristotle identified praxis as one of the central activities, along with *theoria* and *poesis*, of human life (Aristotle, 2004). Praxis refers to practical knowledge with the end goal being action, whereas *theoria* refers to theoretical knowledge and a search for truth and *poesis* to poietical knowledge with an emphasis on production (Aristotle, 2004). Within education, the concept was elaborated on by Paulo Freire (1970), who viewed praxis as a liberatory act, involving a combination of reflection and action upon the world "in order to transform it" (p. 36).

Researchers who have been concerned with taking critical stances on important social issues have described praxis as "critical and collective inquiry, reflection and action focused on 'reading' and speaking back to the reality of the world" (Cammarota & Fine, 2008, p. 2). In this sense, the concept of praxis requires scholars not just identify or describe social problems but also become actively involved in challenging existing conditions and "speaking back" to inequities and injustice. For many researchers, this demands more than just theorizing about issues and problems but also suggesting

*Practical Knowledge ——— action*

solutions or alternatives, ideally in dialogue and collaboration with community members and marginalized populations. Authentic critical praxis often also involves active participation by researchers on behalf of ameliorating social problems. Many researchers have spotlighted the collaborative nature of praxis and its merging of theory and practice. In their description of community-based action research (CBAR), Howard Rosing and Nila Hofman (2007) define praxis as "an integration of community-based research for the purpose of empowering community partners, their stakeholders, and our students" (p. viii). In their view, praxis "can take place only when theory and practice are integrated in particular cultural—that is, economic, political, and historical—contexts" (Rosing & Hofman, 2007, p. viii). It is also important to acknowledge that these contexts both enable and confine the resources available to participants and the activities they engage in (Glass, 2001). Praxis is "marked by . . . [a] dialectical interplay between the way in which history and culture make people even while people are making that very history and culture" (Glass, 2001, p. 16).

In CBQR, praxis means that researchers engage in reflective practice on their experiences related to the issues and topics under study, as well as on those relative to the experiences and perspectives of participants and community members. In addition, researchers engaging in praxis connect the issues at the heart of their study—be they youth civic engagement, early literacy development, or housing—to local conditions and resources, as well as to the larger social and historical contexts in which they are situated. Praxis also necessitates that researchers take active stances within the research process and participate in the development of solutions to educational and social problems. This sort of praxeological learning develops "in the course of being reflexive of ongoing events and changes of human lived experiences" (Hwang & Roth, 2005, p. 9), as well as part of realizing "possibilities inherent in lived experiences" (Hwang & Roth, 2005, p. 19).

## Communities as Intellectual Spaces

The notion of communities as intellectual spaces (CIS) is similar to funds of knowledge theories (González, Moll, & Amanti, 2005), as described in Chapter 1, that view households and families as rich storehouses of knowledge and skills that can be used to inform instructional content and practices within schools and educational institutions. The CIS concept grew out of discussions among a group of progressive scholars in a variety of areas, including community informatics, educational research, sociology, and Latin@ studies, as well as among community leaders and activists, who were engaged in community-based critical inquiry in the Humboldt Park/Paseo Boricua area in Chicago, Illinois. This group was interested in convening a forum for various individuals and community constituencies to come together and participate in dialogues related to relevant community issues. These discussions were meant to cut across disciplines and explore cultural, social, educational, and/or economic intersections of various issues. Dissatisfied with current approaches to describing community knowledge and inquiry, the group introduced the concept of community as intellectual space:

The concept of "community as intellectual space" is based on the premise that if individuals are to understand and create solutions for problems in complex systems, they need opportunities to engage with challenging problems, to learn through participative investigations, to have supportive, situated experiences, to express their ideas to others, and to make use of a variety of resources in multiple media.

The aim of communities as intellectual space is to bring people from all walks of life together to develop "critical, socially engaged intelligence, which enables individuals to understand and participate effectively in the affairs of their community in a collaborative effort to achieve a common good" [as quoted in John Dewey Project on Progressive Education, 2002]. ("Community as Intellectual Space: Preliminary Program," 2005, Symposium Overview, para. 2)

The CIS concept shares a lot in common with Antonio Gramsci's (1971) notion of organic intellectuals, which he positioned against traditional intellectuals trained in universities and mainstream educational institutions. In elaborating this concept, Gramsci was "arguing for a situation where all human beings are intellectual" (Radhakrishnan, 1987, p. 205), as well as outlining how "different sites of social practice can be transformed into sites of adult learning" (Mayo, 2007, p. 424). The organic intellectual that Gramsci (1971) describes is engaged in transformative education as a form of counterhegemonic activity and views education as a means for subverting the status quo and challenging oppressive social structures.

For those conducting CBQR, the CIS concept instructs researchers to recognize the capacity of communities to participate in collaborative and critical inquiry toward the amelioration of issues and conditions impacting their lives. It demands that researchers think in more nuanced ways about community knowledge and avoid viewing communities as monolithic and homogeneous entities composed of individuals with identical and uniform experiences and perspectives. The concept of CIS goes further than approaches that simply acknowledge or respect community knowledge and regard community members as capable of identifying issues and problems but as lacking in the type of intellect or skills to address these issues sufficiently. Rather, communities need to be recognized and embraced as sites of learning and often as "spaces of resistance" (Rinaldo, 2002) that regularly engage in counterhegemonic activity and counterstorytelling, where individuals draw from their experiences to provide an alternative narrative to mainstream and majoritarian narratives (Solórzano & Bernal, 2001). As part of CBQR projects, researchers need to integrate structured and situated forms of and opportunities for critical inquiry and discussion into the project, as well as ensure that multiple voices, experiences, and expertise are part of these dialogues.

## Engaged Learning

Central to any CBQR project is the notion of engaged learning, whereby learning occurs as part of authentic participation in "real-life" settings, which usually refers to settings outside of a typical classroom. Although there is not a common definition or sole theory/theorists associated with engaged learning, the concept is rooted in Vygotskian theories of social learning (Vygotsky, 1978), John Dewey's progressive philosophy of education (Dewey, 1916/2009), and experiential learning theories (Kolb, 1984). To provide some clarity, Stephen Bowen (2005) offers up a taxonomy that provides four ways of thinking about student engagement, particularly as related to college course work: "engagement with the learning process," "engagement with the object of study," "engagement with contexts," and "engagement with the human condition" (p. 4; Duster & Waters, 2006).

According to engaged learning theories, learning is more meaningful when it is connected with and practically applied to current activities and events; when learners are involved in collaborative learning activities and interactions with others; and when individuals have opportunities to be involved in projects that address and develop solutions to complex problems and issues. Engaged learning has become a central tenet of many university and college curricula and offerings as higher education institutions have often been faulted for being insulated from reality, offering decontextualized learning experiences, and lacking engagement with the communities that surround them. Within engaged learning, learners are viewed not as passive consumers of information but as active participants in creating new knowledge. Engaged learning theories are affiliated with instructional approaches such as small group work, service learning, and project-based learning.

Within CBQR studies, researchers serve as engaged learners at all steps of the process. Students involved in community-based studies have multiple opportunities to apply concepts toward understanding and addressing actual problems in authentic settings. Rather than learning about research methods "in a vacuum," students are acquiring research skills within ongoing research activities. Researchers involved in these projects are gaining knowledge about a variety of topics and issues through active participation in community projects and dialogue with community leaders, stakeholders, and residents, as well as those with expertise and firsthand experience related to these issues.

## Elements of Community-Based Qualitative Research

CBQR projects can take many forms, and certainly no formula exists for conducting a study. As we learned in the previous section, some guiding concepts should be attended to throughout the project. In addition, researchers should be mindful of how their project integrates certain essential elements, which are common to all CBQR studies. Although the research design, topics and issues addressed, data collection and analysis approaches, and day-to-day research activities of each project are unique and varied, some shared aspects differentiate these types of studies from other qualitative models. This section reviews some of these elements.

## Collaborative

CBQR studies are inherently collaborative, involving dialogue and debate among research and community partners. Authority within community-based projects is shared, and the viewpoints and contributions of all members are valued and sought through formal and informal means to inform the design and implementation of the project. A few guidelines for ensuring that projects are collaborative and that input from group members is integrated into all stages of the project are as follows:

- Research members are viewed and regarded as *equal partners* at all stages of the project; the distinct knowledge and skills of research group members are used to improve understanding of various dimensions of the topic under study.
- *Opportunities for discussion and dialogue* are provided throughout the project. Differences of opinion that will inevitably arise are not considered impediments or obstacles, but they are valued as helping to highlight the complexities of specific social and educational issues.
- *Leadership in the project is shared*, although it may be helpful to have one person designated to manage activities. Group members should be called on to share their expertise and oversee specific project elements. Decision-making processes should adhere to a consensus model, where all members of the group have the opportunity to voice their opinions and inform and influence decisions.

## Critical

Community-based qualitative researchers maintain a critical stance on the topics and issues they study. However, this does not mean that everyone working on the project must view the topic in the same way but that members must resist the urge to posit simplistic explanations to multifaceted issues and problems. Some principles that can help guide research group members in this critical process are listed as follows:

- *Challenge status-quo narratives* related to the topic under study; this requires that research group members question dominant discourses that often view individuals as solely responsible for their economic conditions and for social inequities, as well as shun deficit-oriented thinking related to low-income and minoritized families and communities.
- *Provide alternative voices* through processes of counterstorytelling (Solórzano & Bernal, 2001), which entails searching for and eliciting multiple perspectives related to the topic and examining how intersections of various factors and characteristics, such as race, gender, class, religion, sexual orientation, and/or age, function to shape individuals' perspectives and experiences.
- *Connect what is happening in local communities to larger societal conditions*, and investigate how broader policies, global events, and historical shifts impact conditions and resources available to community residents.

### Transformative

A primary goal of CBQR projects is to use findings to enact changes and make improvements in programs and policies related to the issue under study. In addition, projects aim to have an impact on perspectives and practices of research group members. Such transformations can be achieved by incorporating the following principles and practices into the project:

- Engage in *transformative pedagogies* where research group members have opportunities for teaching and learning at all levels. Learning and teaching should occur as part of a bidirectional process, where all research group participants are viewed as capable of both sharing expertise and acquiring new knowledge and skills.
- Bring about *changes in perspectives and practices of research group members*; participation in research projects and involvement in community settings should also lead to enhanced and amplified understandings of concepts relevant to the study.
- Be *action-oriented* throughout the project and remain conscious of the ways that research findings can contribute to improved conditions and resources for community members and community organizations involved with the project. As much as possible, projects should also focus efforts on developing products and materials that can be used by community partners after the project has officially ended.

## Community-Based Qualitative Research Models, Projects, and Initiatives

There is no "one way" to conduct community-based research projects. Some might take place as part of a formal study, such as funded research, or research for a dissertation or thesis project. More often, CBQR projects are undertaken through formalized university–community partnerships, through an institute or an initiative founded to conduct and promote this sort of research, or within college course work, where community-based research activities are integrated into course activities and assignments. This section outlines a few course-based models and share project examples that can help inform the design and implementation of CBQR studies.

### Description of Course Models

Many college courses, across social science disciplines at the undergraduate and graduate levels, include research and fieldwork experiences that involve students in working with community organizations and partners. Some courses might mandate that students complete fieldwork hours, whereas others could require that students compile a final community-based project. Projects might be conducted individually or as part of teams. Students might be exposed to particular community organizations or partners through presentation in class sessions or community visits; in some cases, students might be expected to identify a community institution with which to work. These types of community-based "add-ons" are part of an **experiential course-based model** to CBQR.

Another model is called the **immersive course-based model**, which exposes students to community resources, organizations, and issues. These courses are held within community settings, thus, facilitating multiple opportunities for students to be engaged with community residents. Class sessions might also include guest speakers from the community and/or scheduled fieldwork. This immersive model is much more intensive than the experiential approach because it includes the surrounding community as a classroom for the investigation of multiple issues.

## Project Examples

Each CBQR project is unique as it is developed in response to particular community interests, needs, and conditions. As the chapters that describe research design (Chapter 4) and data collection (Chapters 5–6) will demonstrate, a formula for how to conduct a project does not exist. A few examples of projects follow, which provide a sense of the range of possibilities for CBQR studies; these sample studies are drawn from actual studies completed for immersive course models and as part of partnership research.

### *Assessing Instructional Technology Resources*

Two doctoral students enrolled in an immersive summer community-based research course were interested in completing a project in the area of instructional technology with a focus on youth attending a local alternative school. They interviewed community leaders and youth about technology needs and talked to a teacher at the school about technology resources related to her teaching. They also mapped out community locations where technology resources were available to residents and youth. From these interviews and discussions, they found that students attending the school did not have regular access to computers and that they were primarily using smartphones for computing. They thus identified a need for support for students' use of web-based resources to conduct research for assignments, complete assignments, and manage and share projects. They developed training modules and job aids that could help students use technology resources more effectively, as well as helped teachers develop a site for an e-portfolio, which could assist seniors at the school in preparing, organizing, and submitting elements for their final senior portfolio, which was required for graduation. Although the collaborative project was able to create some concrete deliverables for the school, some challenges associated with this project included staff turnover and a shift in the focus of the senior portfolio. It is not uncommon in a CBQR project for the staff members that researchers are working with to leave the organization for another position as staff and teacher turnover in the intense, and often stressful, settings of community-based organizations and alternative schools can be high; pay and compensation are usually low in such organizations, leading to issues in retaining quality staff.

### Supporting Urban Agriculture and Science Initiatives

A doctoral student in adult and higher education who also held a position at a center dedicated to supporting the development and capacity of nonprofits and governmental agencies was enrolled in an immersive summer community-based research course and intrigued by the community's efforts in the area of urban agriculture. In 2006, a report identified the community as a food desert or as lacking in food security for its residents (Gallagher, 2006). Other research in the area of public health documented high rates of diabetes and obesity in the community (Whitman, Williams, & Shah, 2004). These reports spurred community efforts to establish community gardens; students at the school conducted their own research project and submitted a grant and received funding to build a greenhouse on the roof of the school. As part of her project, the doctoral student worked with the science teacher at the school to understand better how the teacher integrated hands-on science activities into instruction and how students were involved in community science projects, such as the greenhouse and the community garden. She regularly observed classes and met with the teacher, and helped organize visits to the school by university engineering professors and students who presented on their work in the area of solar and water energy in South Africa; she also planned visits by the students to campus for further discussions with engineering faculty and students. She identified grants that might help support the school's urban agriculture curriculum and projects. The project allowed the graduate student/researcher to gain insights into the implementation of project-based learning and how to use the surrounding community as a classroom for the application of science topics and the exploration of a variety of health and social issues. The project also enabled the initiation of some university–community partnerships and facilitated academic mentoring of high-school students, exposing them to postsecondary options in the area of science and engineering.

However, despite these successes, the researcher encountered some challenges, including difficulties in communicating with school staff; for example, one campus visit needed to be rescheduled at the last minute because of a school nonattendance day, an oversight on the part of the teacher that caused frustration for the graduate student/researcher who had spent considerable effort planning and coordinating events for the day. Some grants and requests for proposals that the researcher forwarded to school staff were not applied for due to time constraints. These sorts of issues can be pervasive in some projects, especially if community partners are overwhelmed by their current workload and do not have adequate time to devote to the research project. It is important at the outset of the project to establish procedures for communication and to ensure that the project is not an additional burden for community partners. It is also helpful to designate one person to be "in charge" of communication and scheduling, someone who can send out and follow up on e-mail messages, as well as make sure the deadlines are met.

### Intergenerational Mentorship and Advocacy for Young Mothers

A professor who had been conducting ethnographic research at a nearby community-based organization and grassroots alternative school wanted to build on some

High school students presenting their work in the area of urban agriculture to local educational leaders.

of her previous research findings from studies with young mothers attending the school to develop programming and initiatives that could further support this group. To this end, she met with the assistant principal of the school, who also oversaw the program for parents at the school. They identified a need for additional support and motivation for enrolled parents, particularly authentic mentors who have had similar experiences. They collaboratively designed and implemented an intergenerational mentorship program for young mothers at the school, which entailed recruiting program graduates to serve as mentors for current students. These mentors provide presentations to parents at the school that detail their familial and educational experiences, as well as share challenges they have faced as a young mother; mentors are also matched with a student whom they work with throughout the year, and they meet monthly with their mentee to offer additional support and encouragement. Sessions might entail simply going out to lunch and discussing postsecondary goals; mentees have also shadowed their mentor at their job or college site. Some sessions are more social in nature, involving a family outing to a local museum. Throughout the project, the academic researcher worked with the director to convene focus groups to gather insights from students related to what they were seeking in a mentor; they also elicited regular feedback from mentors regarding their work with their mentee. They developed and provided training for mentors, created program materials and handouts for mentorship sessions, and organized and oversaw program activities and events. The professor-researcher also applied for grants and funding to help provide financial support for the program; she received a sizable grant that allowed the program to provide stipends to mentors and funded training activities and family events. At the end of the school year, mentors and mentees were interviewed by another member of the research team, a doctoral student in clinical psychology concurrently completing a master's degree in educational research and who was conducting CBQR for her final project.

Young mothers involved in the Atabey mentorship program at graduation.

Since the mentorship project was ongoing when this text was published, challenges are still being assessed. However, throughout the initial year of the project, coordination of some mentor/mentorship sessions was problematic. School staff needed to provide ongoing follow-up with some mentees due to persistent communication issues; one mentee did not show up for a scheduled meeting, whereas a few others canceled sessions a few times. These inconsistencies are not surprising given the often turbulent lives of young mothers and the many responsibilities they are faced with; they often lack transportation resources and may not have regular access to a phone. Furthermore, some mentorship pairs "clicked" better than others. The research team provided orientation activities at the school site so that mentors and mentees could get to know one another in a group setting before meeting individually, but this did not always assure that individual sessions would be successful.

### Related Projects

The areas of community informatics and CBAR share much in common with CBQR and, thus, offer some other examples of projects that would be appropriate for the CBQR project. For example, Ann Peterson-Kemp's (formerly, Ann Peterson-Bishop) work in community librarianship spawned many projects in line with a community-based research approach; in collaboration with the Puerto Rican Cultural Center (PRCC) and Dr. Pedro Albizu Campos High School (PACHS) in Chicago, she helped develop several community-focused projects: youth attending PACHS were trained in cataloguing methods and helped catalog the PRCC's extensive library collection (Bishop & Molina, 2004); another project involved community activists and residents working with a graduate student from the University of Illinois to create a book-to-prisoners project that developed a procedure for sending books to incarcerated family members of local residents (Bishop & Bruce, 2009).

At DePaul University, students in Rosing's (2007) applied ethnography class conducted a study that involved community-based research at corner stores in the Austin neighborhood of Chicago. The project built on an existing university–community partnership in the area of food systems and work by a campus center focused on service learning (this initiative is described in the following section). Students conducted regular observations at local corner stores as a way of gaining insight into their function within the community, as well as "their distinct role in processes of social, economic, and racial inequality in the U.S." (Rosing, 2007, p. 3). Students also interviewed owners of the stores and prepared a final report that was shared with community partners. These projects "served as a means to inform and think critically about policy decision-making and grassroots efforts towards improving food access in a neighborhood that has long been underserved by the corporate retail sector" (p. 1).

## Initiatives

Many CBQR projects are supported by institutional centers and initiatives that can provide important and essential instructional and financial resources. Although many such initiatives exist—and the number is growing—some that standout as exemplary in the field are described as follows.

### IRWIN W. STEANS CENTER FOR COMMUNITY-BASED SERVICE LEARNING AND COMMUNITY SERVICE STUDIES, DEPAUL UNIVERSITY, CHICAGO, IL

The Steans Center grew out of the Office of Community-based Service Learning, which was founded in 1998. The center takes an interdisciplinary approach to academic service learning through the establishment of collaborative community partnerships with organizations across Chicago, as well as in other locales (for example, students studying abroad have been able to engage in community-based research with local organizations, such as nongovernmental organizations [NGOs], in Merida, Mexico). The mission of the center, as stated on its website, is to develop "mutually beneficial relationships with community organizations to engage DePaul

*(Continued)*

(Continued)

students in educational opportunities grounded in Vincentian values of respect for human dignity and the quest for social justice" (https://steans.depaul.edu/About/IrwinWSteans/Mission). The types of collaborative learning that they offer to the student, and to partnering organizations, encompass the following types: direct service, where students provide direct services, such as tutoring, to the organization; project-based service, which involves student in a direct effort that "results in a tangible product" of use to the organizations at the end of the project, such as a website or strategic plan; community-based research, where students contribute to an organization's research efforts; and advocacy, which entails students participating in ongoing campaigns "addressing critical social, economic and political issues in Chicago and internationally."

The center has received recognition for its work with the Puerto Rican Cultural Center from the Jimmy and Rosalynn Carter Partnership Award and The Washington Center for Internships and Academic Seminars' Civic Engagement Award. The center also provides faculty fellowships to support faculty projects and facilitate the integration of community-based research into their courses. In addition, they offer a minor in community-service studies.

## INSTITUTE FOR COMMUNITY RESEARCH, HARTFORD, CT

The Institute for Community Research, or ICR, was founded in 1987 by Jean S. Schensul as a nonprofit research institute "to develop research partnerships" and conduct applied and action research with communities and organizations in New England and beyond" (http://www.incommunityresearch.org). The ICR's website specifies that the institute employs 40 full- and part-time staff, including youth researchers, professional researchers, and community professionals. The mission of the ICR is to conduct "research in collaboration with community partners to promote justice and equity in a diverse, multiethnic, multicultural world." It works to support community-based research partnerships and to conduct a variety of forms of research to address complex issues, promote positive changes, and help communities "access resources and develop the skills needed to direct and control their own futures."

The types of research that are conducted by the ICR include basic research, intervention research, participatory action research, and cultural conservation and development. Projects have covered topics such as HIV/AIDS risk and infection patterns, depression among older persons, and sexual identity and support of lesbian, gay, bisexual, transgender, and queer (LGBTQ) youth. The ICR has developed training materials for its community-based PAR approach with a focus on work with youth and girls. In 1996, the ICR created the Youth Action Research Institute (YARI), which emerged from its previous work on youth-led action research. The institute provides training to youth in ethnography-based action research, as well as support for their development of research projects for investigating issues of importance to their lives. YARI also works with teachers and other educational practitioners to help them integrate action research methods into their instruction and programming.

The ICR has received funding from private foundations and federal grants to support research projects, and it has been recognized as leader in the field of collaborative and participatory research. Researchers and community partners have published research articles, reports, and training materials; presented work at conferences; and convened and hosted forums, youth summits, and exhibits devoted to a variety of issues and topics, from youth drinking to Bosnian weaving.

## COMMUNITY INFORMATICS, GRADUATE SCHOOL OF LIBRARY AND INFORMATION SCIENCE, UNIVERSITY OF ILLINOIS, URBANA–CHAMPAIGN, IL (UIUC)

The field of community informatics (CI) seeks to explore and understand how "communities access, create, organize, and share information" as well as examine "the types and qualities of connections between and among communities" (http://www.lis.illinois.edu/academics/degrees/specializations/ci). At UIUC, a certificate in CI provides graduate students and faculty in the area of library and information sciences the opportunity to engage in CI course work and research within community settings through various partnerships with organizations in East St. Louis, Missouri; Chicago, Illinois; North Champaign, Illinois; and rural Illinois, as well as in West Africa. The program takes a project-centered approach, which "helps students apply what they are studying to real-world situations that involve community partners in meeting local needs." Students also can develop sustained relationships with community partners, continuing projects after course work has ended.

Students enroll in core course work in CI, as well as complete electives on topics such as community engagement, civic entrepreneurship, and social justice in the information professions. They conduct collaborative projects with community members and other students and faculty that focus on the development of information services and networks that can meet the diverse needs of a wide range of community partners. One particular project that emerged from this CI work was the development and use of software tools to create community inquiry labs, or ilabs, which could help community residents and leaders collaborate with researchers and students across spaces, and address particular issues and concerns (Bishop & Bruce, 2009). A particular initiative that has emerged from the CI program has been the Youth Community Inquiry (YCI) project, which involves work with youth in diverse underserved communities (Bruce, Bishop, & Budhathoki, 2014). Through various projects, youth conduct research, develop podcasts, produce video documentaries, and use GIS/GPS technologies to examine and address a multitude of social issues.

## THE PUBLIC SCIENCE PROJECT, THE GRADUATE CENTER OF THE UNIVERSITY OF NEW YORK. NEW YORK, NY

The Public Science Project (PSP), directed by María Elena Torre and Michelle Fine, was borne out of decades of PAR work at the City University of New York (CUNY) and has tackled a range of issues, from heteronormative violence to educational inequity, through the design and implementation of research meant to push at the boundaries of existing power hierarchies and challenge status quo explanations of inequality. Initially organized as the PAR collective, the PSP brings together diverse groups of individuals and stakeholders—youth, activists, community leaders, elders—to impart knowledge and challenge one another within the inquiry and research process. Although the PSP uses both qualitative and quantitative methods, and is most associated with PAR/YPAR designs, its projects possess many elements of CBQR. Projects are deeply rooted in the community and often situated within schools and community-based organizations; most projects have diverse and robust advisory boards composed of community members, youth, elders, and activists that help ensure that researchers and projects are "accountable to the needs and desires of local communities" (http://publicscienceproject.org/about/history/).

The project hosts a series of methods camps and seminars to share knowledge and experiences and "develop a shared critical language of social theory, feminist theory, critical race theory and methodology" (http://publicscienceproject.org/about/history/). Participants immerse themselves in appropriate and relevant readings, and they collaboratively develop research questions and identify appropriate methods and approaches for data collection and analysis. These approaches include in-depth interviews, participant observation, web-based research, slam books, focus groups, and problem identification webs. One PSP research project, The Fed Up Honeys (described in Chapter 1), involved young women on the lower east side of New York City in examining and challenging stereotypes about women that proliferated in their neighborhood. Another project collaborated with youth pushed out of their high school to examine the politics of the GED. The Morris Justice Project brought together mothers within a community in the Bronx, New York, along with other community members who were concerned with the unjust policing of their sons, to investigate and document community members' experiences with the police and challenge discriminatory policing policies and practices (http://morris justice.org/research-b). The PSP's studies and projects have resulted in numerous publications and other products, such as manuals, "back-pocket" guides, curricula, presentations, and ad campaigns. Details and findings from various projects are featured on the PSP's website.

The PSP also offers summer institutes in critical participatory action research, aimed at graduate students, scholars, and members of community-based organizations and designed to introduce participants to the theory, practice, and ethics of critical PAR to help them integrate it into their scholarship and organizing. PSP projects and activities receive funding from a variety of sources, including local and national foundations.

*[handwritten top margin: integrate students with Puerto-Rican culture/events in the community]*

## PASEO BORICUA RESEARCH GROUP/COURSE, NORTHERN ILLINOIS UNIVERSITY, DEKALB, IL/CHICAGO, IL

The Paseo Boricua Research Group (PBRG) grew out of my own effort to provide immersive community-based research experiences to my graduate students. By building on my existing relationship with The Puerto Rican Cultural Center, located in Humboldt Park, Chicago—where I had worked as a practitioner, researcher, and activist—in 2008, I offered a summer research course at the PRCC. This course provided students with the opportunity to conduct ethnographic fieldwork in a variety of community settings, including a café, a newspaper, an aerobics program, and an Afro-Caribbean music group, to understand better the processes of knowledge and skill acquisition at each site (Johnson, Stribling, Almburg, & Vitale, 2015). In addition to completing fieldwork at a particular site, students were introduced to community programs and organizations; interacted with local residents, community leaders, and youth; and participated in various community settings and activities, such as the annual Puerto Rican parade. They interviewed community leaders and key personnel and participants at each site. In class sessions, discussions focused not only on what they were learning at each site but also on their roles as researchers within the community. After the class officially ended, students wanted to continue some of their work and presented their experiences as researchers at an urban ethnography conference in Philadelphia, Pennsylvania.

*[handwritten right margin: Not just research → also participation]*

The course continued to be offered in subsequent summers, and over the years, the focus of the class shifted to include more participatory approaches and the development of research projects that could foster reciprocal research relationships with the community and community-based organizations. Of particular interest were the ways that graduate students in the course could support the community's efforts and work with youth. Enrolled students participated in discussion groups with community youth to learn about their experiences and challenges, as well as interviewed teachers and practitioners who regularly work with community youth. Students then worked individually or in teams to develop proposals and projects that addressed topics relevant to youth such as community engagement, social-emotional learning, transitions to postsecondary educational and professional activities, and intergenerational mentorship. *[handwritten: Paying attention to a community's specific needs and then gethe research to help address them]*

Students were encouraged to continue their involvement with their projects after the class through volunteer activities and opportunities to enroll in an independent study to implement projects. Each year, a few students enrolled in the class joined a group, called the Paseo Boricua Research Group, which sought to document course activities and successes and understand better the design and delivery of course work in community-based research. In 2012, this group conducted a series of focus groups with former students, which has resulted in two article manuscripts and numerous presentations at national and local conferences.

© Elias Carmona

Photo of "Sea of Flags," a mural by local artist Gamaliel Ramirez, on Paseo Boricua, Chicago.

## Chapter Summary

This chapter reviewed the core concepts and key characteristics of CBQR. We learned about how concepts such as praxis, communities as intellectual spaces, and engaged learning inform the design and implementation of community-based research activities and projects. We also became aware of important elements within CBQR and learned that to be in line with a community-based approach, projects must be collaborative, critical, and transformative for all partners involved in the project. This chapter also provided examples of projects that use a community-based qualitative approach and of institutional initiatives and programs that support the design and implementation of community-based qualitative projects and that purvey ongoing training to those interested in conducting such research, including graduate students, faculty, youth, and community partners.

## Key Terms

Experiential course-based
    model  27

Immersive course-based
    model  27

# ● Activities for Reflection and Discussion   *seeking to understand*

1) Evaluate the sample projects described here by using some of the core concepts detailed at the beginning the chapter. How did the project embody principles of praxis? In what ways was the project mindful of the notion of communities as intellectual spaces? How did the project demonstrate engaged learning? Could you also apply these concepts to a project you are currently involved in?

2) Consider a memorable learning activity in terms of the elements and attributes of community-based qualitative research projects and activities. How was it collaborative, critical, and/or transformative?

3) For a project you are interested in conducting, reflect on how you will integrate core concepts into design and list key collaborative, critical, and transformative activities that will be included as part of the project. See Handout 2.

4) Examine the institutional websites from some of the initiatives described in this chapter. What information is included about the history and background of the initiative? What sorts of details are provided about the design, implementation, and findings of particular projects and studies? How are the voices and perspectives of community partners highlighted?

# HANDOUT 2
# CBQR Core Concepts and Elements (Example)

| | Design | Data Collection and Analysis | Dissemination/ Write-Up |
|---|---|---|---|
| Praxis | | | Use research to address social problems and issues |
| Communities as intellectual spaces | Researchers attend community events; identify skills and knowledge | | |
| Engaged learning | | Research activities take place in authentic settings in the community | |
| Collaborative | Develop research questions collaboratively | • Develop interview questions with groups of teachers and staff<br><br>• Conduct interviews as teams<br><br>• Analyze data in teams | |
| Critical | | Researchers connect findings to larger structural factors and conditions | |
| Transformative | | Provide opportunities for discussion and reflection of how research has transformed researchers' points of view and perspectives | Use findings to create new programs |

# HANDOUT 2
## CBQR Core Concepts and Elements

| | Design | Data Collection and Analysis | Dissemination/ Write-Up |
|---|---|---|---|
| Praxis | | | |
| Communities as intellectual spaces | | | |
| Engaged learning | | | |
| Collaborative | | | |
| Critical | | | |
| Transformative | | | |

# The Role of the Researcher in Community-Based Qualitative Research

## Introduction

This chapter discusses issues related to researcher role, positionality, and ethics within CBQR, a type of research in which the role of the researcher is highly involved. Community-based qualitative researchers are not working with existing data sets, like many researchers conducting large-scale quantitative research studies, but are seeking to conduct research in concert and collaboration with community organizations, leaders, and residents, and thus, they need to build productive and communicative relationships with various individuals and **stakeholders**. This section focuses on issues related to the background and role of the researcher and how to be mindful of these issues at all stages of the research process. Reflections are used to illustrate the importance of researchers conducting community-based research to examine and interrogate their background and be reflexive throughout the research process. This chapter also discusses ethical concerns and issues related to conducting research within community settings.

## Learning Objectives

After reading this chapter, students will be able to:

1. Recognize and better understand the importance of researcher background, positionality, and self-reflexivity within all stages of community-based qualitative research (CBQR) studies.

2. Identify different forms of privilege, and explain how these figure into the process of building rapport and relationships with research co-participants.

3. Examine general ethical issues and concerns related to conducting research with human subjects and the more specific ethical issues and responsibilities entailed in collaborative and participatory community-based studies.

4. Describe certain characteristics and various roles of community-based qualitative researchers, and indicate why these are important to the implementation of a CBQR project.

# Examining Our Own Background, Experiences, Assumptions, and Biases

At the outset of a community-based research project, it is essential for researchers to examine their backgrounds and perspectives—often referred to as **positionality**—as our personal, educational, and professional experiences greatly inform our viewpoints on a host of issues and phenomena, often including the ones that are the focus of our research. We all possess particular lenses and ways of viewing the world, and to approach the research process as if we are value-neutral does a disservice to our research, to community residents and research participants, and to ourselves. For example, our upbringing and family background impart us with particular values that may or may not align with others with whom we are collaborating as part of the research project. Factors and characteristics such as race, class, gender, sexual orientation, religious affiliation, and age all play a central role in shaping our identities, as well as in how we orient toward the communities in which we conduct research and the topics we choose to study. In addition to these background characteristics, our educational and professional backgrounds and experiences are integral in the formation of various beliefs and notions, such as how individuals best learn and what it means to be a good worker. For example, those who work in fields such as medicine might be accustomed to diagnosing, and then curing or fixing, problems or ailments, and they could enter a community with that diagnostic and interventionist mindset, which may or may not be welcomed or appropriate. Individuals who have been educated or have worked in a highly structured or hierarchical environment might be less comfortable in educational and professional settings where learning takes place *in situ*—or on site and less formally—or where authority is shared rather than top-down.

This process, of reflecting on one's background and positionality and how it figures into research, is referred to as **reflexivity**: It "is a process that challenges the researcher to explicitly examine how his or her research agenda and assumptions, subject location(s), personal beliefs, and emotions enter into their research" (Hsiung, 2008, p. 212). Different than quantitative research projects, in which there has "long been a tendency to view the self of the social science observer as a potential contaminant, something to be separated out, neutralized, minimized, standardized, and controlled" (Weis & Fine, 2000, p. 34), in qualitative research, reflexivity is an integral part of the research process. Because the qualitative researcher is also the instrument and is responsible for building rapport with participants, conducting interviews so as to elicit participants' distinct experiences and narratives, and making interpretations from data, researchers need to be reflexive at all stages of the research process. Lois Weis and Michelle Fine (2000) have referred to the act of thorough self-reflexivity as "flexing our reflexivities" and have stated that it helps researchers avoid hiding "behind the alleged cloak of neutrality" (p. 34). Others have referred to this process as "disciplined subjectivity" or "the practice of rigorous self-reflection about one's own preferences, prejudices, hopes, and concerns" (Erickson, 1986; LeCompte, Schensul, Weeks, & Singer, 1999, p. 66). Such reflexivity is especially important in community-based research, where the goal is for academic researchers to work collaboratively with community members and build reciprocal research relationships. Strategies for encouraging self-reflexivity throughout the project include creating checklists of assumptions and hunches and maintaining reflective logs and journals (LeCompte et al., 1999).

Our understandings related to background, education, and work are often taken-for-granted beliefs that have remained unchallenged throughout our lifetimes, especially if one has lived and worked in a relatively homogenous and monolithic environment, where family members, peers, and colleagues share many of our beliefs and values. When students and novice researchers prepare to conduct research in an unfamiliar environment, or one that does not "look like" where they live and work, they often experience anxiety and unease. For example, the initial few years that I offered my summer research course in Humboldt Park—an area located on the near northwest side of Chicago and inhabited mostly by Puerto Ricans/Latinos and African Americans—prior to the start of class, many students who hailed from suburban and rural areas sent me e-mails inquiring about their safety. Their perspective on the area was often informed by negative media images and portrayals of Humboldt Park as dangerous and gang infested. One student, a Caucasian woman in her 50s from a rural town who had never taken public transportation, arranged for her husband to drive her on the first day. Another student, Diana, who lived in a more affluent Chicago neighborhood, organized a carpool for fellow students who lived in the suburbs. In the following excerpt, a student discussed her initial fears about the community and about how the perspectives of family members informed some of her views:

So I grew up in . . . a nearby suburb, and as a family we would come into the city a lot but more downtown and touristy kinds of things and museums. I live in the West Loop so I don't live too far from Humboldt Park. And I've actually spent a lot of time in the Wicker Park area just east of Western and had lots of people who were either looking for apartments or just making recommendations about the area say, "well it's safe up until Western. You don't want to go west of Western." That's just something that you hear a lot. . . . So again, it's like there's just in my mind a geographical boundary where, I guess I kind of felt comfortable because people made a statement like, this is an appropriate place for someone like you to be. No one actually said that but that's the message I got. . . . But probably one of the biggest things for me was my husband's family, so both my husband's mother and father grew up in Humboldt Park. They both lived on Division Street . . . their experience was that the area was very safe at one point when it was mostly European immigrants and then their perception is that the neighborhood became very unsafe and dangerous and that their properties were worth less money as more people from Puerto Rico came into the area. And so I knew mostly about Humboldt Park through, frankly, some of their prejudices.

Another student, a reading specialist, shared her expectation for the research class, that she would teach "underprivileged" children to read:

I prepared myself for my journey into the "foreign neighborhood" as many would . . . reflecting on all the things that the people there did NOT have that my family and I were fortunate enough to enjoy daily. *otherizing → Focus of differences / prejudice*

One year, two students in the course one year were nurses interested in community health issues, who entered the community with the intention of conducting a needs assessment; initially, this orientation toward assessment and deficiencies kept them from exploring some of the existing initiatives in the area of community health and wellness.

Reflecting on our experiences and their relationship to our research settings and participants does not mean merely focusing on differences. Although, as mentioned, there may be many areas of divergence between academic researchers and participants in community-based research projects, there are often as many similarities and points of connection. In taking stock of one's background, researchers should be wary of the danger of "**otherizing**" and focusing solely on differences (Abu-Lughod, 1993; Fine, 1994). In addition to explicitly identifying the ways that your experiences might set you apart from potential research partners, it is as important to reflect on possible intersections with your experiences and viewpoints, related to characteristics such as gender, life experience, family status, religion, and sexual orientation, so that "we may be better able to perceive similarities in all of our lives" (Abu-Lughod, 1993, p. 27). Several students who have enrolled in summer research classes I have instructed grew up in the community, or in similar communities in Chicago, and were thus interested in taking the course to integrate their formative experiences in the community with their new roles as graduate students and academic scholars; some have explicitly stated a desire to "give back" to their respective communities and acquire ideas and models that can inform their community work. Other students have discovered unexpected and surprising connections to their autobiographies and identities. For example, one student, Nicole, realized that her new husband had grown up in the area where she was now conducting research. She reflected on this realization and the insight it provided her on her husband's experiences: "That was a big part of him that I didn't know. And so . . . just having this recognition in this community of someone I'm now sharing my life with that before, I just wasn't aware of some of those things." Another student, a Puerto Rican male who had grown up in the neighborhood, shared some of the pejorative and pessimistic messages related to his chances for success that he received as a student at the local high school. Now enrolled in a master's program at the university where I teach, he enrolled in the class as a chance not only to fulfill elective requirements for graduation but also to do something for his community.

Another student, an African American woman who had grown up on the south side of Chicago, described how the Puerto Rican parade reminded her of an event in her neighborhood:

> During the Puerto Rican People's Parade the atmosphere along Division Street was electric. I was quickly reminded of summers I spent as a child in on Chicago's South Side at the *Bud Billiken Back to School Parades* held each year in the African American community. It was evident that the residents of the Humboldt Park community were anticipating something special and I was eager to witness the parade. Before the parade I strolled down Division Street, this time on foot, and had the opportunity to mingle with the residents of the community. I met Juan, a Puerto Rican man who made me laugh heartily with his quick wit and comparisons of James Brown dance techniques and traditional Puerto Rican salsa. Juan "schooled" me about the connections between the African-American and Puerto Rican communities. His lesson was about not only dance technique but of historical solidarity and bloodlines. I met members of an Afro-Caribbean dance studio who were warm and eager to share their knowledge of Afro-Caribbean music and dance and invited me to enjoy the parade from the front of their shop. Additionally, they gave me a quick run-down of the events of the day and the best places to eat traditional Puerto Rican food. Humboldt Park felt like home to me . . . I met people I would have never met had I come back to Chicago and travelled to my familiar South side and West side neighborhoods.

This student's reflections demonstrate how she was able to forge links with members of the community; although she initially assumed she would have nothing in common with community residents, during the parade, she discovered points of connection with various aspects of her identity—in addition to discovering ties to her ethnic identity, she took photos of Puerto Rican youth with Gay Pride flags that resonated with her identity as a lesbian. Her experiences illustrate the many roles and identities we take with us into a community-based research project and how we can be both an insider and an outsider relative to our research topics, settings, and participants. **Insiders** are those that have a preexisting relationship with the community or

© Elias Carmona

Participants in the Puerto Rican People's Parade, Chicago, Illinois.

institution in which they are conducting research, or that share significant commonalities with research participants. On account of this insider status, these individuals often possess "local knowledge" or **emic** understandings of the setting and relevant issues (Cochran-Smith & Lytle, 1992; Geertz, 1973; LeCompte et al., 1999). In contrast, **outsiders** are not familiar with the setting prior to conducting the research and have little to nothing in common with the participants; outsider perspectives have often been referred to as **etic**. However, instead of viewing the insider/outsider role as a dichotomous binary, many researchers have instead advocated for viewing our role as situated along a series of insider–outsider continua (Hellawell, 2006). In other words, rather than labeling the researcher as either insider or outsider, it is more instructive to reflect on the ways we are both insiders and outsiders relative to our settings, a view that acknowledges the multifaceted nature of our identities and the varied textures and characteristics of the communities within and with which we do research. As David Hellawell (2006) points out, this insider–outsider continuum is fluid and dynamic, and "the same researcher can slide along more than one insider-outsider continuum, and in both directions, during the research process" (p. 489).

In the following excerpt, an international student from Taiwan reflected on her multiple layers of identity at different points of her study:

"Where are you going?" The taxi driver, a man with black-grey hair and wrinkled face, asked me in an Asian accent. "Please drive me to Division and California, the Puerto

Rican Cultural Center," I said. "Do you speak Spanish, Miss?" "No!" I laughed. The taxi driver: "So why do you go there?" I answered him: "There is a festival today." This was June 13, 2008, Friday afternoon on the West Side of Chicago: An outsider of Puerto Rican community (me) being challenged by another outsider (the taxi driver). There are indeed assumptions of linking the language with culture, race and territory. My research experience with *Bomba* musicians has led me to rethink the relationships among language, ethnicity, community and identity.

As a Taiwanese student in the United States for a few years, I have traveled through several cities and states but have never been in this area of the Chicago. Both the native Puerto Rican community and Humboldt Park/Puerto Rican community seemed remote to my native culture. Was I a sensitive tourist/outsider who was curious and interested in everything, an eager student wanting to learn the music of *Bomba*, or a researcher who took on a mission to make sense of cultural practice in this community? Being a mixture of all these roles during this research project pushed me out of my comfort zone. Not only because I had to filter through several cultural layers to understand the context of Chicago's Humboldt Park Community, but also to change my habit from passive observation to active participation.

This student's reflection illustrates how researchers conducting community-based research studies often initially grapple with their sense of belonging within a community, as well as how they might have to contend with others' narrow and limited

© Elias Carmona

Musicians at a Bombazo or Afro-Caribbean music event/performance.

understandings of a particular community (for example, that one needs to speak Spanish to have a reason to visit). Part of the challenges this student also faced involved examining her purposes for conducting research and interrogating her orientation toward the setting. These are important reflective processes for all community-based researchers to engage in throughout their research projects.

## "Check Your Privilege": Being Mindful of Race, Class, Gender, and Other Advantages

As prospective community-based researchers reflect on their backgrounds and assumptions, it is vital to be critical of how our backgrounds and experiences are related to larger social and economic conditions and systems that often privilege some characteristics and backgrounds at the expense of others. For example, the legacy of slavery and long history of racism in the United States has disadvantaged African Americans, while affording certain advantages to Whites, what Peggy McIntosh (1998) has referred to as an "invisible package of unearned assets" (p. 188). Throughout U.S. history, various groups of immigrants have also been discriminated against and systematically exploited in ways that have advantaged others. In her seminal piece on White privilege, McIntosh (1998) reflects that she "had been taught about racism as something which puts others at a disadvantage, but had been taught not to see one of its corollary aspects, white privilege" (p. 188) and how it put her at an advantage. She encourages other Whites to reflect on a list of conditions and factors that purvey advantages in their daily lives, such as being able to be sure that people of their race are represented positively in the media and that curricular materials reflect their race.

Although **White skin privilege** has been the focus of much of the writing about privilege, there are many other forms of privilege and advantages that researchers may possess, and they are often much less visible than Whiteness, including, but not limited to, gender, class, educational level, sexual orientation, language, and religion. Many community members whom I have worked with as part of the summer research class I instruct in Humboldt Park have been clear that when outside researchers and college students enter the community to do work or conduct research, they become conscious of their privilege, what they refer to as "checking your privilege." **Checking privilege** is akin to the aforementioned idea of examining what might be in our "backpack" of advantages. Community members who have interacted with college students and researchers have recommended that any sense of superiority or feelings of expertise on the part of the student or researcher be left behind or "checked" at the outset of entering the community and then constantly revisited throughout the project. One community member, who works closely with youth, drew on her experiences as a community resident who has had to confront stereotypes of Latinos/as and youth as she proffered advice for outsiders for working respectfully in the community:

> Understand that we are educated and are able to understand the issues with our community . . . we [as Latino/a youth] have an opportunity to learn things differently

because we understand things differently and [for researchers] to understand that it is not the same for everybody.

Checking privilege requires the researcher to respect and value all voices and opinions and to acknowledge the privilege that may come with his or her skin color. One community member described it this way:

Just be willing to, like, check your privilege . . . and realize that there are people here that don't have what you have. You can be a part of it if you want. Just be open to what we have to offer.

Some have also described White students and researchers entering a low-income community of color with "White knight" syndrome or the belief that they will swoop in to "save" the downtrodden. This sort of missionary standpoint assumes that there are no existing resources in the community or that residents need—or even want—the help and assistance of outsiders. Community members suggest an alternative to the "White knight" that involves being aware of extant community resources, ideologies, and interests, as well as being conscious of your purposes for conducting research in the community and being amenable to others questioning or challenging you about your role. As one community member stated, "[Y]ou have to be able and open to have discussions about your participation. What you want to do here. What you want to get out of it."

Checking one's privilege also means supporting the daily work and life of the community, often in small ways. One community member exhorted those interested in conducting research in the community also to "lend a hand" and engage in small, everyday tasks that might be considered "menial" and not directly related to the research task at hand. For example, students in my summer research class have helped with cleanup at a community festival and distributed community papers with youth. This sort of work should never be viewed as "beneath" the academic researcher but as part and parcel of any community-based research project. First and foremost, participating in everyday community work helps an academic researcher gain insight into community life, as well as to build relationships with residents. It also communicates to community members that the researcher values and respects the community beyond just how it might serve as a site for research. And, especially important in a collaborative research project, engaging in everyday work and tasks alongside community members helps break down any existing power relationships between academic researchers and community residents, and it promotes more equitable and reciprocal partnerships. I encourage students in my summer research classes to attend various community events, in addition to those that are part of class, and frequent area restaurants and businesses (in fact, going out for lunch at local cafes is a mandatory part of fieldwork). This involvement also helps researchers identify issues and concerns of importance to the community. One community member articulated her expectations for those interested in working on the community:

To be involved with what the community does. Because I have seen a lot of people who come here to do work and have agendas, but they are not willing to engage in the small things that we do here. So if you are here in the community to do research here. Go to events. Talk to people . . . and just be willing, to like, give your time. That's really what I expect. It's giving of your time, to be active in the community. Lend a hand. That's really what I expect.

## Characteristics of Community-Based Qualitative Researchers

Although anyone can conduct community-based research, it is certainly not for everyone. To undertake such a project, and implement it genuinely and successfully, the best-suited researchers have certain recommended traits and characteristics. A group of students who completed my summer community-based research course led focus groups with other students who had enrolled in the course, in which they shared some of their experiences in the course, and discussed the qualities of community-based researchers. One of the most prominent characteristics mentioned was the need to be *open-minded.* Students and researchers who enter a community with fixed and intransigent notions of community, research, and learning will have a difficult time taking in new ideas and information. To build successful and productive relationships with community members and institutions, one must be willing to step out of one's existing comfort zone and be open to new experiences and ways of viewing the world. Furthermore, particularly as related to the design and implementation of research projects, researchers must be prepared to confront "unknowns" as there is often not a clear path for these sorts of projects. Thus, the research process can be riddled with anxiety for some, especially those who are used to research that begins with a hypothesis and follows a predetermined and unwavering plan for data collection and analysis. In courses that use a community-based research model, students who are used to prescriptive assignments or rigid rubrics might feel uncomfortable not being given a distinct direction for research and allowing topics and issues to emerge from participation in a community setting or through dialogue with community members. One student in my summer research class discussed her experiences in the course with other students:

I think the biggest thing for me is to have students be open to the experience. . . . that first day, you know you don't really know exactly what it is that you're going to, you know what your research interests are, but you really don't know how you're going to incorporate that or what you're going to do, but I think that being open to the experience is really key. I hear so many people talking about, just in this group about the challenges or the apprehension that you had coming in to the class but the fact that you were open to the experience I think really led to success in the class and so that would be my major point of advice from the beginning is just to be open to what, what the class can bring, to be willing to experience it, even though you don't really know what the outcome is.

Because of the emergent nature of community-based qualitative research (CBQR) projects, it is also advantageous if researchers are *flexible*. Many times, an initial idea for a research project might emerge and then need to be changed due to shifting participant interests or priorities. Or maybe an initial line of inquiry does not pan out and another topic materializes as more salient or timely. Furthermore, since community-based research does not always adhere to conventional norms of research, a certain amount of *creativity* is useful, especially as it relates to developing innovative methods for recruitment, data collection, and dissemination. For example, researchers might need to identify participants and co-researchers at parks, local stores, or salons, or through social media, rather than at traditional educational institutions. To engage youth in projects, forms of popular culture and expression, such as hip-hop and spoken word, and social media might be used to collect data and to share research findings. Related to the notion of being aware of one's positionality and checking one's privilege discussed in previous sections, it is also important that community-based researchers employ *nonjudgmental* attitudes and a *humble* demeanor.

In the area of nursing and health education, there has been attention called to the need to develop **cultural competence** among those individuals preparing to provide care to an "increasingly multilingual and multicultural U.S. population" (Mendias & Guevara, 2001, p. 256). Some researchers have also applied this notion of cultural competence to research and scholarship in the area of health and medicine, and they have developed criteria for evaluating research as culturally competent (Meleis, 1996), as well as for measuring cultural competence among practitioners (Geron, 2002). Aspects of cultural competence that are instructive for community-based qualitative researchers include an "awareness of identity and power differentials" and a sensitivity to context and divergent communication styles (Meleis, 1996; Mendias & Guevara, 2001, p. 256). Those in the field of teacher education have articulated the notion of culturally responsive teaching and pedagogy, which is defined as "using the cultural characteristics, experiences, and perspectives of ethnically diverse students as conduits for teaching them more effectively" (Gay, 2002, p. 106). In this sense, being culturally responsive means possessing rich and expansive cultural knowledge and being able to engage in appropriate cross-cultural communication (Gay, 2002). Although these traits and characteristics were developed to help promote culturally competent care and teaching, these can certainly also be employed to foster culturally competent community-based researchers.

## Researcher Ethics and Responsibilities

This section reviews and discusses ethical issues entailed in conducting CBQR with a focus on the ethical responsibilities of the community-based researcher and how those engaging in this type of research can address and negotiate institutional requirements for research. The section ends with a description and discussion of various roles and stances that community-based researchers might adopt within the research project.

## Institutional Review Boards and Informed Consent

As novice and seasoned academic researchers, we are accustomed to discussions of research ethics, usually related to institutional review board (IRB) approval and informed consent procedures. **Institutional review boards** are groups at colleges and universities and other institutions where research is conducted (such as school districts and prisons) tasked with reviewed research protocols to ensure that they follow ethical research procedures, in particular, those related to treatment of human subjects. **Informed consent** is the process whereby researchers obtain approval from individuals, often referred to as "subjects," to participate in the study. Basic elements of informed consent include a statement of research purposes and goals, what participants will be expected to do (such as participate in an interview), any potential risks and/or benefits to participants, and a disclosure that participation is voluntary and participants might withdraw at any time. These procedures were enacted largely in response to egregious treatment of vulnerable populations by researchers, most notably and infamously, the Tuskegee Syphilis Study, an experiment that took place from 1932 to 1972 in the United States, under the auspices of the U.S. Public Health Service, in which African American men living in the rural South were uninformed that they had the disease, and not treated for it, even though penicillin was developed during the study period (Heller, 1972). As a result of the lack of treatment, many of the study's subjects died, and men transmitted the disease to their partners, many of whom gave birth to children with congenital syphilis. In 1979, the Belmont Report was created to offer direction for researchers on "ethical principles and guidelines for the protection of human subjects of research." These guidelines pay special attention to the treatment of vulnerable populations within research and were accompanied by the Common Rule, which established consistent federal policies and regulations for agencies and institutions.

## Representational Issues:
## Ethical Injunctions and Responsibilities

Although IRBs provide important ethical oversight to academic researchers, many scholars have spotlighted other, more informal, ethical responsibilities of the researcher, what some have referred to as "good manners" (LeCompte et al., 1999, pp. 64–65). Weis and Fine (2000) have referred to the ethical challenges as "speed bumps":

> Our bumps range from finding our political investments and identities nestled too intimately inside the narratives of men and women whom we have interviewed, to the troubles of gaining ethics approval from committees seemingly more concerned with institutional liability than the work at hand to the struggle of (co)constructing narratives that challenge—rather than reproduce—dominant discourses. (pp. 67–68)

These responsibilities include being respectful of those who participate in our research and being mindful of the ways that they represent the communities and settings in which they do research, as well as the participants and organizations with which they are working (LeCompte et al., 1999; Weis & Fine, 2000). Weis and Fine (2000) have described this set of responsibilities as "ethical injunctions" (p. 62) and have eloquently articulated the ethical dilemmas that they continually grapple with as they conduct research:

> We continue to struggle with how to best represent the stories that may do more harm than good, depending on who consumes or exploits them: stories that reveal the adult consequences of child physical and sexual abuse; stories that suggest that it is almost impossible to live exclusively on welfare payments, encouraging many to lie about their incomes so that they self-define as "welfare cheats"; stories in which white respondents, in particular, portray people of color in gross and dehumanizing ways. . . . To what extent are we responsible to list "Warning! Misuse of data can be hazardous to our collective national health"? (pp. 47–48)

This concern for representation is especially important given the negative and damaging ways that many low-income communities and people of color have been depicted in the media. For those who believe that research should be used to improve conditions and inform, and transform, policies and practices, a heightened concern exists to the ways that research findings might be misused or result in damaging and detrimental perspectives of particular communities and people.

© Elias Carmona

Community meeting space.

This attention to misrepresentation does not mean that one should romanticize all attributes of a community or leave out negative or destructive features and elements of particular beliefs and experiences. Rather, this sort of ethical work demands that researchers be acutely aware of how these portrayals might contribute to stereotypes and, thus, be vigilant to contextualize experiences and behaviors, as well as able to turn the spotlight on oneself to examine personal circumstances, beliefs, and behaviors. When conducting research in close contact with community members and institutions, "good" and "bad" stories will certainly emerge and tensions regarding the use of these various narratives will arise (Weis & Fine, 2000). It is incumbent on the research team to make sure that such information is used for productive ends and to enhance understanding rather than just titillate, provoke, or critique for critique's sake. Within our analysis process, this means looking for examples of the mundane and for everyday tasks, rather than focusing solely on the most salacious and scandalous bits and excerpts (Weis & Fine, 2000). It also requires that we interrogate our reasons for sharing particular vignettes: Do they advance an analytical argument? Do they shed light on a specific process? Do they provide a more nuanced explanation of a process? Do they offer multiple viewpoints on a particular event?

Because community-based research studies involve collaboration at all stages, one would assume that these representational issues would not arise as community members—in their roles as co-researchers—would have the opportunity to critique and provide feedback on how their community is being portrayed. However, the collaborative and collective nature of CBQR projects makes such vigilance related to representation even more paramount as the research team needs to ensure that all voices are being heard and that multiple perspectives and experiences are incorporated at all stages of the project. Because knowledge is co-constructed within these projects, academic researchers need to be careful that one voice does not dominate discussions and silence divergent perspectives. And academic researchers must carefully inspect their role in the dialogue process and how they might be inadvertently replicating unequal power relationships within discussions and project activities. For example, Kysa Nygreen (2013) provided a frank and thoughtful reflection on her role in a participatory action research (PAR) study with youth. After reviewing her transcripts, field notes, and memos, she realized "the extent of . . . [her] privilege in the group and its harmful effects on . . . [the] work": "What I saw was that, in many ways, my own actions contributed to the reproduction of power inequalities, the silencing of youth voices, the perpetuation of my own agenda, and the confirmation of my own sense of entitlement" (Nygreen, 2013, p. 17). Although it is unfortunate that such a revelation occurred after the research had culminated, with some distance, Nygreen (2013) was able to subject her own role and participation in the group "to the same type of critical analysis to which [she] . . . subjected the words of the youth" (p. 17). The painful lessons she shares about her experience offer instructive reminders for other researchers interested in engaging in collaborative and participatory research with communities and youth. Some strategies to avoid such missteps and oversights include deliberately incorporating an explicit and ongoing critique of processes and an evaluation of power sharing as part of the project design. In addition, maintaining a reflective journal related to one's role as a researcher can assist in spotlighting areas where inequities are being reproduced.

## Institutional Review Boards and Community-Based Qualitative Research Projects

Educational institutions assert that ethical procedures and protocols exist to protect human subjects within research. This is certainly a goal of IRBs and other ethical bodies, but some also point out how these boards are in place to protect the institution, as well as to safeguard their legal interests, sometimes at the expense of the genuine research interests of a community and academic freedom (Hessler, Donald-Watson, & Galliher, 2011; Tierney & Corwin, 2007). For some vulnerable populations, such as marginalized youth—those whose voices are largely not part of academic scholarship—the IRB process can end up as "obscuring, silencing, and not protective" (Weis & Fine, 2000, p. 80). The processes can be particularly problematic and obstructionist for those conducting practitioner research and for participatory research teams (Boser, 2007; Pritchard, 2002). Susan Boser (2007) has highlighted how the processes of obtaining informed consent and ensuring confidentiality puts all responsibility and power in the hands of the researcher "with a limited view of the potential for human agency among participants in the study" (p. 1063). This sort of top-down power is at odds with participatory and community-based research studies, where shared power is a central and essential feature and that often take place in a "unique, complex, and evolving milieu" (Boser, 2007, p. 1065).

In CBQR studies, research purposes and activities are developed collaboratively and constantly negotiated throughout the project within collective and reciprocal processes not easily accommodated by IRB protocols, which usually require that research procedures be determined at the outset of a project. Furthermore, because those who would traditionally be considered research "subjects," or participants, are also co-researchers, the process of informed consent can be complicated. Many IRBs require that all members of a research team complete human subjects training, which can involve attending an all-day workshop or completing a lengthy online course. This can be burdensome for some community members and youth, whose schedules might not allow for a training on campus or who do not have access to a computer. Moreover, as the trainings are aimed at academic researchers and graduate students, some of the language used in the materials can be technical and esoteric and pose problems for high-school students and adults with limited formal education. An oral history project that I was involved in as a graduate student—which trained young Latina mothers in oral history methodology to conduct interviews with their female forebears on the experiences of migration, work, and motherhood—ran into a roadblock when the academic institution sponsoring the research required that the young Latina mothers complete an online training so that they could appropriately obtain informed consent from their female relatives. This requirement was an impediment as most of the women had no access to computers and some had very low reading levels in English, and because the course took nearly 5 hours to complete, it would have been onerous for many of the single mothers to fit into their already busy schedules. Fortunately, we were able to negotiate with the institution to waive this requirement; many institutions have since exempted oral history projects from IRB review. However, this example is telling regarding the ways that regulations and protocols purported to protect research participants can pose obstacles to research and knowledge generation; it was also puzzling given that we believed that the young women could provide a more authentic explanation of the purposes of the research, while ensuring that their relatives would not be exploited or misused within the research project.

Although we cannot dismiss with IRBs and the attendant mandated procedures, we can educate boards at our institutions about the work that we do and about the dynamic and emergent processes entailed in conducting CBQR. Research questions and initial protocols should be drafted collaboratively with research partners; although this can mean a lag in the startup of the project, it helps one comply with the IRB requirements and ensures that the initial design is representative of community interests and concerns. Many IRBs will allow you to submit interview guides after the project has commenced and to submit revisions and amendments as interview guides are developed and when changes are needed. The human subjects training requirement for co-researchers is harder to negotiate and can be problematic. In my work with teachers at an alternative high school, this mandate proved difficult for some to finish in a timely fashion as they were already overloaded with the demands of an intense workplace. A suggestion for expediting the training is to offer supports and incentives for individuals to complete training. This should be accompanied by a petitioning for the loosening of certain IRB requirements to facilitate participation by some key stakeholders.

## Roles and Stances of the
## Community-Based Qualitative Researcher

Within a CBQR study, the academic researcher can assume many roles. First and foremost, the researcher is a co-researcher investigating, teaching, and learning alongside research participants. Initially, academic researchers might spend a considerable amount of time observing and listening to key stakeholders to identify key issues. As the project develops, one might take on a more active role in relation to the community and its concerns; these roles can continue after the project has ended. This section discusses a few of these roles and provide examples from prominent studies that take a community-based or participatory approach. It should be noted that these categories of roles are not mutually exclusive and contain many overlapping elements. Furthermore, researchers can inhabit shifting roles throughout the course of a project or serve in multiple roles simultaneously.

### *Teachers and Facilitators*

Community-based qualitative researchers often begin their projects as teachers. Sometimes academic researchers arrange to teach a class at a local high school or community center as a way of gaining access to and building relationships with youth to initiate a research project. A notable example is Jason Irizarry's (2011) work with students at a high school nearby his university; his regular instruction of a research course became the context for a PAR project examining the educational conditions and experiences of Latinos/as. Other times, existing classroom teachers—often attending graduate school in addition to teaching—might develop a research project with their students. Within CBQR projects, academic researchers are typically serving as teachers and trainers, instructing co-researchers in particular methodologies and approaches.

### Ambassadors and Allies

Many graduate students and academic researchers make such powerful connections with communities in which they conduct research that they carry with them to other settings. Often their experiences in a particular community challenge preconceptions about this community and transform negative notions into positive ones. Students who have enrolled in my summer class have had specific interactions with community residents and youth that have resonated with them in myriad ways. After the class has ended, they often take it upon themselves to serve in the role of **community ambassadors**, disseminating information about the community in a variety of other external contexts, such as workplaces, college courses, and civic organizations. This role can help spread the word about community efforts and successes, as well as work to dispel myths and misconceptions about particular communities as dangerous and unwelcoming. They might present their experiences to colleagues or bring their own classes for a tour of the community. This is especially important for those who work in settings where individuals might have limited knowledge of certain areas; for example, many students enrolled in my classes work in suburban and rural areas and are unfamiliar with many urban communities. Individuals can also function as **allies**, which involves offering solidarity and support for the life and work of the community. This might include frequenting local businesses, attending and volunteering at community events, or providing monetary support for particular initiatives. Students who have been enrolled in my courses have purchased children's books in Spanish for their literacy and reading courses at a local bookstore; others have purchased needed books and other resources or provided information on available grants for local organizations and educational programs. Students who had previously been wary of venturing into the area went out of their way to have brunch at a local restaurant or attend the annual Puerto Rican parade. Although these may seem like small and insignificant gestures, the support of ambassadors and allies can play an important role in "spreading the word" and expanding the reach of the work of a community.

### Advocates and Activists

Often, as a result of being involved in a research project, academic researchers take a more active role on behalf of community programs and issues. Because of their participation conducting research alongside community members and their intense involvement in community efforts, they become especially invested in certain causes and issues. Their involvement leads them to continue with the work after the official research has ended, often marshaling together various resources toward the benefit of community programs and efforts. For example, a researcher might use research findings to work on achieving additional changes and enacting legislation or help in the establishment of new programs by writing grants for funding. This role of "researcher as mediator or broker" (Dyrness, 2011, p. 202) can be useful in extending the research into other arenas; some community-based projects often explicitly include advocacy efforts as part of their dissemination plan, and thus, these take place in collaboration with community co-researchers.

In other cases, academic researchers take on more activist stances possibly mobilizing for and speaking out at demonstrations and protests related to certain causes. This is especially the case within PAR studies, which are often focused on promoting activism as part of the design of the project. Some academic researchers are activists prior to the initiation of a project, and this role provides the impetus for the study. Some notable examples of academic researchers serving in an activist role include David Stovall's (2006) work with youth and parent-led educational grassroots movements. In his work, Stovall positions himself as both "participant researcher" and "concerned community member" and identifies his research as deeply rooted in his experience as a community organizer (2006, p. 97). Alongside conducting research, Nolan Cabrera (2011) played a pivotal role in demonstrations and civil disobedience to protest Arizona's dismantling of ethnic studies programs.

Andrea Dyrness (2011) has differentiated between "activist research" and "participatory research," and she has elaborated a "policy-oriented activist research model," in which "researchers lend their research products and expertise to the service of marginalized groups seeking specific, winnable policy changes" (p. 201). This model aligns with the advocacy role described earlier. On the other hand, Dyrness (2011) articulates her view of participatory research—and this is the approach she uses in her research—as that which seeks to transform research relationships and "expand the capacity of participants to make change in their own lives and communities" (p. 201) rather than through the sole efforts of an individual researcher. Within CBQR projects, researchers can take on policy-oriented advocacy roles, as well as function as more radical, community-based activists and in participatory ways that promote empowerment and transformation from within. Although there might be occasions for solitary advocacy work on the part of the researcher, or where researchers might serve as a liaison or broker between the community and external entities, the primary goal in CBQR is to foster collaborative efforts toward community changes and transformation.

## Researcher Autobiographies and Vulnerabilities

Within community-based research projects, academic researchers are obviously inhabiting multiple roles, interacting with community residents in various ways, and acquiring multiple experiences within the setting. This chapter has discussed at length the distinct histories and backgrounds that individuals carry with them into a setting and project, as well as how these inform researchers' lenses and perspectives. As they are amassing new experiences and being exposed to different ideas and perspectives, researchers' existing notions are being challenged and, in many cases, transformed. Students in the summer research classes that I have instructed have often been confronted with community narratives, experiences, and perspectives that cause them to reflect on and rethink their own experiences and question some of their previous practices and beliefs. Sometimes, their interactions with particular community members bring into focus their role in destructive processes impacting the community. For example, after interviewing a community activist about her antigentrification work, one Caucasian female student became more aware of, and subsequently questioned, her previous view of gentrification as a positive and somewhat benign process. The young Puerto Rican woman's recounting of how her family's displacement due to urban renewal and rising rents, and the threat that gentrification posed to the stability of the Puerto Rican community, had such an impact on the student during the interview that she broke down in tears.

Noted anthropologist Ruth Behar (1996) has written about how acts of bearing witness within the immersive sort of fieldwork required in ethnography can intersect with aspects of the researcher's autobiography and provoke vulnerabilities and emotional responses on the part of the researcher. She is critical of the sort of objectivity and

© Elias Carmona

New condominium development in Humboldt Park, Chicago.

detachment called for in much research and advocates for a more vulnerable and reflective role that acknowledges the "emotional and intellectual baggage" that researchers inevitably bring with them into research settings (Behar, 1996, p. 8). Within CBQR studies, dialogue about these sorts of vulnerabilities and autobiographical intersections should be part of the project, and research teams should not shy away from discussions about intersections and tensions, points of connection and areas of divergence, or differing perspectives and understandings of particular phenomena. Rather than detract from the research, these discussions can highlight key elements of community issues and experiences and can help the research team better understand the broader conditions and contexts influencing community issues and concerns.

Many times academic researchers' experiences within a community resonate with them in such a way that they reexamine some of their previous experiences and practices. For example, one student in a research class, a Caucasian mother who lived in a far-flung suburb, described the impact of her experience with a group of young Latinas through her fieldwork at a summer enrichment program:

> The words that I use to describe the inner sense of these girls and their community connection are *loyal, committed, dedicated* and *empowered.* I would use none of these words to adequately describe my own sons' community connection. Even though we as a family take part in many community events, volunteer at numerous community agencies, and have lived and attended school in the same community all of our lives, the ownership these girls had of their Humboldt Park neighborhood was unmatched. . . . I questioned these girls about this: Where had I failed my own children? Why didn't they have the love of community that these girls emanated on a daily basis? . . . At the end of eight weeks I was not only inspired by the girls and their inherent defense and love of their neighborhood, but sorry that my boys had not been brought up to have these same instincts.
>
> Ultimately what I thought I was going to bring *to* this experience—inspiration for the downtrodden people I expected to meet—became what I brought away from the experience. I was so inspired by the protective nature and pride these girls displayed toward their community and specifically toward the people they work with at the Teen Club called the *Batey Urbano.* . . . I was transformed—I learned a lot about research, yes, but I believe more importantly I learned more about my own beliefs about me. I learned about being a better mom and I learned that five teenage girls from Humboldt Park have changed the world for this middle aged, blonde, suburban woman in a most positive way.

This student attested to the transformative effects of her involvement in the community and with this particular group of young women on her role as a mother. Other students were also transformed: A student began biking more often after completing a project at a community biking initiative; another student's experience with an Afro-Caribbean music organization caused her to reevaluate her previous beliefs about the teaching, learning, and performance of music. These revelations are a few examples of how CBQR can yield not only programmatic changes but also transformations in researchers and their practices.

© Elias Carmona

Chairs festooned with flags in preparation for an alternative high-school graduation.

## Chapter Summary

From this chapter, we have learned the important and myriad roles and responsibilities of academic researchers within CBQR projects. Researchers need to be cognizant of their backgrounds, privileges, assumptions, and biases prior to entering a research setting, as well as of how they are both insiders and outsiders in relation to topic, setting, and participants. It is essential that throughout a community-based research project, members of the research team engage in dialogue with co-researchers regarding their changing beliefs, as well as to share tensions and differences of opinion.

Ethical requirements imposed by institutions can provide important safeguards and protections for certain populations of research participants, but they can also pose challenges for collaborative and community-based research, where the conventional distinction between "researcher" and "subject" does not usually apply. Thus, research teams often need to grapple with how to meet these requirements and still be true to the collaborative and participatory nature of CBQR projects. Finally, we learned that academic researchers can assume multiple stances and roles within a research project, including teacher, ally, and activist.

## Key Terms

| | | |
|---|---|---|
| Allies  56 | Informed consent  51 | Positionality  41 |
| Checking privilege  47 | Insiders  44 | Reflexivity  42 |
| Community ambassadors  56 | Institutional review | Stakeholders  40 |
| Cultural competence  50 | boards  51 | White skin privilege  47 |
| Emic  45 | Otherizing  43 | |
| Etic  45 | Outsiders  45 | |

## ● Activities for Reflection and Discussion

1) Educational autobiography: Write a reflection on your educational experiences, including elementary through postsecondary experiences, and nonformal educational experiences. Respond to the following prompts/questions: What events/experiences stand out? What are your strongest educational memories/experiences, positive or negative? How have your experiences informed your views of teaching and learning or your worldview? In class or a research setting, share your educational autobiography with a partner (either a classmate or another member of the research team). What are similarities and differences between your educational experiences?

2) Before initial experience in the community setting, respond to the following writing prompts:

   a) What are your goals for research within the community? What skills/knowledge do you hope to gain? What do you hope to accomplish?

   b) What are you excited about in relation to this course?

   c) What challenges do you anticipate? What might you be anxious about?

   d) What existing knowledge/information do you possess about this community? Where did you obtain this knowledge?

3) Select a particular topic and issue of interest to you (for example, reading instruction, youth civic engagement, health education, and adult learning). Make a list of your relevant experiences, assumptions,

and biases related to this topic. Share these experiences, assumptions, and biases with a partner or research team.

4) Examine your backpack of privileges imparted by your background and characteristics. How might an awareness of these privileges help inform and facilitate the implementation of your research project?

5) Of the researcher roles and stances that are described in this chapter, which ones do you foresee taking on as part of your research project? Are there roles you would feel comfortable inhabiting? Are there roles you would feel uncomfortable with? Are there other roles that you expect to assume as part of your project?

# Project Design, Data Collection, and Analysis

# PART 2

# Project Design

## Introduction

This chapter provides guidelines and information for initiating and designing CBQR projects. Areas to be covered include the development of relationships with community members and local organizations, identifying and refining research interests and purposes, and charting a plan for data collection. Although the design of community-based studies is flexible and emergent, and often dependent on the changing and dynamic community contexts within which the projects take place, researchers nevertheless need to begin the project with a clear plan for data collection, acknowledging that this plan could change. Before beginning a project, academic researchers need to spend time familiarizing themselves with the community and community-based organizations and getting to know leaders and residents.

## Learning Objectives

After reading this chapter, students will be able to:

1. Recognize the importance of developing relationships with community stakeholders, and describe several approaches to learning about a community and building rapport with residents.

2. Understand the purpose and role of research questions within community-based qualitative research (CBQR) projects, and create research questions for a potential project.

3. Identify different forms of data collection within CBQR projects, and explain how these different forms can be used to explore phenomena within a project.

4. Develop a plan for data collection for a potential project.

# Gaining Community Access and Developing Relationships With Community Members and Institutions

Community-based qualitative research (CBQR) projects usually do not just "happen" or emerge on their own, but they require a certain amount of planning and intention on the part of academic researchers and community stakeholders. Although some research projects arise from community organizations interested in documenting and/or evaluating their efforts, or by certain civic groups wanting to learn more about and/or address a particular community issue, more frequently they are initiated by academic researchers, such as faculty or graduate students, who possess a desire to conduct research in collaboration with a community, or who have an existing relationship with a particular community. However, desire and intention on the part of the researcher are not usually sufficient to get a project underway; some time and energy is required on the front end to develop relationships with key stakeholders and learn about the community. This process of gaining access to and building relationships with community organizations and partners is essential; it is unlikely that a researcher who knows nothing about a community could just waltz in and start conducting research. First off, it is improbable that community members would talk to a complete stranger or to someone who had not gained entrée through a community insider. Second, without community input and collaboration, the project would be inauthentic and might not reflect the key concerns and issues significant to the community.

An academic researcher, or group of researchers, can gain access to a community in several ways to plan and conduct a CBQR project. If one member of the prospective research team is also a member of the community, or has an existing relationship with an organization in the community, this individual might set up an initial meeting with community stakeholders to introduce research team members and discuss plans and possibilities for a research project. Stakeholders are those who have a vested interest in a particular issue or concern and are critical to understanding the issue and how it impacts various groups. Academic research teams with no preexisting connections with a particular community should first make contact with key organizations involved in work that aligns with their research interests as a way of identifying stakeholders. For example, a researcher or group interested in youth civic engagement might identify afterschool programs or organizations working with youth, such as the YMCA or Boys and Girls Club. Those who want to explore environmental issues might inquire at the local park district; groups interested in investigating health concerns might contact community clinics and hospitals. Although mainstream organizations, such as public schools, public libraries, and hospitals, can seem like sensible starting points for gaining access to a community and making contacts, they often are centralized; thus, to conduct research, one often needs to obtain approval from larger entities, such as a district office or corporation, and to negotiate with multiple gatekeepers to initiate a project. In community-based research, **gatekeepers** are individuals who control access to a program or site and its material and human resources; these individuals could include school principals, executive directors, and community leaders. They are often the people "in charge" and those who supervise programs and staff and are essential to the success of a project. Even if a researcher has secured buy-in from a youth group or project coordinator, it is important to check in with those responsible for overseeing a program or project as they can often "make or break" a research study.

In contrast to large mainstream organizations, smaller nonprofits and community-based grassroots organizations usually possess less layers of bureaucracy that potential researchers will need to wade through to begin a study. Furthermore, these smaller organizations often employ many individuals living in the surrounding community, thus, providing greater insight into relevant community issues and concerns. Because they are community-based, rather than part of a larger centralized or corporate entity, they tend to be closer "to the ground" regarding relevant issues significant to the community. They might also be more open and receptive to the sorts of innovative research approaches and projects that are at the heart of CBQR. Furthermore, grassroots organizations might require less negotiation with gatekeepers, although researchers still need to talk to the people "in charge" before beginning a project. A project could also work with multiple sites and types of institutions, although this would require more coordination to bring together research team members. Research projects and teams might also be convened outside of a conventional organizational structure, such as among homeless youth, but some leaders and group members may be available to serve as liaisons to the group.

## Orientation Experiences

As academic researchers are making contact with institutions and organizations within the community, it can be helpful to engage in **orienting experiences** within the community. This approach helps members of the research team, particularly those with limited knowledge of the community, become familiar with community issues and concerns. These orienting experiences could include tours of the community led by community leaders or insiders; many communities have organizations, such as chambers of commerce or historical societies, that lead tours for a small fee. These tours can provide important background information and furnish an overview of the history and layout of the community, as well as offer an entrée to particular organizations. I usually begin my summer research course with a small tour led by a community leader or a member of the local business development organization. If it is not possible to arrange a formal, structured tour, groups should consider a self-guided orientation experience, which might involve research team members exploring the community on their own and locating and mapping landmarks, organizations and cultural centers. I have instructed students in my classes to walk through the community and identify sites and resources related to their topic. Along the way, they need to collect brochures and information; I also encourage them to take photographs and talk to organizational staff and community residents as they explore their topic in the community. Other orienting activities could include using a community map to plot out various organizations and resources. For example, research groups interested in health issues could locate and chart grocery stores, community gardens, hospitals and clinics, and parks and exercise facilities in an effort to account for existing resources and to become familiar with what is currently available to residents. Research groups could also use virtual resources, such as websites and online archives, to learn more about the history and resources of the community. Local and citywide foundations and cultural/arts organizations and museums are often great resources; for example, in Chicago, the Chicago History Museum maintains an online archive that includes information on particular neighborhoods and an on-site reading room/library for researchers and teachers and The Chicago Architecture Foundation offers tours and lectures on a variety of Chicago neighborhoods. A local architecture and arts organization, Architreasures, has also created a self-guided tour of murals in Humboldt Park by using QR (quick response) codes. Community-based research teams should seek out similar sorts of resources and materials in the communities within which they are conducting research (or possibly create these as part of their research projects).

Other orienting activities might include attending local events, which offer great opportunities for building knowledge about a community and getting to know community members. For example, community parades and festivals can often provide a useful overview of community life, and insight into cultural traditions and practices, as well as introduce key organizations that work in the community. My summer research class usually commences with the annual Puerto Rican parade. After a course introduction and initial discussion, students experience the parade on their own and complete a writing assignment, which requires that they provide a description of the community and reflect on their experience at the parade. Some years, the beginning of the class has fortuitously coincided with a community conference that brought together academic scholars and community leaders and activists to explore and discuss salient community issues and topics. Although not all communities might furnish such rich opportunities for orienting oneself, members of the research team should seek out and attend local events and celebrations whenever possible.

Background readings and resources can also provide important information about a community and/or population. Other researchers may have conducted studies within the community that could provide useful insights to the research team. Reports and statistics on poverty, housing, educational attainment, and health outcomes can offer a window into the community context and conditions for residents, as well as point to significant needs and areas for developing community-based research projects. If the research project is being developed as part of a class, the instructor might invite guest speakers or panels to address particular community experiences and concerns. For example, I usually ask the executive director of the hosting organization to provide an overview of the community and the primary projects of his organization; I also have organized panels of local teachers and youth to share their experiences and offer opportunities for dialogue and discussion. These panel discussions have often served as important starting points for the development of collaborative community-based projects. These sorts of formal interchanges can also be arranged for research groups convened outside of a class structure.

Orienting activities can play an important role in not only furnishing knowledge about the community but also in helping dispel or counteract negative images and stereotypes about low-income communities of color. For example, one student, a reading teacher who lived in the Chicago suburbs and enrolled in a summer course I instructed, described her limited experience with Chicago, as well as her initial views of the community in which the class was located:

> I didn't know that this was part of Chicago. Because Chicago to me was Michigan Avenue and Lake Shore Drive. It's the museums. It's Navy Pier. And when I go in for a show. And that's kind of all I really—that was my context for Chicago before. So I thought this was Humboldt Park, Illinois, not knowing that it was part of Chicago. But once you hear something like that, like anything, then I was being barraged with things on the news, like "shooting in Humboldt Park" and this and that in Humboldt Park, and, you know, carjacking in Humboldt Park. I'm like I've never heard of Humboldt Park before, why am I know so hypersensitive to hearing about it. And that was kind of my scary, beginning feeling of it.

Through tours of the community and other course experiences, this student became more aware of community resources, in particular a community bookstore, which she repeatedly returned to after the course ended to purchase resources for her classes.

## Developing Rapport and Identifying Resources

As research group members are initiating and developing projects, it is important for academic researchers to engage in activities and interactions that can help them build rapport with community members and potential members of the research team. **Rapport**, which stems from the French word *rapporter* meaning "to carry something back," refers to building close relationships of mutual understanding with others and to developing understanding of others' beliefs and values, finding areas of commonality whenever possible. One way to begin building rapport is simply to "show up," to be present and volunteer at program and community events. Many of these activities can provide opportunities to engage in informal conversations with community residents and can help residents learn about academic researchers. Exchanging personal information about family and hobbies can be useful in helping to identify common experiences and mutual interests. Social activities can also function to promote rapport among academic researchers and community members; for example, going out for lunch or coffee can help break down perceived barriers and open up lines of communication.

Within the initial stages of a community-based research project, university resources can be instrumental in helping to identify community partners and build research relationships. For example, many universities and colleges have a community partnership office, which maintains a list of local organizations and may have existing relationships with certain organizations. These offices could serve as collaborators for a project or even provide funding for start-up and orientation activities. Some campuses have departments or programs that focus on civic engagement or centers dedicated to service learning, which could be helpful in providing community contacts and in recruiting interested students to work on the project. Similarly, student groups and resource centers devoted to particular identities and causes, such as Latino/a, African American, and lesbian, gay, bisexual, transgender, and queer (LGBTQ) centers, often have relationships with community groups and organizations, and can offer access for academic researchers interested in designing projects focused on related issues.

## Identification of Goals and Project Purposes

As academic researchers are building rapport and research relationships with community residents, they are amassing a list of appropriate and relevant research topics. Through orienting activities and research team meetings, researchers should be identifying goals and the purposes of research project and developing an overall design for the community-based research study. This section provides some guidelines for designing projects, including writing purpose statements and research questions.

It is essential that research goals and purposes for community-based research projects be developed collaboratively with the input of academic researchers and community partners. Although qualitative research projects are flexible and dynamic, with purposes often dynamic and shifting to address changing interests and needs, projects should begin with a research purpose statement and research questions. A **research purpose statement** is a broad statement that provides an overall direction for the study. **Research questions** offer a more specific and narrow focus for developing data collection tools and instruments. Research purpose statements usually include the identification of the **central phenomenon** or issue under study, such as youth civic engagement, educational attainment, or access to health resources, as well as some general information about setting and participants.

A basic format for a qualitative research purpose statement follows. This is just one format and should not be viewed as a template or be used prescriptively:

> The purpose of this study is to VERB (examine, investigate, explore) PHENOMENON/ISSUE among PARTICIPANTS in SETTING.

Along with the purpose statement, the research team should develop three to five research questions (or RQs), which will help narrow the focus of the study. These questions should be open-ended and not answerable with a simple "yes" or "no." They should also be free of jargon and written for the "layperson" or understandable to an individual outside of the specific field under study. This is particularly important in CBQR projects when individuals involved in the project have divergent experiences and various levels of expertise related to the project. It can also be off-putting to use academic jargon within a project as it can reinforce power hierarchies between academic researchers and community residents and serve to privilege academic knowledge over that of the community. By using insider terms, or terminology that is only understandable to a small group people, or only to those with intimate knowledge of the topic or setting, the project will be less accessible to others. In addition, purpose statements and research questions should not include hypotheses or assumptions about the topic or setting, nor should they attempt to determine causal or correlational relationships among variables. The goal of a qualitative project is to reveal and uncover new knowledge and describe multiple experiences and perspectives on an issue rather than test existing hypotheses or determine a single answer to or cause of a problem.

To summarize, when writing research questions, members of the research team should write questions that are as follows:

- Open-ended: Cannot be answered with a "yes" or "no" or single-word answer.
- Free of jargon: Avoid academic jargon and use layperson's terms whenever possible.
- Free of hypotheses and assumptions: Avoid words and phrases such as "test" or "determine if . . ."
- Focused on revealing participants' perspectives: Reflect an acknowledgment of multiple experiences of and perspectives on a particular phenomenon or issue.
- Free of causal or correlational relationships: Do not use words and phrases such as "relationship between," "affect," or "effect on."

Some examples include the following:

Purpose statement: The purpose of this study is to explore youth civic engagement among Latino/a and African American youth.

RQs:

1) How do community youth define and view community?

2) How do community youth describe the community they most identify with? In what ways are they involved in this community?

3) What opportunities (activities, projects, initiatives) exist for community youth to be involved in their community? What roles do community youth and other participants take on in these activities? According to youth, what skills and knowledge do youth gain through their involvement in these activities?

Purpose statement: The purpose of this study is to examine experiences and relationships between generations of Latino/a mothers (mentors and mentees) who had children during adolescence involved in a community-based mentoring program.

RQs:

1) How do mentees describe their experiences as young mothers? What challenges do they identify? What resources and sources of support?

2) How do mentors describe their previous experiences as young mothers? What challenges do they identify? What resources and sources of support?

3) How do mentors describe their postsecondary educational, professional, and personal experiences? What experiences do they share with mentees?

4) How do mentors/mentees describe their relationships with one another? What sorts of conversations and activities do they engage in?

5) What activities and events are offered through the mentoring program? What roles do participants take on during these activities? What sorts of information and knowledge are shared?

Purpose statement: The purpose of this study is to investigate the efforts of a community nutrition and health initiative in expanding community residents' knowledge and awareness of their health, as well as of broader health concerns.

RQs:

1) What activities and services are currently offered in the community to address health issues and concerns, such as obesity and diabetes?

2) How do staff members in the program describe the services provided? What are the goals of the work? What are the successes? What are the challenges?

3) How do participants in the program describe their health? According to participants, what health challenges have they faced?

4) How do participants in the program describe the services provided? According to participants, what knowledge, skills, or practices have they gained from the program?

# Data Collection in Community-Based Qualitative Research

After the researchers have decided on a purpose statement and three to five research questions, they should develop a plan for data collection. The purpose statement and research questions provide an important direction for deciding on what sorts of data to collect. For example, if a project aims to examine how LGBTQ youth in a transitional home describe their experiences in school, the researcher(s) should design a guide to interview individual youth, and/or a group of youth as part of a focus group. If a research question focuses on examining behaviors, practices, and/or interactions among specific groups of participants, then participant observation within relevant settings would be an appropriate means of data collection. The point of collecting data is to gather information that can help answer research questions; in addition, researchers should aim to collect different types and forms of data, across participants and settings, to provide insight into a phenomenon. The use of multiple forms of data within research is referred to by many as **triangulation**, which is borrowed from a navigational term that refers to using multiple measurements and points to determine a single point in space. This process of using more than one method of data collection and different data points strengthens findings and enhances the credibility of a study. For example, observations of community settings and events can provide support for conditions, behaviors, or practices described within individual interviews. Discussions within focus groups can offer insight on observed activities and incidents. Artifacts, images, and other documents supply visual and textual representations of belief systems and perspectives expressed in other contexts. In addition to substantiating converging patterns and thematic points, this use of various forms of data can also provide evidence of divergent viewpoints, as well as document contradictions and tensions within and across settings and participants. The remainder of this section provides an overview of types and forms of data that can be used in CBQR; each of these will be discussed at length in subsequent chapters.

## Kinds of Data in Community-Based Qualitative Research

As stated, it is recommended that researchers use multiple forms of data collection, although there may be a central focus; for example, individual in-depth interviews may be the primary means of data collection in a study exploring homelessness among LGBTQ youth with program artifacts and observations of events providing supporting data. The aforementioned study, examining youth civic engagement, included interviews with students and observations of classes and community activities, and it devoted equal weight to both types of data. Employing multiple forms of data collection in your study will furnish you with a richer and more nuanced data set, as well as allow you to develop assertions substantiated across data types.

### Interviews and Focus Groups

One-to-one interviews are common methods of collecting data in all qualitative studies. In community-based projects, they can offer essential background information, especially during the initial stages of the project, as well as provide important insight on perspectives and experiences. Most interviews in community-based research studies will take place as scheduled meetings, using a semistructured interview guide, but they can also occur as part of more informal interactions. Interviews with adults usually last between 45 and 90 minutes long, whereas interviews with teenagers are often shorter; interviews with children rarely last more than 20 minutes. The central goal in individual interviews in qualitative research is to elicit extensive and descriptive narratives from participants related to particular experiences and issues rather than one-word or brief responses. Interviewers are encouraged to ask follow-up questions that build on participants' distinct experiences and help them further elaborate definitions and viewpoints.

Focus groups are used when researchers want to gather many perspectives at once, and they can be helpful when there is less time available to schedule individual interviews. Focus groups are appropriate when researchers want to encourage debate and discussion across participants related to particular issues and experiences. Focus groups are best when composed of five to eight individuals and can be homogeneous—a grouping of individuals who share many characteristics in common—or heterogeneous—where there might be significant divergence on certain characteristics, such as age or gender, and roles. Most focus groups use an interview guide that includes central guiding questions, as well as follow-up questions. Although focus groups can allow for the amassing of multiple perspectives over a short time, they require careful planning upfront and often necessitate more material and personnel resources than individual interviews (and these are discussed in detail in Chapter 5).

### Participant Observation

Observation of activities and particular settings can provide researchers with deeper understandings of community life and practices, and it can help them get a sense of significant community issues and concerns. These observations can take place as part of formal, scheduled events or, more informally, in response to impromptu activities. The types of activities that researchers might observe, as participant observers, include workshops, classes, meetings, performances, demonstrations, community-service activities, school assemblies, and cultural events. Researchers can also conduct regular observations of particular settings, such as community businesses and workplaces, or spend time observing the activity of broader community contexts, such as parks and urban gardens.

The role that researchers can take on within these observations can vary and can range from passive to active participation. For example, a more passive role might mean that a researcher is observing a classroom from the periphery and not engaging with students and other participants; if the researcher is taking a more active role, she or he would be participating in classroom activities and discussions rather than just taking in activities from the sidelines (the many roles that researchers can take on as participant observers will be discussed in Chapter 6). Within all types of observations, researchers should have some way of documenting interactions and behaviors and of depicting settings and participants, such as video or audio recording or note taking. These will help researchers in preparing formalized field notes and/or observation transcripts.

### Surveys and Questionnaires

Although surveys and questionnaires are more common in quantitative studies, they can be useful within CBQR as a way of providing a broad overview of certain participant characteristics, beliefs, or attitudes. Surveys can include multiple-choice and scaled items, as well as open-ended questions. Questionnaires can also be used alongside open-ended interviews as ways of collecting demographic data from participants. Surveys can also help researchers identify individuals that meet certain criteria that they would like to interview more in depth. However, although surveys and questionnaires can provide important descriptive information about participants, they should not be the primary data source with community-based qualitative studies, or be employed to establish causal or correlational relationships among variables, as these measures are only appropriate for quantitative studies.

### Other Data

Although interviews, focus groups, and observations often provide the largest source of data within qualitative studies, many other types of data can be used within community-based qualitative studies. For example, **visual data**, such as photographs of community settings and activities and posters and advertisements for services and events, can document community activities and highlight significant community issues. **Documents**, including student journals, program brochures and policy statements, and meeting notes, can provide insight into participant perspectives, reveal institutional values and priorities, and substantiate beliefs and practices observed elsewhere. Increasingly, **websites** and **social media sites** are being used to examine individuals' beliefs and viewpoints related to particular issues and concerns. Within community-based qualitative studies, community portals and program websites can offer information on initiatives, services, and events. Comments and postings on program pages and Twitter feeds and hashtags often provide a window into current perspectives and debates on relevant community issues and controversies. Many other visual, textual, and digital sources of data can be used to support developing thematic and theoretical points related to a study's central phenomenon or issue (and these are described more fully in Chapter 6).

## Chapter Summary

In this chapter, we learned about how researchers can orient themselves to a particular community as they prepare to conduct CBQR. These orienting experiences are important to building a foundation for the research study and to building relationships with community organizations, leaders, and residents. Once these relationships are established, researchers need to develop a design for the study and a plan for data collection, acknowledging that this plan can change as the study responds to changing interests and needs. Many different data collection approaches can provide insight into a study, and this chapter introduced some prominent approaches, including interviews, focus groups, observations, and the gathering of visual/textual documents and artifacts. Although the exact types of data collection used within a study are determined by the research questions, it is important to employ multiple forms of data collection to offer rich insight on a study's phenomena/central issues.

## Key Terms

## ● Activities for Reflection and Discussion

1) Generate a list of potential orienting activities for learning about a specific community: What organizations would you visit? Who would you need to talk to? Plan a community walk/tour for this specific community.

2) Identify community resources and institutions relevant to your research interests. Examine brochures and web pages to identify what sorts of services and programs they provide.

3) Write one purpose statement and three to five research questions for a community-based qualitative research study. What sorts of data collection activities would be most appropriate for this purpose statement and its research questions?

| TABLE 4.1 ● Learning About a Community |
|---|
| Orienting activities |
| Community tours |
| Research on community organizations and institutions |
| Interviews with community leaders |
| Speakers |
| Videos |
| Readings |
| Building rapport activities |
| Discussion groups |
| Lunches and meals |
| Attending cultural events |
| Panels of community youth and residents |
| Resources |
| Websites |
| Chambers of commerce |
| Cultural institutions |
| Libraries |
| History museums and archives |

| **TABLE 4.2** ● Types and Uses of Data in Community-Based Qualitative Studies | | |
|---|---|---|
| **Type** | **Some Uses Within CBQR** | **Examples** |
| **Interviews** | • Obtain background information on community and/or organization<br>• Elicit participants' experiences and beliefs related to particular issues<br>• Follow up on behaviors/practices examined elsewhere | • Interview a director of a health program about the history, mission, and work of a community health initiative<br>• Interview youth about their involvement in community projects |
| **Focus groups** | • Foster discussion and dialogue among a group of participants on a shared experience<br>• Help clarify group norms and practices<br>• Identify divergent perspectives on an issue or shared experience | • Convene a focus group of young Latina mothers to discuss experiences in school and the challenges of being a student-parent<br>• Talk to community activists about antigentrification efforts |
| **Observations** | • Gain insight into community life, activities, and practices<br>• Describe community settings and contexts<br>• Examine participant roles and behaviors, as well as interactions among participants | • Participate in/observe demonstrations to save a community mural<br>• Observe training workshops for prospective mentors in a youth mentoring program |
| **Visual documents** | • Identify relevant symbols and images<br>• Provide visual representations of settings, activities, and participants<br>• Offer substantiation for observed practices and beliefs | • Examine photographs of signage at an alternative high school to identify images related to success<br>• Look at community websites |
| **Textual documents** | • Identify significant language and metaphors used to describe practices and policies<br>• Provide substantiation for perspectives articulated in interviews or observed in other contexts | • Examine program brochures for language used to describe goals and mission<br>• Look at training guides to identify purposes and strategies for preparing mentors |

# HANDOUT 3
## Data Collection Plan

|  | When (date/time/ duration) | Status (scheduled, completed, canceled) | Completed (✓/date) |
|---|---|---|---|
| **Observations: What?** |  |  |  |
|  |  |  |  |
|  |  |  |  |
|  |  |  |  |
|  |  |  |  |
|  |  |  |  |
|  |  |  |  |
|  |  |  |  |
| **Interview(s): Who?** |  |  |  |
|  |  |  |  |
|  |  |  |  |
|  |  |  |  |
|  |  |  |  |
| **Artifacts: What?** |  |  |  |
|  |  |  |  |
|  |  |  |  |
|  |  |  |  |

# Interviewing

## Introduction

This chapter covers aspects of the interviewing process in CBQR, including selecting participants, writing questions, identifying an appropriate interview method, and conducting the interview. The chapter also reviews different types of interviews researchers might use within their study, including individual interviews and focus groups.

## Learning Goals

After reading this chapter, students will be able to:

1. Identify different types of qualitative interviews, and determine when and how they might be used in a community-based qualitative research (CBQR) study.

2. Create and develop interview guides for various types of interviews, including individual interviews and focus groups.

3. Explain how to prepare for various types of interviews, and identify approaches used by researchers to conduct interviews.

4. Describe the role of the researcher within interviews, and discuss how to elicit additional information from interviewees through follow-up questions.

# Types of Interviews

Interviews are a primary way of obtaining information in all qualitative research, and they are especially important within community-based qualitative research (CBQR) studies as they enable researchers to gather pertinent background information on the community and particular institutions that might not be accessible via other means. Community leaders often possess a storehouse of information and knowledge that has not been published elsewhere. Furthermore, individual and group interviews can help researchers delve into the particulars of specific activities and events and probe participants' perspectives on certain issues and concerns. This section reviews some key types of interviews used in CBQR and how they might contribute to the construction of knowledge within the study. Interviews are important within qualitative research because they provide insight into participants' behavior, perspectives, and attitudes and emphasize the telling of stories and elicitation of rich narratives. Irving Seidman (2013) describes interviews as possessing "an interest in understanding the lived experience of other people and the meaning they make of that experience" (p. 9).

## Formal and Informal Interviews

Interviews within CBQR studies can take place formally or informally. Formal interviews are scheduled interviews usually occurring face to face and using an interview guide; informal interviews can be more impromptu and emerging from regular interactions with community members and research participants, and they usually do not employ an interview guide, although a research team might develop some guiding questions to gain insight into community life and practices. There are generally three types of interviews used within research studies: structured, semistructured, and unstructured. **Structured interviews** are used within quantitative studies and survey research, and they rely on a prescribed and standardized interview guide with closed questions and a fixed set of responses, although some open-ended items might be included. Questions are all asked in the same order and in the same manner, and there is meant to be no opportunity for interviewees to veer from the guide or share the details of particular experiences and viewpoints. In contrast, **unstructured interviews** do not make use of a guide, and they may only have areas or topics for discussion, such as "family life," "education," "community," or "work." Questions are meant to emerge from the experiences of interviewees, and they are developed and posed within the context of the interview. These sorts of interviews are appropriate for life history interviews with participants and when researchers might be interested in gaining broader insight into the background of the community and experiences of participants.

**Semistructured interviews** use an interview guide but one composed of open-ended questions that allow for interviewees to share and narrate distinct experiences related to the research topic or focus. Follow-up questions may be asked that are not part of the initial interview guide, thus, providing the opportunity for questions to be generated that build on the unique perspectives of research participants, as well as for the research to be taken in new and unexpected directions. Interviews using a semistructured guide are the most common in qualitative research studies, and they are a key way to gather information within CBQR projects.

Interviews in CBQR studies usually occur face to face as this is often the best way to build rapport with participants; because interviews in community-based studies often take place within the community, they can also be great opportunities to learn about community life and practices. However, there might be some occasions when a telephone interview is more convenient, although this should only be used if a face-to-face interview cannot be arranged. Gestures and other cues, which often suggest interviewees' frame of mind or viewpoints on an issue, are inaccessible over the phone. Increasingly, interviews within qualitative research studies are also occurring in online environments, such as through e-mail or via video chat. Although these methods can be essential for researchers conducting research from afar, or who cannot access a location or participant, they are not recommended for CBQR studies, except as a form for conducting follow-up interviews. The sections that follow review types of interviews that can be conducted formally or informally by using unstructured or semistructured interview guides.

## Background and Foundational Interviews

In the initial stages of a study, background and foundational interviews with community leaders can serve an important function and provide essential historical and background information on the community and particular institutions. In some cases, this information can help furnish a direction for the study especially when researchers are beginning the project with a broad area of interest rather than with a specific research focus. Much of the information provided in these interviews might not be published or available elsewhere, and thus, it can be integral to gaining information for the study.

Specific content that might be covered in background interviews might include the history of a particular organization or community or an overview of an organization's primary services and projects. Individuals who might be targeted for these interviews could include local politicians and prominent community leaders, executive directors of community organizations, and local historians. These interviews would usually be scheduled as formal interviews, and they use an unstructured or semistructured guide. An unstructured guide would be especially appropriate for interviews aimed at obtaining an overview of the community or a particular organization. Semistructured guides are necessary when researchers are interested in specific issues or want to gather background information on particular projects, incidences, or events.

## Individual Interviews With Leaders, Practitioners, and Community Residents

Throughout the project, researchers should be gathering perspectives and experiences related to the topic/issue from a variety of participants. This can be done as part of formal interviews, as well as through informal conversations within research activities. Different from background interviews—where the interview is used to establish foundational information and possibly determine a direction for the study—these interviews are intended to provide insights that can contribute to developing study findings and/or informing the creation of new programs and initiatives. In community-based research projects, it is important to gather multiple perspectives, including those in leadership roles; practitioners, teachers, and individuals who are "on the ground" and responsible for implementing programs and initiatives; and community residents and those who use specific programs or attend particular events.

These sorts of individual interviews are usually formal interviews employing a semistructured interview guide. However, follow-up interviews might take place more informally, and questions could potentially be posed over the phone or via e-mail. Content that might be covered includes individuals' familial, community, and professional experiences as a way of better understanding community issues and concerns. Interviews would also focus on eliciting participant perspectives on specific issues.

## Focus Groups

During a study, it can be helpful to bring together groups of particular individuals for a focus group. This allows for the sharing of common or divergent experiences and discussion of key issues. Focus groups can be particularly useful when researchers are interested in gathering perspectives from a large number of participants in a short time or when it is difficult to set up individual interviews. Focus groups are also appropriate when researchers are interested in fostering discussion and debate around particular issues or topics. Groups can comprise homogeneous or heterogeneous groupings. In **homogeneous groups**, participants are grouped because of a common characteristic, such as age, gender, professional role, or membership in an organization, and help researchers tap into group norms and practices. For example, a researcher might be interested in exploring youth perspectives on civic engagement and community involvement in a Latino/a community, and convene a group of students 16 to 20 years of age attending a local alternative high school that promotes community involvement. **Heterogeneous groups** bring together participants who might vary on a specific characteristic and can facilitate debate across groups and characteristics. For example, a research team might want to explore the issue of food deserts and insecurity from various age perspectives to get a sense of generational issues related to access to food and nutritional practices.

Focus groups are generally organized as formal interviews as they often require prior planning and coordination. They usually use a semistructured interview guide and require a facilitator, and sometimes an assistant, who starts off asking central questions and then probes to elicit additional information and encourage discussion and debate.

## Panels

Panels are similar to focus groups, but they entail direct presentations by three to five participants, in possession of knowledge or experiences related to the topic, to a group of researchers, who then ask follow-up questions and engage in discussion. Panels are particularly appropriate for undergraduate and graduate classes assigned to conduct community-based research. They can be a great opportunity to provide introductory information to a research group to identify key concerns related to a specific issue and/or sector of the community. For example, in a summer research CBQR course that I teach, I regularly organize a panel of youth from an alternative high school in the community. One year, the presentations and discussion focused on youth civic engagement; another summer, the emphasis was on postsecondary transitions to college and work. Discussions allowed graduate students to gather information related to their projects and to refine their research focus.

In planning panels, researchers should target individuals who have key experiences and knowledge related to the topic, instructing each participant to present more generally about his or her background and experiences for 10 minutes, and then allowing for discussion and more targeted questions. Researchers should prepare two to three questions, but they can also ask questions in response to information shared by panelists. Panels can bring together those who have fairly similar experiences or roles, such as the youth panel described earlier, or might involve individuals with varying roles on a project or initiative, such as teachers, youth, and staff involved in a local sex education initiative. These panels, as well as focus groups, can also help identify individuals you might want to interview individually and more in depth.

CBQR studies often make use of multiple interviewing formats and approaches throughout the course of the study to gain insight into the central phenomenon or topic. For example, background interviews with community leaders and panels comprising community youth could be employed at the beginning of a study to gather information and develop a more specific focus; later, individual interviews with particular participants and focus groups will help researchers identify important perspectives and issues related to this focus. Throughout, informal interviews with participants can help researchers follow up with particular participants and expand on experiences and clarify viewpoints. The following sections provide researchers with more detailed information on how to prepare interview guides and conduct various types of interviews.

## Writing Interview Guides and Questions

As mentioned, many interviews in qualitative research use a semistructured interview guide. These guides include mostly open-ended questions, allowing for follow-up questions and probes that are not on the guide but generated in response to participants' experiences and narratives. This section provides guidelines for writing and generating questions for individual interviews and focus groups, as well as include some sample guides.

Semistructured interview guides include a list of guiding questions to be asked during the interview to ensure that researchers are gathering useful information across participants throughout the study. For the most part, interview questions should be aligned with a study's research questions, although there may be background questions and follow-up questions that do not directly relate back to a particular research question but provide important contextual information to the study or take the study in new directions. Although there is flexibility entailed in all qualitative research studies, and particularly in CBQR projects, interview guides provide an essential structure for the interview, as well as help researchers stay on task within the interview. Although each interview is unique and based on the distinct experiences of participants, it is important that studies obtain some common information across participants to identify patterns and themes during the analysis phase.

Interview guides in qualitative studies should predominantly comprise **open-ended questions**, which cannot be answered with a yes/no answer (these are referred to as closed questions). They should be questions that elicit extended descriptions of particular experiences and perspectives rather than one-word responses. They often begin with broad "Tell me about . . . " questions as a way of drawing out narrations from participants, and then they include more specific follow-up questions that focus on the particulars of experiences or on helping participants define or describe key concepts, beliefs, and practices. The questions should avoid leading the interviewee down a particular narrative pathway, which may seem an obvious point, but it can be difficult to remove our biases and assumptions from questions. For example, a question such as "Don't you think group learning is the best way to teach youth?" obviously contains an assumption about the best pedagogical approaches (and is a yes/no question). However, a question/prompt that may seem open-ended, such as

"Talk about food deserts as the biggest problem in the community," also contains a central assumption about the role of food deserts, which may or may not be shared by the interviewee. Within the interview, it is important that perspectives and viewpoints originate with the interviewee rather than be suggested or identified by the interviewer. A researcher can also lead the interviewee by only focusing on one facet or property of an experience. For example, it is fine to ask participants to identify their favorite aspect of a particular experience, but this should be followed up with a question that asks them to share a less favorite feature or something that they would improve and change. Sometimes, it can be difficult for participants to identify less favorable elements of an experience or program particularly if they believe the interviewer might have a personal stake in the program or there are power differentials between researchers and interviewees. For example, when I have interviewed youth about what they would change at their school, some have seemed reticent and reluctant as they identify me as a teacher, although I am not a teacher at their school. In these cases, I ask participants how they would prepare someone about to attend the school. This can provide insight on what they find as valuable, or less valuable, about the school or program without interviewees feeling like they are being critical or disparaging of the interviewer.

Furthermore, questions that focus on concrete and particular instances and examples are more likely to yield detailed descriptions than general questions. For example, "Tell me what you like about your job," may be used to start off a discussion about an interviewee's professional role, but this should be followed up with "Describe a project at work that was particularly enjoyable for you" or "Describe a day at work when you felt especially successful." Other ways to obtain specific details about a particular event would be to ask participants to pretend they were being followed by a video camera. Questions that ask how participants define particular concepts or offer exemplars can also be useful in generating knowledge and perspectives on topics central to the study. For example, a study on community/civic engagement would want to ask all participants to provide their definition of a community; a project exploring community food insecurity and health issues might ask participants to describe what it means to be a "healthy person."

For questions that aim to identify more abstract values and beliefs, it can be helpful to ask participants hypothetical questions or to create an ideal exemplar or model. For example, rather than ask young parents what their educational philosophy is, I often ask them to create their "ideal teacher," one they would want for their child. Researchers interviewing program directors and staff at a health program could ask them to imagine their ideal health education program or ask them to imagine they were in charge of a fully funded new health education program. In community-based qualitative studies, researchers are often interested in the roles and positions that participants play in a setting and in the tasks, activities, and responsibilities associated with these roles. Interviewers might ask participants to describe a typical day or their morning routine. Or they could ask participants to offer a job description that includes tasks and responsibilities. See Figure 5.1 for a summary of types of interview questions.

**FIGURE 5.1  ●  Interview Question Examples**

- Tell me about . . .
- "Spectrum" questions: What is your favorite thing about your community? What is your least favorite thing about your community? What would you change?
- Typical day/routine: What is a typical day like for you?
- Definition question: What is your definition of technology?
- Recall a specific event (instance): Tell me about the last community project you were involved in.
- "Video camera" question: If I were to follow you with a video camera during the last community event, what would I see?
- Referral/recommendation question: How would you prepare someone to attend this program/school? What advice would you provide someone about to begin a job here?
- Response to prompts/scenarios

It is also essential that the guide not contain "double-barreled" questions or a single question that includes more than one question. For example, questions such as "What do you like most about this community and what do you like the least?" and "How would you describe yourself and how would others describe you?" are questions asking for two different responses. Often, the interviewee gets confused by the double-barreled question and may ask the interviewer to repeat the question or may just respond to one part of the question. It is suggested that multipart questions be divided up into separate questions. They can also be included as follow-ups on the guide.

Questions should also avoid academic jargon unless it can be assured that participants are familiar with particular terms. Such jargon can be off-putting to participants, especially if interviewers have a higher level of education than participants. Some jargon may be appropriate, and even expected, if it is regularly used by participants within the community setting. For example, a term such as *socio-emotional learning* might not be a familiar one for high-school students at a community alternative high school, but it might be one regularly used by members of the social work staff at the school. Similarly, trained staff members at a health/diabetes initiative are likely familiar with specific public health terminology, whereas clients who use the services are less acquainted with these terms. Researchers should also be sensitive to cultural norms and preferences, and they should avoid derogative and pejorative terms. For example, when conducting interviews with formerly incarcerated individuals, a researcher would want to avoid the term *ex-con*; when interviewing staff at a juvenile detention facility, interviewees should not use the term *juvenile delinquent* to describe the youth. In the communities within which I research, the term *Latino/a* is preferred over *Hispanic*. Furthermore, in certain professions and fields, there are often agreed-upon terms for specific roles and positions, and researchers should be attentive to these when developing and refining their interview guides. For example, in the early childhood field, there has been much work to professionalize the field and to move away from the notion that teachers are "just babysitting" children; therefore, terms like *caregiver* have been eschewed in favor of *early childcare professional*. Although researchers might believe that they are aware of appropriate and respectful terms, it is advised that researchers show their interview guide to a community insider to gain insight on terminology. A rule of thumb is to avoid language that labels interviewees in terms of a perceived pathology or deficit. However, as the examples shared underscore, certain terms can connote orientations or viewpoints toward particular groups and there are many other subtleties and nuances that play a role in how a particular term or phrase might be received by a participant.

When developing an interview guide, researchers should pay attention to the ordering of questions. I usually recommend beginning an interview with a broad, warm-up question. This often helps "open up" the interview and put the interviewee at ease. It is also helpful to ask the more benign questions toward the beginning of the interview and to save questions touching on sensitive issues or controversial topics for later on in the interview after researchers have developed a sense of trust with interview participants. If questions cover a wide variety of topics, it is suggested that researchers group questions by topic area, such as family, education, work, or community.

## Follow-Ups and Probing Questions

Interview guides should also include follow-up questions to elicit additional information from participants; these can be especially helpful for less talkative participants and if interviewees are initially not forthcoming with information. In addition to follow-up questions created for the guide, researchers might need to ask probing questions, which are developed in the moment in response to information shared by interviewees, that can help clarify or expand participants' experiences and perspectives. Some basic types of follow-up and probing questions and their purposes are discussed in this section.

Some follow-up questions are meant to *clarify* information shared by participants. This can be important if an interviewee does not directly respond to the question or if information shared is unclear to the interviewer. Clarification questions can involve the rephrasing of the question or asking the participants to repeat a portion of their response. This rephrasing can assist the interviewee in better understanding the question. In some cases, requesting that participants describe or explain a place, event, practice, or occurrence to the researcher as if they were outsiders, or had never been to the setting, can help clarify the details of responses. This approach can be particularly useful if researchers are insiders to the setting and participants assume shared knowledge and experiences and, thus, do not provide detailed accounts as they might to an outsider.

Another strategy for asking follow-up questions involves getting participants to *expand* their response. This can help provide additional details on an experience and/or flesh out the particulars of an instance or event. The interviewer can very simply ask, "Can you tell me more about that?" as a way of probing participants to share more information related to their response. Often, researchers are also interested in concrete examples and illustrations of a practice or event. Follow-up questions such as "Can you provide an example of a time that happened?" can help participants further *illustrate* beliefs and practices, which helps researchers further understand their meaning or significance.

Throughout the interview, researchers might also need to ask interviewees to *define* particular terms and concepts. These definition questions can help identify and refine the meaning participants attribute to specific concepts. These could include specialized terms, such as *food desert* or *project-based learning*, as well as more general and commonly used terms that could have multiple and various meanings, such as *success*, *community*, or *identity*. An example of a definition question would be as follows: "You earlier stated that you wanted youth attending the program to be successful. What does it mean to you to be successful?" Definition questions could also be part of central questions in an interview guide, especially when researchers want to explore definitions of a concept across participants. For example, a study investigating youth's perspectives on civic engagement could ask all youth being interviewed, "What is your definition of community?" as a way of establishing knowledge and perspectives on a particular concept. Researchers should also pay attention to "**markers**" which Robert Weiss (1994) defines as "a passing reference made by a respondent to an important event or feeling state" (p. 77). These refer to events that the interviewee deems as significant to his or her lives but that might not be directly related to the study topic. For example, an interviewee might mention a recent "breakup" or the death of a loved one or an argument or disagreement with someone in the workplace that may not be immediately significant to the topic at hand but that could provide some insight on issues impacting the mindset of an interviewee. Sometimes these are offered directly, whereas on other occasions, they can be suggested more obliquely. For example, a participant might say that "a lot was going on at that time." Researchers could view this sort of statement as insignificant, or feel uncomfortable about probing further, but these markers can often provide further information about the conditions and context related to the study's phenomenon or topic.

At times during the interview, there may be the need to ask questions that *redirect* the interviewee, especially when the conversation is veering too far off topic. Some questions or statements that may help redirect an interview include "Earlier we were talking about . . . can you tell me more about that?" or "What you are sharing is very interesting, but I want to make sure that we have time for all of the questions on the guide." It is fine during an interview to get a bit off topic and to allow for tangential conversation as it can help build rapport and make the interviewee feel more comfortable; sometimes these sorts of conversations can also lead to unexpected discoveries and take the research in new directions. However, if the interview goes too far off course, researchers may end up not getting all areas or topics addressed.

Another technique that can be helpful when conducting interviews for CBQR studies include the use of **elicitation devices**, such as **mapping exercises**, responses to scenarios or lists, or **freesorts (also called free pilesorts**; Schensul, 1999). For example, a study examining health and food insecurity might ask participants to mark on a map stores where they can obtain nutritious food. Requesting responses to lists of items or scenarios can also be an important way to spur discussion of particular topics. For example, a list of cultural proverbs related to childrearing commonly used among Puerto Rican families might be used to initiate discussion of how they have been used in participants' families. Descriptions of stereotypes of homeless people could be used to explore perspectives on homelessness within a particular community. Freesorts involve the use of index cards on which are written various items or cultural domains that participants can group or sort into categories. For example, a project interested in community housing issues might have participants sort problems with housing, such as cost, safety, or quality, by order of importance. In using such elicitation techniques, researchers should be careful that they are not leading the interviewees down a particular narrative path. Many of the topics and items for lists and freesorts can also be generated from interviews and other forms of data collection, which will make sure that they are salient and relevant to the setting and participants.

## Focus Group Guides

When developing interview guides for focus groups, researchers can follow many of the aforementioned guidelines suggested for writing questions for individual interviews. However, focus group interviews are meant to encourage discussion and debate, and thus, questions are often more targeted toward shared experiences rather than individual narratives. Pranee Liamputtong (2011) recommends the following structure for focus group interview questions: Introductory, Transition, Focus, Summarizing, and Concluding (p. 76). Introductory questions help generate knowledge about participants' experiences and perspectives, whereas transition questions narrow the focus and prepare for key questions related to topic/phenomenon of study. These focus/key questions are more closely related to research questions. Summarizing questions restate main points and provide a chance for participants to discuss important issues; concluding questions offer a final opportunity for participants to weigh in on the topic and cover ground not yet addressed in focus group. For example, Liamputtong (2011) suggests that the focus group facilitator end with "Is there anything we didn't talk about?"

Elicitation strategies such as the mapping and freesort activities described earlier can be extremely helpful for generating discussion within focus groups. For example, at the beginning of a session, in a project examining civic engagement, youth could be asked to locate on a map organizations and/or places where they hang out in the community. These could then be placed on a larger map and employed to initiate a group discussion on resources for youth in the community.

# The Interview

This section focuses on preparing for and conducting the interview. In particular, it provides helpful information for scheduling and planning interviews, as well as guidelines to assist in the facilitation of the interview. These aspects of the interview process are as important as the design of the interview guide. Proper planning and facilitation—which includes paying attention to participants' demeanor and behavior—can often "make or break" the success of an interview. The first two sections provide information applicable to individual interviews, whereas the last section provides additional guidelines for implementing focus groups.

## Preparing for the Interview

Once researchers have developed an interview guide and have selected appropriate individuals to interview, they need to go about scheduling interviews and attending to logistical concerns related to the interview process. These details are not insignificant as aspects such as convenient and comfortable location and proper equipment provide the conditions for a successful interview. The following guidelines can help researchers with individual interview preparation.

### Scheduling

Scheduling interviews can be more time-consuming than one might imagine as it requires coordinating busy schedules of interviewers and interviewees. When planning interviews, it is important that researchers open up their schedules so that they can accommodate the availability of interviewees. Since researchers are asking participants to dedicate their time and energy to participate in an interview, they should not be rigid in offering days and times. Especially in community-based research, where participants often work for hectic nonprofit organizations, there may be limited time for conducting interviews. Those working for schools and education programs may not be able to participate in an interview when students are on-site; if interviewing students, researchers may have to interview after a class or program has ended. Some participants may serve in an organization or initiative as a volunteer, and thus they are trying to balance full-time paid employment with volunteer responsibilities. Therefore, researchers need to be sensitive to these issues when setting up interviews.

### Location

Another concern when arranging interviews involves the location for the interview. It is often most convenient to conduct the interview at the participant's workplace or primary research setting, such as the school or community-based organization. However, issues such as privacy, noise level, and comfort level must be considered when scheduling interviews. For example, although a participant's workplace seems like a good choice for the interview, if there is no private office available, it would be inappropriate for an individual interview. An interviewee's home can sometimes be a suitable setting for an interview and can provide additional insight into the home life and setting of a participant; however, there may also be interruptions that could disrupt the interview. Thus, although convenience is a major factor in the scheduling process, researchers need to be mindful of potential distractions and/or impediments posed by various settings.

### Dress

In planning the interview, researchers should also consider how they might dress for the interview. Although this could be viewed as a somewhat superficial concern, one's attire can play a significant role in developing rapport with an interviewee. For example, professional dress can indicate respect for the interviewee, whereas dressing sloppily suggests a lack of concern or care for the interviewee. On the other hand, in some cases, overly formal attire can make a participant uncomfortable or uneasy, in particular, if researchers possess more power in terms of education level or class. Although a business suit could be appropriate dress for an interview with a local political leader, it would likely make one overdressed for an interview with youth attending an afterschool program, when business casual attire would be sufficient.

### Language

The language of the interview should be a language of fluency for the interviewer and interviewee. Although particular researchers may believe that they speak a language well enough to conduct an interview, they should be fluent, as asking follow-up questions and probes requires a sophisticated knowledge of a language and its nuances. Participants may also deem their language skills as "good enough" to complete the interview, but researchers should explain the importance of being fluent and conversant in the target language for the interview. If none of the researchers can conduct interviews in a language of fluency for interviewees, researchers should hire an interpreter to participate in interviews (and keep in mind that researchers would also need to translate interview guides).

### Make a Checklist

Once interviews are scheduled, researchers should develop a checklist of supplies and materials for interviews to ensure that they have everything they need to conduct interview. Materials that researchers would want to bring to an interview include a copy of the interview guide, a digital voice recorder or video camera (depending on how researchers plan to record interviews), and copies of the consent forms (projects would usually provide one for the interviewee and keep a signed one for the project, but the particulars are contingent on the institutional review board protocol for the project). Researchers might also want to bring a notebook for taking notes during the interview. Remember to test the equipment before the interview, as well as to bring extra batteries and/or a back-up recording device; there is nothing worse than having to reschedule an interview because of equipment malfunctioning.

## During the Interview

Robert Bogdan and Sari Biklen (2006) exhort qualitative researchers that good interviewing involves "deep listening" (p. 106), and Irving Seidman (2013) identifies listening as "the most important skill" (p. 81) for qualitative interviewing. The same holds true for interviews within CBQR studies. Important qualities to exhibit during interviews include "respect, interest, attention, and good manners" (Seidman, 2013, p. 99). Interviewees who believe that researchers are interested in what they have to say and respect their beliefs and viewpoints will likely be more forthcoming in sharing information. Robert Weiss (1994) recommends developing a "research partnership" with interviewees, which can be initiated by plainly explaining the purpose of research and further developed and maintained by being an engaged and respectful listener.

At the outset of the interview, researchers should emphasize that there are no right or wrong answers and that all responses are valid. During the interview, interviewers should take notes on important points but also try to maintain eye contact throughout the interview, if culturally appropriate. As noted in the previous section, researchers should also ask for clarification of terms and definitions, as well as be mindful of "markers" (Weiss, 1994, p. 77). However, in asking these follow-up questions, researchers need to be careful not to interrupt the interviewee. When an important term or concept is used, researchers should take note of it and ask the participant after he or she has completed response. If participants are interrupted in the middle of a response, they may lose their train of thought and overlook important details related to a particular experience or event.

Although the interview should proceed like a great conversation, the interviewer should be in control throughout the interview. It is fine to engage in "friendly chit-chat" not directly related to study—particularly before the formal interview begins—as it can help build rapport. However, throughout the interview, the interviewer should be asking the majority of questions, and most of the talking should be done by the interviewee. It is important for the interviewer to be in charge of the interview but not so overly controlling that the participant feels manipulated. Throughout the interview, researchers should carefully manage transitions by preparing the interviewee for shifts to new topics; I usually recommend setting up the interview at the beginning by explaining to the interviewee what areas the interview will cover and then informing participants as the interview moves from one topic to another.

Within the interview, provide participants with sufficient time to collect thoughts and prepare their response. At times, researchers will need to "tolerate silence," such as awkward pauses (Seidman, 2013, p. 95). Researchers should resist the urge to try to "help out" the interviewee by immediately rephrasing the question or suggesting responses as this can sometimes interrupt their thinking or lead the interviewee.

If participants are struggling in their response, grasping for a word or phrase, do not be tempted to finish their sentences or offer a phrase. It is fine to restate the question if they continue to labor; sometimes it is also helpful to repeat an earlier portion of their response. Researchers should also be mindful of any sensitive questions or areas. Some questions might evoke painful experiences or memories for participants; if researchers anticipate some potential emotional areas, they should have Kleenex on hand. If interviewees are very upset, provide them with the opportunity to end the interview. In interviews I have conducted with young mothers, women have recounted horrific instances of domestic violence, sexual abuse, and losing loved ones to gang violence. Unfortunately, these experiences are part of their lived realities and provide insight into issues that need to be addressed within educational and social programs. Researchers need to be careful not to counsel participants or engage in what Seidman (2013) refers to as a "therapeutic relationship" (p. 109). Researchers may need to refer participants to counseling services (and most institutional review boards require that researchers have a list of resources and services on hand for referrals).

When interviewees share their experiences, researchers can react in various ways, and these reactions can influence participants' further responses. Some qualitative methodologists urge interviewers to remain neutral in the face of participants' opinions and perspectives so as not to lead the interviewee or convey preference for a particular viewpoint (Seidman, 2013); they view the use of "OK" and "yes" as responses to interviewees as reinforcing their responses, as well as potentially altering them (Seidman, 2013). However, those researchers employing a participatory approach within their projects might share the researcher role with participants and, thus, opt not to remain neutral; in many cases, then, they serve as advocates on behalf of issues important to participants. Especially when participants share painful experiences, it can be helpful to acknowledge these emotions and/or express some sympathy for particular challenges. If interviewees feel as if they are emoting to an impassive and expressionless "brick wall" and not receiving any response from the interviewee, they might refrain from further disclosure. Within CBQR studies, researchers are often playing more of an advocacy role, or they might be members of the community; thus, some sensitivity and/or empathy could be appropriate. I view the neutrality issue within interviews as occurring along a continuum; the level of compassion that is fitting needs to be decided by the researchers and often depends on the topic and the design and purposes of the project.

It is also important to avoid evaluation or judgment of information shared, in particular, when discussing divisive or controversial topics or issues. Sometimes participants might disclose beliefs or opinions that challenge the researcher's thinking or that the researcher disagrees with; in these cases, researchers need to be careful not to pass judgment on participants' beliefs and practices as this could discourage them from being honest and forthright in their responses. Statements that express shock and surprise, such as "Really?" or "You did WHAT?" as well as body language and facial expressions, can indicate disapproval of or disagreement with a particular viewpoint. Researchers are encouraged to keep an open mind throughout the research process and to be respectful of participants' experiences. The goal of most community-based research studies is not to evaluate practices and programs as "good" or "bad" but to understand better a phenomenon or issue from multiple, and often divergent, experiences and perspectives, which may or may not align with those of the researchers.

Another tricky area involves the amount of acceptable self-disclosure on the part of the interviewer/researcher. Within the field of qualitative interviewing, there is no consensus regarding how much a researcher should reveal about his or her experiences and perspectives. Seidman (2013) has discussed the delicate balance that an interviewer must strike in "saying enough about [oneself] . . . to be alive and responsive but little enough to preserve the autonomy of the participant's words and to keep the focus on his or her experiences, rather than [the interviewer]" (p. 98). Weiss (1994) believes that self-disclosure "complicates an interview situation by shifting the respondent's attention to the interviewer and altering the respondent's relationship with the interviewer" (p. 79). In some cases, sharing too much of one's opinion on an issue could bias participants or make them hesitant to share their perspectives. For example, if researchers are interviewing various residents, of different income levels and ethnicities, in a community about housing and gentrification issues, they might not want to reveal their opinions. However, a certain amount of self-disclosure could help build rapport or make the interviewee more comfortable divulging information. When I have interviewed teen mothers, I have often shared my role as a mother of a young child as I believed it might serve to bridge the age gap between us and build a sense of commonality.

Some participants might be interested in the researcher's experiences and ask pointed questions during the interview; if the interviewer avoids or tries to shake off their queries, they may feel a lack of reciprocity on the part of the interviewer. Thus, in some cases, it may be fine to respond to participants' questions when the interview has ended if researchers believe that doing so won't prejudice the interview and compromise study findings.

## Ending the Interview and Afterward

Researchers should remain mindful of keeping to time allotted for the interview; if the researcher has told the participant to expect a 45- to 90-minute interview, he or she should not exceed this allocation. Toward the end of the interview, if it seems that there will not be enough time to ask all of the questions, the researcher can ask if the participant can extend the interview or schedule a second interview. If neither of these are a possibility, the interviewer should try to complete as many questions as possible in the remaining time. When the interview has ended, it is important to thank the participant for his or her time and to ask whether the interviewee has any additional questions. I don't recommend turning off the recording device until after the participant has asked any questions as these can often furnish interesting insights related to the study's topic. Researchers should also be sure to obtain current contact information for each participant in case they need to ask additional follow-up or clarification questions or need to set up follow-up interviews or focus groups.

Although some CBQR projects may have funding to compensate interviewees, many projects do not have sufficient funds to provide remuneration for participation in research. Monetary compensation might include a stipend, a giftcard or gift certificate, or a small gift. In projects I have conducted, I have purchased gift certificates at a local café, writing journals, and sweet treats. In addition to monetary gifts, there are other ways to reward participants for their involvement in the study, such as the offering of a service. For example, teachers might appreciate help with curriculum planning or some resources for the classroom. A community-based organization might need assistance with identifying and/or preparing grants for a particular initiative or project. Youth could use support and guidance from researchers in writing personal essays for college or completing the college application process.

After the interview has ended, researchers should listen to the interview as a way of critiquing or evaluating the quality of the interview guide and skills of the interviewer, especially toward the beginning of the study when researchers have just begun the interview process. This can help researchers call attention to occasions when they might have asked better follow-up questions or when they might have been inadvertently leading the interviewee. Often, researchers are unaware they were interrupting a participant or evaluating information shared. Careful listening to each interview before conducting the next interview can help researchers strengthen and improve their skills as they progress through interviews, as well as help researchers refine the interview guide.

In most qualitative research studies, researchers prepare **verbatim transcripts** of interviews. This means completing word-for-word printed renderings of interviews for analysis (which is covered in detail in Chapter 7). Transcripts should be completed as soon as possible after each interview, and sufficient time should be allotted for the transcriptions as they can be time-consuming (allow 4–6 hours per each hour of interview). Tools and resources that can be helpful in transcribing include foot pedals for more precisely rewinding recordings and transcription software that can assist with keyboard shortcuts for rewinding and slowing down recording; although some programs and voice recognition software claim to transcribe automatically, these usually yield sloppy and inaccurate transcriptions. Projects with monetary resources may opt to pay professional transcribers, but researchers should still listen to audiotapes before sending them out because of the aforementioned points about being able to critique interviewing skills. Furthermore, when transcribing interview recordings, one becomes much more familiar with interview data, which will be extremely beneficial in the analysis phase. If completing all of the transcriptions is too onerous and unrealistic for a project, researchers might consider farming some of them out to a professional service but still transcribing a portion of the interviews.

## Focus Group Implementation

Many of the recommendations for the implementation of interviews are also applicable to focus groups. However, because the focus group interview involves group facilitation and encouraging debate among participants, some additional approaches for preparation and implementation can be useful to achieving a successful and productive focus group. The following suggestions are related to focus group implementation:

- **Offer incentives**: To ensure that researchers will have sufficient participants for the focus group, incentives should be provided. These could include small stipends, gift cards, or a raffle. For youth, a pizza party can be a great way to incentivize participation.
- **Consider transportation and child care:** Another way to ensure full participation is to provide transportation and/or parking stipends and childcare (especially if researchers are focusing on parents within their research project). If funding is not available for this transportation, researchers should try to convene the focus group in a convenient location. An alternative to providing childcare stipends would be to offer childcare on site (I have found this imperative when conducting focus groups with young mothers).
- **Provide refreshments:** Offering food and/or refreshments can help create a convivial atmosphere and make participants more comfortable. It also provides an additional incentive for participants. Food can be available at the beginning of a session as a way of orienting participants into the session and of allowing for late arrivals; refreshments might also be served as part of a mid-session break.
- **Use nametags or tents:** This is especially important if participants are unfamiliar with one another. Supplying name tags or tents can help participants learn and use each other's names, as well as assist the facilitator in remembering participants' names. It is also helpful to ask focus group members to state their name when they speak as this eases identification of participants during transcription.
- **Sit in a circle around a table if possible:** To encourage discussion, it is crucial to provide conditions that facilitate conversation and dialogue. This includes making sure that participants are facing one another and are close enough to hear other participants. A table is not essential but can provide a steady surface for participants to take notes and a place for researchers to place the recorder/microphone. Furthermore, a table can sometimes make shy or anxious participants feel less exposed and vulnerable.
- **Work in pairs:** Because there are a lot of components entailed in setting up and managing an effective focus group, it is recommended that researchers work in at least groups of two. One researcher can serve as the facilitator, while the other can take notes and be in charge of consent forms and recording devices. Having at least two people also helps guard against important details being overlooked. Projects that are being conducted by one researcher only could make use of a graduate assistant or volunteer from a community partner.

The role of the facilitator in a focus group is to help foster dialogue and make sure that all participants get a chance to share their perspectives. It can be detrimental to the group if one particularly strong opinion dominates the discussion and silences other voices. Researchers should explore differences and disagreements *in situ*, or at the time they are being shared, without provoking arguments or conveying preference for a particular viewpoint. Some questions that might be used to promote discussion and make sure diverse viewpoints are expressed include "Does anyone have another experience to share?" or "BLANK seems to think X. Does everyone agree with that? Are there other opinions?" If one person seems to be dominating the discussion and/or interrupting others, facilitators can remind participants of ground rules for focus group.

## Chapter Summary

In this chapter, we learned various strategies for the design, planning, and implementation of individual interviews and focus groups within CBQR studies. Interviews are a central form of gaining information and data in CBQR studies and require careful planning. Whereas individual interviews focus on eliciting rich and detailed narratives and descriptions from participants, focus groups emphasize dialogue and debate among participants on shared and divergent experiences and viewpoints. In addition to developing an interview guide that includes open-ended, nonleading questions, researchers should ask follow-up questions and probes that build on participants' distinct experiences. "Deep listening" and respect for others' opinions and perspectives are important qualities for interviewers to possess. Researchers need to ask follow-up questions that can expand and clarify responses and help participants define important terms and concepts.

## Key Terms

Elicitation devices  90

Freesorts (also called free pilesorts)  90

Homogeneous groups  84

Heterogeneous groups  84

Mapping exercises  90

Markers  89

Open-ended questions  85

Unstructured interviews  82

Semistructured interviews  82

Structured interviews  82

Verbatim transcripts  96

## ● Activities for Reflection and Discussion

1) **Interview guides:** Develop an interview guide for a proposed community-based qualitative research study. Trade your guide with a partner, and check each other's guides for the following:

   a) *Open-ended questions:* They should not be able to be answered with a yes/no or a single word/phrase.

   b) *Free of leading questions:* Check questions for implicit hypotheses or suggested responses.

c)   *Free of academic jargon:* Review questions to make sure that language is clear and will be understandable to interviewees.

d)   *Culturally appropriate terms and language:* Check questions for terminology and labels; take note of any terms that should be changed.

2)   **Practice interview:** Conduct a mock interview with a partner. Develop/use a basic interview guide that focuses on educational background or professional experiences. Remember to ask follow-up questions that help clarify and expand responses, as well as define important terms. Each individual should get 10 minutes to ask questions. After the interview, discuss areas of strength, as well as where better follow-up questions could have been asked.

3)   **Transcript reflection:** Review a transcript from an individual interview or focus group (either one you have conducted or a research team member). Identify places where the interviewer exhibited strong interview skills, and label them STRONG. Identify places where interviewer could have had stronger skills, and label them IMPROVE. Identify good follow-up questions, and label them STRONG FOLLOW. Identify weak follow-up questions, and label them WEAK FOLLOW. Find markers, and label them MARKER. Circle or highlight insider terms/concepts.

4)   **Focus group fishbowl (for classes or research teams):** Assign three to five members of a small group (about six to eight) the following roles: "Gets off topic," "Agrees with everyone," "Interrupts," "Does not share or speak," and "Dominates discussion." Make sure that you have a few group members who have no assigned role; these individuals should just act normally. Designate another individual to serve as the facilitator. Provide a basic interview guide (of about five questions) to the facilitator on a topic that all group members have knowledge of and experience to respond to (for example, for a group of graduate students, questions might focus on experience in a program). The rest of the class or group should observe the focus group while they go through the questions (allow about 10–15 minutes). Afterward, discuss how the facilitator handled problematic behaviors. Point out successes and where the facilitator might have addressed issues differently. This activity can also be adapted for smaller groups; assign less of the behaviors/roles, and make sure there is at least one member with a "normal" role.

# HANDOUT 4
## Sample Interview Guides

**Sample Interview Guide: Worker at a Community-Based Organization**

1. Tell me about your educational experiences.

2. Tell me about some of your work experiences.

3. How did you find out about the program?

4. What are your responsibilities in the program?

5. What types of training did/do you receive? Were there any training materials provided?

6. Describe a typical day for you. What activities are you involved in? If you were to write a job description for your position, what would it include?

7. How do you know if you are successful? Describe a particularly successful moment.

8. What are challenges in this work? Describe a challenging moment, or when you weren't successful.

9. What have you learned from your participation at (name of site)?

10. If you were to describe the program to someone else, what would you say?

11. What are your goals in 1 year? 3 years? 5 years?

**Interview Guide for Mentors in an Intergenerational Mentorship Program for Young Mothers**

1. Tell me about your educational experiences.

2. What was your first reaction when you discovered you were pregnant? Who did you tell? How did he or she react?

3. What were your experiences as a student-parent?

   a. What were your challenges?

   b. What support and resources did you use/receive?

   c. Describe a particular memory as a student-parent that stands out.

4. What were your goals when you graduated?

   a. Educational?

   b. Professional?

   c. Personal?

5. Tell me about your activities/experiences since graduating from high school.

   a. Educational?

   b. Professional?

   c. Personal?

6. What challenges have you faced since graduating?

7. Why did you want to become a mentor for other young mothers?

8. What skills do you believe you bring to your role as a mentor?

9. What are your goals as a mentor?

10. Tell me about your work with your mentee. What do you do? Talk about?

11. Describe your mentee.

12. Tell me about an interaction with your mentee that stands out.

13. What have you gained/learned from your experience as a mentor?

14. What have been some challenges of your mentorship work?

15. What changes would you make in the mentorship program?

16. What advice would you provide to other young mothers?

17. What advice would you provide to others interested in mentoring young mothers?

**Interview Guide for Youth on Community Engagement**

1. What does community mean to you?

2. Describe the community that you identify with the most.

3. What things are you most proud of about your community? The least proud?

4. What do you think about community involvement?

5. What does an active community member look like?

6. What is your first memory of this community?

7. How would you describe the community to someone who has never been there?

8. How do you think outside people perceive the community?

9. Have you been involved in any community projects in the past year?

   a. How were you introduced to community service/civic engagement?

10. If you were in charge of a new community project, what issues/needs would it address? Why?

*(Continued)*

(Continued)

11. What information do you share with your family/friends about your involvement in the community?

    a. What do they say about your involvement in the community?

12. Tell me about the school's role in your community service?

13. What do you think your community will look like in 10 years?

**Questions for Focus Groups With Students in a Community-Based Research Course**

1. Please introduce yourself. Include program, degree, and professional role.

2. What motivated you to enroll in the class? How did you find out about course?

3. What did you know about the class before attending? Instructor?

4. Prior to attending the course, what did you know about the community?

5. What do you remember about that first day of the course?

6. What are your strongest memories from the course experience?

7. How was this course different than others you have taken?

8. What did you gain from taking this course?

9. What challenges did you face in taking this course?

10. How could the course be improved?

11. How would you describe the course to others?

12. How would you prepare other students about to take this course?

# Observations, Fieldwork, and Other Data Collection

## Introduction

This chapter describes approaches for conducting observations and fieldwork, along with other data collection methods that might be used within a CBQR study. This chapter also includes student reflections on the challenges entailed when conducting fieldwork, as well as examples of different sorts of visual and/or electronic documents and artifacts that can serve as a source of data within CBQR.

## Learning Goals

After reading this chapter, students will be able to:

1. Describe different types of participant observation, and determine when certain participant observation approaches are most appropriate within community-based qualitative research (CBQR) studies.

2. Discuss some of the issues and challenges entailed when conducting field work.

3. Identify different types of textual and visual data and artifacts that might be used within CBQR, and describe how they can be used to support other forms of data.

4. Explain how websites and social media posts might be used as a source of data within CBQR studies.

# Observations and Fieldwork

Conducting observations and engaging in fieldwork are important components of data collection in community-based qualitative research (CBQR) projects. Early on in a study, they can help researchers become acclimated to the community, familiarize them with community events, and help them build rapport with community members. Throughout the study, fieldwork provides insights on community life and practices and helps researchers tap into and better understand interactions among participants.

## Types and Levels of Participant Observation

**Participant observation** is a central data collection approach within anthropology and other fields such as sociology, psychology, and education; it involves either formal or informal observations of settings, activities, and/or events, such as classrooms/classes, meetings, performances, tutoring sessions, workshops, protests and demonstrations, daily rituals, and workplaces. The goal of these observations is to learn "the explicit and tacit aspects" of the life routines and culture of a particular group (DeWalt & DeWalt, 2011, p. 1). Formal observations are usually set up in advance and are often of nonpublic activities, such as classes, meetings, and workshops, whereas informal observations might be more impromptu.

Within these observations, researchers can adopt various roles in relation to settings and participants. James Spradley (1980) outlines different levels of participation that might occur within participation observation, from passive to complete. A *passive* participant would maintain no membership within the setting, serving as a bystander and not interacting with participants. In CBQR studies, these sorts of observations might include initial observations of relevant community settings—such as parks, playgrounds, and central business districts—or events such as community parades and festivals. *Moderate* participation would entail that the researcher maintains a balance between being an insider and outsider within the setting and adopts a more peripheral role. The researcher might observe a classroom or workshop from the corner and occasionally interact with participants, but for the most part he or she remains on the sidelines.

Researchers might also take on *active* membership as a participant observer, where they seek "to *do* what other people are doing . . . to more fully learn the cultural rules for behavior" (Spradley, 1980, p. 60). An active role requires that researchers fully participate in setting activities. For example, a student enrolled in a summer community-based research course I instructed conducted fieldwork at a community café to understand better how employees learn at this workplace and the role of the café in community life. Instead of observing from the outside, as in passive or peripheral membership, the student donned an apron and worked the front counter of the café. This role allowed her to gain greater insight into the processes of knowledge and skill acquisition and the routines at the café than if she had been sitting in the corner observing passively.

*Complete* or full membership is a role assumed by individuals who are already participants in a setting. This would be appropriate for research partners conducting research in settings and contexts within which they actively participate and are thus familiar. Some researchers caution that it is more difficult to notice tacit rules and taken-for-granted routines when one is a member of the setting. However, the insight that a complete member can provide is often invaluable to a project; in CBQR studies, such insider knowledge and experiences are essential to better understanding community issues, beliefs, and practices.

Within one research study, researchers can take on multiple roles and levels of membership as participant observers. For example, researchers investigating a community agriculture initiative might assume a moderate role for observations of planning meetings, taking notes and asking questions when appropriate; during a planting event for a community garden, it would be more appropriate for researchers to participate alongside program staff and community residents in the activity, taking on an active role.

Within CBQR, the concept of *observant* participation might be more meaningful than participant observation. Although participant observation occurs along a continuum, the term emphasizes observation rather than the active participation in community settings that is the hallmark of most CBQR studies. In some cases, a more peripheral role might be appropriate. But, in many other instances, taking on the role of bystander might actually hinder a researcher's ability to learn about a particular setting. For example, Kathy, who conducted fieldwork at a community bike shop as part of a summer research course, initially attempted to collect data standing in the corner with a notepad. She shared that she felt awkward and out of place and that participants at the site seemed to view her as an intrusion—in fact, one bike shop member teased her by asking who she was an informant for. After what she viewed as a fieldwork disaster, she returned to the site, brought her bike, and participated in a fix-it workshop, finding this to be a more natural and effective approach for learning about the processes of knowledge acquisition and transmission at the shop.

Kathy's experience illustrates the need for researchers conducting CBQR to make decisions regarding the level of participation in observations based on what makes sense and is appropriate in particular contexts, as well as keeping in mind the purpose of the observation. Community-based qualitative researchers usually take a more active role in observations and include complete members as part of the research team, but there may be occasions when a more passive or moderate role is warranted within observations. The following section discusses issues related to conducting observations.

## Conducting Participant Observation

Although observations within CBQR studies can emerge informally, there is often planning required for conducting observations. First and foremost, as detailed in Chapter 4, researchers should decide at the outset of the study what sorts of events and activities will be helpful to providing information and insight related to the project's research questions. It is also important to determine the type of role that researchers will play in observations before conducting observations. For example, researchers should agree to their level of participation in each observation and discuss this role, along with the purpose of observations, with key stakeholders and/or gatekeepers beforehand as this can help the research team avoid confusion and misunderstandings. For example, if a researcher plans on adopting a moderate role within an observation of a science class where an urban agriculture project is being introduced, this should be clearly articulated and agreed to beforehand with the teacher. Otherwise, the teacher might view the researcher as potential "extra help" within the classroom or involve the researcher in the classroom as an active member. Conversely, the researcher might want to take on an active role within a particular setting but then is excluded and treated as a passive observer by participants because the role was not negotiated at the outset. Furthermore, researchers should inquire about any rules that apply to the setting—such as dress codes or cell phone use—to prevent violating any of these. Especially in situations where adults might be in positions of authority over youth or children, the role of researchers within the setting should be mutually agreed to beforehand.

As illustrated in Kathy's "sticking out" in her observation of a bike shop, regardless of the level of participation chosen for an observation, researchers should attempt to "blend in" as much as possible. This acclimatization can be achieved through appropriate clothing/dress, stances, and/or materials. Researchers should dress in ways that are suitable given their role and the setting. For example, if researchers are actively participating in a community cleanup, formal attire, such as a suit, would not be appropriate; however, if they are serving as passive observers of a school board meeting, they might want to dress more professionally. Researchers can also blend in as far as stances and orientation. Particularly in the beginning of a project or when tackling a controversial or divisive topic, researchers might want to keep their viewpoints and stances somewhat neutral as expressing strong opinions within the observations might silence divergent voices or bias participants' perspectives.

Researchers should also plan for how they will document information from observations. Many fieldworkers take field notes (and these are discussed in more detail in the following section) to detail descriptions of setting and record interactions, dialogue, and behaviors, although in some instances, this sort of "in the field" note taking can be viewed as intrusive. An alternative option is to take notes immediately after the observation, but the level of detail will be compromised. Sometimes audio and video recording is used to facilitate this documentation, but this can also be an invasive element, and it poses additional risks to confidentiality, which can make institutional review board (IRB) approval more cumbersome.

The role of the researcher within observations should be evaluated and negotiated throughout the project by members of the research team, as well as through ongoing discussions and dialogue with research partners and participants. As much as possible, researchers should make attempts to reciprocate participants for the opportunity to observe them.

## Field Notes

There are two primary types of field notes: descriptive and reflective. **Descriptive field notes** provide in-depth descriptions and depictions of particular settings and events, as well as the participants, objects, activities, behaviors and interactions that make up these contexts. **Reflective field notes** contain reflective commentary and are often focused on the role or stances of the researcher in relation to the setting and participants, providing the opportunity for researchers to "step back" from the setting and explore moments of discomfort or discontinuity, reflect on ethical dilemmas, discuss methodological challenges and obstacles, detail revelations and epiphanies, and/or examine researchers' experiences and beliefs in relation to research participants. This section will be focused on descriptive field notes as these are the type of notes most often used as a part of a data set, although reflective field notes can serve as important data to offer insight into the research process and researchers' changing stances and beliefs. (See Figure 6.1 for a summary of information in descriptive and reflective field notes.)

As mentioned, it is important to establish a method of documenting information and insights gained within observations. Many fieldworkers take **jotted field notes**, traditionally in a notebook but more increasingly by using laptops and other technology such as tablets and phones. When it is not possible to take notes *in situ*, researchers might make notations immediately after the observation, while information is still fresh. Audio and video devices can also be employed to support researchers' memories during an observation (and the following section provides more explanation of how to use audio and video recording to prepare transcripts of observations). Many researchers insist that field notes be written "contemporaneously" as perspectives change over time and because of the importance of "preserving experience close to the moment of occurrence" (Emerson, Fretz, & Shaw, 2011, p. 17). After the observation, these jotted

---

**FIGURE 6.1  ●  Information in Descriptive and Reflective Field Notes**

---

**Descriptive Field Notes**

- Descriptions of participants: Physical characteristics, clothing and accessories, gestures and facial expressions, role within setting or activity
- Description of setting/context: Physical context, organization and layout of the setting, decorations, signage, materials, and specific items
- Discussion and dialogue: Members' terms, dialogue, descriptions, stories, definitions, forms of address and greetings, and everyday questions and routines; capture direct quotations when possible
- Accounts of behavior and activities: Roles and behavior, reactions and responses; avoid abstract words of actions
- Observer's behavior: Researcher's physical location in the setting, behavior, and interactions with participants

**Reflective Field Notes**

- Reflective commentary
- Role or stances of the researcher in relation to the setting and participants
- Moments of discomfort or discontinuity
- Ethical dilemmas
- Methodological challenges and obstacles
- Revelations and epiphanies

---

notes should be written into **formalized field notes** to create a fuller and more detailed rendering of activities and events and to produce a more seamless narrative than is possible with jotted notes, although field notes can never serve as an omniscient version of what has occurred. Most researchers strongly urge that these formal field notes be written immediately after the observation; Annette Lareau (1989/1997) recommends strict adherence to her 24-hour rule for completing field notes. Otherwise, one cannot trust the accuracy of the information included in the notes and they may not include the same level of detail. If it is not possible to write up formal field notes within a day, researchers might consider dictating field notes to create "talk notes," although eventually these will need to be transcribed if they are to be used for analysis (Emerson et al., 2011, p. 49).

When conducting CBQR studies, researchers should always carry a notebook with them even if they have not scheduled ans observation. This will enable them to take advantage of impromptu opportunities for participant observation and to record notations of spontaneous events and displays. For example, members of the research team might be out for lunch and come upon an activity relevant to their research topic, or they may observe an interaction that provides insight into their topic. Students enrolled in summer classes I have instructed on CBQR have taken note of organized groups exercising in the park and newly added healthy offerings in local restaurants as evidence of the role that a community health initiative was playing across community settings. Students attending a community parade included not only rich detail of parade floats but also accounts of what took place before the parade, such as descriptions of community residents dancing on the sidewalk, and noted comments made to them and questions asked by passersby. One student even recorded in her field notes a discussion she had with the taxi driver who drove her to the area.

In writing field notes, researchers should attempt to identify and describe indigenous and local meanings and develop "an understanding of what [participants] . . . experiences and activities *mean to them*" (Emerson et al., 2011, p. 16). Field notes should include detailed descriptions of the setting, as well as of participants. Field notes from initial observations of a site might also feature maps and drawings of site/setting or classroom layout. These descriptions should be as fine-grained as possible, including vivid details that will evoke visual images. When describing people, include descriptions of features and characteristics such as hair and skin color, body type, attire, jewelry and accessories, and tattoos. In the early stages of the project, researchers should create such character sketches to provide them with a sense of key actors and participants in particular settings; as they become more familiar with individuals within the research context, they may not need to include these detailed physical descriptions in every field note entry. Researchers should also take in the physical context, noting details about the organization and layout of the setting, as well as decorations, signage, materials, and items. It is important to "map the scene" not only to capture these details but also to examine spatial arrangements and gather data on social relationships (DeWalt & DeWalt, 2011). Within CBQR, in addition to descriptions of specific sites, researchers might provide descriptions of the broader community. This community mapping can be used as a "means of defining the study area, understanding and analyzing the geographical description of community members, [and] describing the activity spaces" (DeWalt, & DeWalt, 2011, p. 84).

Alongside these depictions of the physical elements of the setting and community, field notes should include accounts of social and interaction processes. As researchers observe interactions and dialogue among participants in the setting, they should take specific note of details that contextualize talk, as well as of members' terms, descriptions, stories, definitions, forms of address and greetings, and everyday questions and routines. The sorts of language and terms that participants use can provide researchers with insights into how various individuals in the setting view the topic and their stances related to community issues and events. The ways that individuals interact with one another within the setting can indicate relationships among participants; researchers should be especially sensitive to participants' roles and power hierarchies within particular activities and contexts. In pursuing members' meanings, researchers should pay attention to the ways in which members' react to specific events and behaviors, as well as to how they "invoke relevant contexts for particular activities and relevant contrasts for some feature or quality of their setting" (Emerson et al., 2011, p. 144). In addition, documenting "members' complex explanations for when, why, and how particular things happen," or their theories of causes, can help researchers better understand participants' beliefs and processes of meaning making (Emerson et al., 2011, p. 149). Whenever you can, quote people verbatim rather than summarizing what they say, although it is not always possible to collect extended direct quotes; thus, field notes should include direct quotations interspersed with approximations and summaries.

When writing up descriptive field notes, researchers should avoid the use of any judgmental or evaluative language, such as "good" or "bad" as a way of describing a behavior or person. Remember that the purpose of participant observation is not to judge or evaluate the behavior and actions of participants but to learn more about experiences, beliefs, and practices. Using adjectives or phrases that label, generalize, or stereotype participants results in vague and objectifying (and often inaccurate) descriptions that pose challenges to analyzing data later in the project. For example, two students enrolled in a summer CBQR course interested in health initiatives within a Puerto Rican community were assigned to walk around in the community and individually take field notes on resources related to health in the community; in a corner store, one woman described the cashier as "African American" and another as "Puerto Rican," and both were incorrect (I knew that the man was from Palestine). Both women had made assumptions about the man's ethnic identity based on his skin color and the community context that provided few specifics about what he looked like and what he did. Instead, they might have written concrete descriptions of his features, what he was wearing, what he said, and what sorts of objects, such as photos and artifacts, occupied his work area, details that would have been much more enlightening regarding the man's identity. Robert Emerson, Rachel Fretz, and Linda Shaw (2011) urge fieldworkers to steer clear of simplistic physical attributes and "common indicators of general social categories"—such as age, gender, and race—and instead "capture distinctive qualities" and create a "*vivid* image" that "depicts specific details about people and settings so that the image can be clearly visualized" (p. 60).

Abstract words, such as *teaching*, *disciplining*, and *leading*, are also not helpful in describing participants' actions and behavior; instead researchers should write detailed accounts of what people are doing and saying. Furthermore, community-based qualitative researchers should focus on what they see and observe, rather than on what's "not there," or what does not happen, as noting what is absent contains an implicit value judgment and assumptions regarding what resources and practices researchers think *should* exist within the setting. Within descriptive field notes, researchers must resist the urge to analyze or interpret behavior, although many would point out that engaging in participant observation and constructing field notes is always an interpretive act as researchers make decisions about what to notice that are always filtered through the particular lens of the researcher. That said, explicit analysis and interpretation should be kept at a minimum and only included as part of an aside or observer's comments. These **observer's comments** can be indicated with bracketed text, such as [OC: ] (Bogdan & Biklen, 2006). Researchers could also include some reflective commentary at the end of their notes.

Although the primary focus of descriptive field notes is on the participants and setting, researchers should also include themselves as a character. This could include descriptions of the researcher's physical location in the setting, behavior, and interactions with participants. For example, researchers should describe their role within the setting and how participants respond and react to them, such as questions they ask or comments they make. It is also important to keep notes organized and establish a consistent system of record keeping for field notes, such as including dates, time periods, and setting in header, and titling each field note with a numbering system (for example, Field01, Field02, etc.).

### Videotaped Observations

Some researchers within CBQR studies might also videotape observations to provide a source of data. For research projects interested in capturing interactions and dialogue in a fine-grained way, recording and completing a verbatim transcription is essential. Videotaped observations can, of course, offer much more detail than is possible in observations that rely on memory and handwritten notes; however, a drawback is that recordings need to be transcribed, which is extremely time-consuming. When this level of detail is not required, video recordings could be used to supplement and support the completion of field notes; in this case, researchers might use recordings to "jog" memory or fill in gaps within notes rather than to complete verbatim transcriptions. Or, researchers could review video recordings and select critical incidents that closely relate to topic or phenomenon and transcribe those more fully, although it can still be a chore to review recordings. Furthermore, it should be noted that video recordings also pose additional challenges in terms of storage and usually require dedicated and ample server space. Gathering data via audio and video recordings also makes IRB approval more cumbersome.

Although one might view video recordings as purveying an omniscient view of a particular setting, there are limitations. Unless researchers have multiple cameras and research team members who can manage the cameras, the video can only offer a "slice" of activity in any particular setting, depending on where the camera is situated and what persons and activities the lens is taking in. Thus, researchers should not rely solely on the video recording and take notes if they can. Furthermore, in some cases, the presence of video cameras can be perceived intrusively and might make participants uncomfortable and reticent to participate authentically in the setting.

## Documents, Artifacts, and Visual Data

In addition to conducting participant observation and completing field notes, researchers might collect textual documents and visual images to provide insight on their topic and setting. These can be identified and gathered within participant observation or even suggested and provided by participants within focus groups and interviews. Some might be physical documents, such as paper brochures, handouts, and posted flyers, whereas others might be found electronically, such as websites and blogs. This section discusses the use of this sort of data within CBQR and provide some examples from community-based studies.

## Use of Documents, Artifacts, and Visual Data

Documents, artifacts, and visual data might be used in several ways within qualitative research studies. In some cases, documents and artifacts might serve as a primary source of data, for example, when researchers might be analyzing archival documents, such as letters or journals, or when they might be examining photographs and images related to a particular topic. Since community-based qualitative researchers are often interested in community members' experiences and perspectives related to a particular issue, it is rare for visual and textual documents to serve as the *sole* source of data within the study. However, there are many cases when they might serve as *a* primary data source, along with interview transcripts and field notes. For example, researchers could examine youth project assignments and materials, such as handouts, final papers, and presentations, related to a community involvement initiative to identify definitions and views of the community. Researchers might closely analyze program materials used to promote neighborhood health programs to explore the sorts of language and terminology used to describe health issues, as well as the types of services offered.

More often, community-based qualitative researchers use documents, artifacts, and visual data to substantiate findings generated from interviews and observations; in these cases, documents and visual data would not be examined as closely as in the previous examples. Photos from a community activity could be used as supportive evidence of youth involvement in community events. Students' poetry and art could serve as exemplars of youth expression and creativity within an after-school arts program. Documents and artifacts can also be used to furnish background information and context related to the setting and issue under study. For example, organizational websites can offer insight into the mission or vision of an organization; community blogs and web portals can be used initially to assess community concerns related to a particular topic.

## Textual Documents

A variety of textual documents might be used within a CBQR study, and the examples discussed here are not meant to be exhaustive. Including documents as a data source can provide significant examples of practices and beliefs described within interviews and observed in various community settings. They can also serve to enliven findings by offering textual demonstrations of how certain beliefs and experiences are enacted and expressed by individuals as well as on an organizational or community level. A primary source of documents is offered through participant produced texts and writings, such as student poetry and creative writing, homework assignments and essays, participants' journals or diaries, and/or notes and lists created for specific purposes. For example, in a study looking at housing issues within a community, a high-school student's poem about changes in the community illustrated how residents are responding to gentrification. In a project on youth civic engagement, a student essay detailing participation in a community beautification project provided insight into specific ways that youth are involved in their community and how such involvement contributes to their notions of community and views of themselves.

Another source of textual documents can be purveyed by program and classroom handouts and materials, such as curriculum guides and syllabi, program brochures, leaflets promoting events, and teachers' lesson plans (see Figure 6.2). These sorts of documents serve as instantiations of particular beliefs and objectives or demonstrate how certain messages and values are being publically transmitted and disseminated. For example, in a project on youth civic engagement, a teacher's lesson plan for a parenting class for young parents served as an illustration of how advocacy skills were integrated into classroom instruction.

Policy documents and materials, such as state educational standards, policy manuals, and organizational mission statements, can help researchers identify organizational goals

---

**FIGURE 6.2   ●   Sustainable Democracy Drafting Organizational History**

*Use the research and bullet points from your group members to fill out this sheet. The paragraph must include:*

1. What is the organization you are working with, and why did its members approach you with their problem?

2. Describe the history of the organization. When and why was it founded? By whom? Include source (Author, Year).

3. What community need does this organization exist to address? Include source (Author, Year).

4. What is the mission, vision, or major goal of this organization? Include source (Author, Year).

5. What does this organization do? List and describe its major activities? Include source (Author, Year).

6. Who is served by this organization? What is the organization's target audience or population? How does it reach out to them? Include source (Author, Year).

7. What effect has this organization made on the community since it started working on this problem? What successes has it had in meeting its goals? Include source (Author, Year).

8. How does the organization collect data on its outcomes? How does it know if it is successful? How does it measure its results? Include source (Author, Year).

---

and objectives, as well as determine broader discourses circulating around participants and setting. In a project interested in social emotional learning at a local alternative school, a researcher examined state guidelines informing the school staff's approach to social emotional learning. A project investigating civic engagement reviewed the school handbook, mission statement, and guiding instructional framework to identify how notions of community activism and social justice were integrated into school policy.

## Photographs, Images, and Visual Documents

Visual images can also serve as an important source of insight within CBQR studies. For example, photographs of classrooms, meeting spaces, and events can provide information on spatial layout and organization of activities. Photographs of signage and posters within settings can suggest significant values and belief systems, as well as indicate broader discourses influencing the setting and participants. These images might also contain text, but the emphasis is on how the text interacts with and supports the visual elements.

Archival photos can also be used within studies to purvey historical context and background, and they might be analyzed to examine past events or activities or to trace changes within the physical setting. For example, in a project investigating gentrification and housing in an urban community, photos of the primary community business district over a 50-year period could provide a visual depiction of the community's economic trajectory and the impact of gentrification on community development and displacement of businesses and residents. Pictures of specific events, such as festivals and parades, can offer insight into the long-term significance and transformation of particular traditions and customs, as well as the import of various issues and concerns within the history of the community.

Advertisements, leaflets, and postcards, either locally produced or part of broader public media campaigns, can also play a role in CBQR studies. Locally produced leaflets or banners can serve as instantiations and expressions of community discourses and beliefs related to particular issues; billboards and advertisements can indicate external messages and rhetoric swirling around context and shaping external and local attitudes related to an issue or population. For example, a project exploring the experiences and civic engagement of young mothers in a community reviewed advertisements and popular media images of teen parents as a way of documenting stereotypes and messages about young parents (see photo on page 116). These images were also used to spur discussion about the mothers' experiences with stigma and discrimination. The mothers then created an alternative ad campaign of posters and public service announcements, which included positive images and messages about the experiences and struggles of young mothers.

## Websites, Electronic Artifacts, and Social Media

As the Internet, digital resources, and social media become more prevalent ways of acquiring and sharing information, they also become important sources of data

Teen pregnancy advertisement.

within CBQR studies. Organizational websites often include a wealth of information about programs, services, and resources, alongside news related to community issues and events. The website for a community alternative high school featured information on a community urban agriculture initiative that was useful evidence for researchers examining youth civic engagement. Community portals and blogs can help researchers tap into various and divergent attitudes related to community issues and concerns. For example, in a study on housing and gentrification, a community discussion board revealed conflicts and tensions between the long-time, predominately low-income Latino/a residents and the mostly White newcomers to the area.

Social media sites, such as Facebook, are an additional source of data within CBQR studies. These virtual communities can serve as windows into community issues and debates. Within a project investigating an intergenerational mentorship program for young mothers, researchers used the program's Facebook page to keep track of postings by members, which helped them identify salient issues and topics within the community. The number of "shares" and "likes" of particular items can also indicate the resonance of specific issues. Comments on postings can be analyzed to offer insight on attitudes and viewpoints related to certain topics. Memes, which are images crafted, transmitted, and transformed by users within social media, contain cultural symbols and social ideas that can be used to trace the evolution of individuals' responses to current events, trends, and particular cultural phenomena. In a CBQR study, researchers might examine memes related to a relevant topic or event, such as a local election or controversy.

Hashtags and Twitter feeds are increasingly becoming a way of exploring significant issues, themes, and narratives within a variety of forms of research. Hashtags are tags, keywords, terms, and phrases prefaced with the pound sign (#) that are included as part of a posting on Twitter, or tweet, or other social media site or electronic communication; these terms can be searched by using the term that will locate all instances of the particular hashtag. Hashtags serve clerical and semiotic purposes as they index and order information, as well as "mark the significance of an utterance" and "create a particular interpretive frame" (Bonilla & Rosa, 2015, p. 5). Community members might employ hashtags to express viewpoints, reference local issues, and/or participate in broader social movements. For example, young mothers attending an alternative high school used the #noteenshame hashtag within public service announcements and posters that sought to challenge stereotypes of young parents and speak back to stigmatizing advertisements and depictions in the popular media. The use of this hashtag connected their efforts with a national movement comprising parent advocacy and policy organizations and other young parents.

Individuals might identify a particular event with a hashtag or even use the name of the community as a hashtag to tag and situate an incident, image, or event. Researchers might search for hashtags to locate posts and photos related to a specific event, such as a community parade or protest, or to gather general images of and posts related to the community. Hashtags such as #blacklivesmatter and #ferguson—the first initiated in response to the 2013 acquittal of George Zimmerman in the 2012 killing of Black teen Trayvon Martin in Florida, and the latter created as part of mass protests in 2014 in Ferguson, Missouri, after the killing of Michael Brown, a young Black man, by a police officer—have been used to document and connect incidences of police violence against African Americans and tally the deaths of Blacks at the hands of the police (Bonilla & Rosa, 2015). Although community-based qualitative researchers are often concerned with issues, activities, and events within a particular geographic locality, the examination of relevant hashtags can be important in demonstrating how local issues and concerns are reflective of and responsive to national and global events and movements, as well as how what happens in a community setting can be connected to occurrences and issues in other contexts.

The hashtag's potential to make intertextual connections across settings and instances can also be a limitation in that a hashtag can link "a broad range of tweets" that may not be related as various users attribute their purposes to a particular term, such as #STL used to refer to traveling to St. Louis to attend a baseball game and as an expression of solidarity with protesters in Ferguson, MO (Bonilla & Rosa, 2015, p. 5). Furthermore, although it is often possible to determine a geographic location of a tweet, other aspects of the context are more difficult to pin down and such posts thus provide a "limited, partial, and filtered" perspective (Bonilla & Rosa, 2015, p. 7). Because it is usually not possible to determine the identity or to follow up with users and participants in various social media spaces, their intent and purposes are difficult to ascertain. Researchers gathering data from social media sites also need to be mindful of the ethical issues and dilemmas entailed in this form of data collection. Although much of the Internet is a public domain, and generally free from processes of informed consent, the line between public and private can be a bit murky. When using posts from those participating in a CBQR study, researchers should make sure they ask for permission to use them for the study and take steps to protect the identities of participants.

## Chapter Summary

This chapter examined the use of participant observation and other forms of data collection within CBQR studies. In particular, the chapter discussed how fieldwork can be used within projects to provide insight into the experiences, beliefs, and practices of community members, as well as offer a window into activities and routines of particular settings and contexts. The role of the researchers within observations can range from passive to active, and it often depends on type of activity or setting being observed. Conducting participant observation usually involves completing formalized field notes after observations, which generally focus on description over reflection, although reflective commentary can be included as bracketed commentary. Often, researchers complete reflective field notes—which can provide opportunities for researchers to reflect on ethical dilemmas or discuss intersections between their lives and those of participants—in addition to descriptive field notes more focused on detailed and microscopic description of setting, participants, and activities.

Textual and visual documents and artifacts are another important form of data employed within CBQR studies. These could include works generated by participants, organizational and programmatic materials, and/or archival images and documents. These sorts of documents are often used within studies to support other forms of data and provide further substantiation of key findings. The Internet and social media sites can also serve as a data source within community-based studies. For example, organizational websites offer valuable information about services, resources, and relevant issues; social media postings and hashtags can indicate resonant topics and debates and demonstrate connections between community activities and events and broader social issues and movements.

## Key Terms

Descriptive field notes   108         Jotted field notes   108         Participant observation   105

Formalized field notes   109         Observer's comments   111        Reflective field notes   108

## ● Activities for Reflection and Discussion

1) Conduct a field observation at a public event (at least 15 minutes), either alone or with a partner. If you conduct the observation with a partner, make sure that you stand in different spots in the setting. Take notes on the physical aspects and layout of setting, as well as on the characteristics of the participants. Pay attention to interactions and dialogue among participants and be mindful of insider terms. After the observation, share notes with your partner. What were the differences/similarities in what you noticed? What was missing? Review notes for any evaluative or judgmental language. If you conducted the observation alone, write a short reflection on your experience of conducting the observation. What were the challenges? What did you learn? What do you want to know more about?

2) Draft a list of textual or visual documents or artifacts related to a topic for a community-based qualitative research study. How would you obtain these? How would they complement or support other forms of data? What insights would these provide to the project?

3) Review social media sites and news feeds related to a certain issue or event. What various hashtags are used to tag the event or issue? Select a few of the more prominent hashtags, and conduct a search for other posts using that hashtag. What do the posts have in common? How do they diverge? What do you learn about the issue or event from these posts?

# Analysis of Data in Community-Based Qualitative Research

## Introduction

This chapter examines methods and approaches for analyzing data in CBQR studies, including how to identify themes and patterns from various forms of data to elaborate findings and develop assertions. This chapter also discusses how to analyze data collaboratively as part of a student research group or in conjunction with community partners.

## Learning Goals

After reading this chapter, students will be able to:

1. Describe and use various strategies for initial analysis and coding of qualitative data within community-based qualitative research (CBQR) studies.

2. Differentiate between inductive and deductive processes for analyzing qualitative data.

3. Identify approaches for constructing findings within CBQR.

4. Discuss how to conduct analysis of data collaboratively, and describe ways to incorporate community perspectives into data analysis.

# Data Analysis Within Community-Based Qualitative Research Studies

Once researchers conducting community-based qualitative research (CBQR) studies have begun collecting data, they need to develop a plan for analyzing these various forms of data. Data analysis can occur throughout the study as part of ongoing and in-the-field approaches, as well as part of formal analytical processes conducted after researchers have amassed a large data corpus. This section reviews basic coding strategies for analyzing qualitative data and discuss stages of analysis within a CBQR study, as well as how to employ these stages to identify patterns and themes within data that can provide insight into the central topic or issue being studied. In addition, this section details specific analytical strategies that can be used for handling particular types of data, such as textual documents and images.

### Initial Analysis and Coding

Analysis of qualitative data can happen on many different levels and at different stages within one project. Margaret LeCompte and Jean Schensul (1999) have identified three levels of analysis, the most basic being at the **item level**, which involves breaking down data into specific, and smaller, units through a process of coding or labeling. At the **pattern level** of analysis, researchers aim to identify "categories of items that seem to fit together" to elaborate patterns and thematic threads within the data (LeCompte & Schensul, 1999, p. 68). The **structural level** entails a broader examination of relationships among certain patterns with the goal of constructing and developing a theory that depicts or explains a particular phenomenon. Johnny Saldaña (2014) portrays the analytical process as moving from real to abstract, from particular to general, as qualitative researchers use coding to group data into categories, identify significant themes and concepts, and generate assertions and theories. Not all qualitative studies are concerned with theory generation, and many CBQR studies remain at the pattern level of analysis by using data to describe thematic patterns and common and divergent community perspectives and practices related to a study's topic or phenomenon. Analysis of qualitative data is often viewed as a "radically inductive" process as qualitative research generally aims for the emergence of conceptual and thematic categories through data collection and grounds theories in the data rather than using the study to test or prove theories selected *a priori*. However, some qualitative work, including CBQR studies, could employ **deductive** processes alongside **inductive** ones. For example, researchers might be informed by particular theoretical frameworks or lenses that are used to make sense of their data. Researchers might build on earlier studies they have conducted to gather further evidence to support theories generated in these previous studies. That said, even if researchers are incorporating deductive processes into analysis, the primary focus of qualitative research is inductive, which

---

**FIGURE 7.1  ●  First-Cycle Coding Strategies**

**Open coding (inductive):** Allow codes to emerge from findings; can be used with any of the coding strategies described later in this chapter.

**Closed coding (deductive):** Use only codes prescribed *a priori*.

**Descriptive/elemental coding:** Label physical attributes and elements of the setting and context; summarize basic topics and activities; describe how participants define their setting and view particular issues; indicate shared rules and norms; describe strategies; depict sequences of events, processes, and turning points.

Examples: "DESCRIPTIONS OF EDUCATIONAL EXPERIENCES," "VIEWS OF COMMUNITY," "DEFINITIONS OF HEALTH LITERACY," "PROCESS OF DROPPING OUT OF SCHOOL," "WORKING TOGETHER".

**In vivo coding:** Use participants' words and terminology as codes.

Examples: "HIDDEN GEM," "FIND YOUR OWN WAY," "BACK IN THE DAY".

**Emotions coding:** Focus on attitudes, emotions, and beliefs during coding.

Examples: "EXPRESSING ANGER".

**Narrative coding:** Code structure of narrative and discourse.

Examples: "CHANGING THE SUBJECT," "I STATEMENTS".

**Methods coding:** Code references to methodological issues; mark instances of rapport building; label observer's comments.

Examples: "VIEWS OF ME," "BUILDING RAPPORT".

---

allows for the emergence of themes from participants' beliefs and experiences and community understandings and practices. Analysis of qualitative data is recursive and iterative in that it involves a back-and-forth, cyclical examination of data.

The process of breaking data into smaller parts and organizing it involves **coding** the data. A **code** is a label, term, or short phrase that "symbolically assigns a summative, salient, essence capturing, and/or evocative attribute for a portion of language-based or visual data" (Saldaña, 2014, p. 3). Codes can be applied to a single word or phrase, a sentence, a paragraph, or an entire page of an interview transcript, a field note, or a textual document; codes can also be used to label and categorize visual images. **Open coding**, commonly used within qualitative research studies, is an inductive approach that involves a line-by-line close reading of data; rather than beginning with a prescribed set of codes, as in **closed coding**, researchers allow for codes to emerge from the data, which can often take research in unexpected directions. This open coding process also helps ensure that codes are grounded in the experiences and perspectives of participants rather than imposed via the biases and assumptions of researchers, or narrow expectations of what they "hope to find" in the research. Many qualitative researchers might draft a list of potential codes as part of precoding activities and based on the study's research questions and theoretical and conceptual frameworks, but they are not limited by these codes and still create and generate codes *in situ* through a close reading of the data.

The many strategies to qualitative coding are each informed by particular theoretical orientations and methodological designs and approaches. Codes can be created based on describing settings, behaviors, and practices; identifying local knowledge, meanings, and terms; locating the significance of particular activities and events; and/or depicting values and emotions. The multitude of potential types of coding schemes and approaches (Saldaña, 2014) that might be used to analyze data can prove overwhelming for novice researchers and, at times, can vex seasoned researchers. Most qualitative researchers use an eclectic approach, combining different schemes in ways that make sense given their research questions and topic. Some basic coding schemes that can be useful for community-based qualitative researchers, especially in the initial stages of analysis, include elemental and basic descriptive methods, which label physical attributes and elements of the setting and context, summarize basic topics and activities, describe how participants define their setting and view particular issues, indicate shared rules and norms, describe strategies, and depict sequences of events, processes, and turning points (Bogdan & Biklen, 2006; Saldaña, 2014). Examples of codes that could be used to label various experiences and viewpoints include "DESCRIPTIONS OF EDUCATIONAL EXPERIENCES," "VIEWS OF COMMUNITY," or "DEFINITIONS OF HEALTH LITERACY." Codes that could be used to organize elements of life histories or sequences of events could include "DECRIPTIONS OF CHILDHOOD" or "PROCESS OF DROPPING OUT OF SCHOOL." Certain behaviors and interactions could be coded as "WORKING TOGETHER" or "TEACHING CULTURE."

Families of codes might also be used to identify values, attitudes, and emotions, which can be helpful for examining community members' emotional reactions and responses to particular issues and occurrences. **In vivo coding** involves using the participants' own words and phrases as codes to describe conceptual categories, which is of particular importance in CBQR as it is focused on gathering and describing local knowledge and community meanings. For example, "HIDDEN GEM," uttered by one community member, might be used to describe statements made by other community members' related to their views on aspects of activities in the community. "FIND YOUR OWN WAY" could be applied when young parents recount ways that they have developed childrearing knowledge *in situ*. Codes can be used to label specific activities, events, strategies, and roles and relationships. Narrative codes might describe the structure of talk and discursive elements, such as "CHANGING THE SUBJECT," which could indicate controversial topics or issues within the community. Researchers can also code references to methodological issues, such as "BUILDING RAPPORT" to catalog instances of researchers developing relationships of trust with community participants; researchers might also code questions that community members ask about research or researchers as a way of documenting interests or concerns related to the research or their growing awareness of the research process.

## Coding Cleanup and Second-Level Coding

As mentioned, analysis and coding occur as cyclical, iterative processes. Coding occurs as part of second, and often third, cycles of developing and applying codes, moving from general and descriptive codes to more specific and interpretive ones. After initial, or first cycle, coding, researchers engage in additional coding and analytical process to delve deeper into data, identify connections within data and among various codes, and elaborate patterns and thematic threads. Between these cycles, researchers need to conduct coding cleanup, which entails renaming, reducing, and/or merging codes, and organizing them by creating overarching categories (Saldaña, 2014). Open coding often produces an unwieldy number of codes, and coding cleanup can help streamline and refine codes. For example, researchers might decide that a few codes describing specific community issues would be more useful merged into a larger "COMMUNITY ISSUES" code. Codes that seem underused might be merged with others or discarded, whereas codes that are more robust might be broken up into smaller, more refined codes. Codes can be grouped together based on a similar topic, such as family, education, or the workplace to assist in the organization of codes.

Once researchers have conducted an initial cleanup and organization of codes, data that have been coded similarly should be examined as part of a second cycle of coding. In the past, many researchers would manually code on paper copies of transcripts, field notes, and other documents, writing in margins and circling and underlining key terms and passages. These documents could be cut (yes, with scissors!) and pieces pasted on butcher paper or notecards, or placed in separate file folders. Technological advances have allowed for less manual means of organizing and grouping data. For example, word processing programs can be used for coding data, using comment bubbles or highlighting tools; separate document files can be created for storing similarly coded data. Also, numerous qualitative data analysis software programs can be used to code and retrieve the data easily, although these programs are often expensive and might be beyond the budget of a CBQR team; they also might require special training for researchers. After researchers have organized the data corpus, then they can examine the data that have been all coded under one code to look for "resonant metaphors" and "repetitive refrains" and to identify patterns and themes (Lawrence Lightfoot, 1997, pp. 193–201). In this process, it is also important to seek out divergent and "deviant voices," as well as discrepant cases that can provide insight into phenomenon (Erickson, 1986; Lawrence-Lightfoot, 1997, pp. 192–193). As opposed to quantitative and positivist research, which disregards outliers in efforts to determine a central tendency within the data, qualitative researchers acknowledge and embrace the existence of multiple experiences and perspectives. For example, a CBQR team might review excerpts from transcripts, field notes, and documents coded as "DEFINITIONS OF COMMUNITY" for common language used by institutions and community members to describe their views of community, as well as for potential contradictions and tensions within and among participants related to the community.

As researchers are coding data, it is important to remember that codes are not the same as themes. Themes are outcomes of coding, but themes are more tacit, reflecting meaning-making and more nuanced processes, whereas codes are less inferential and meant to label data to organize it (LeCompte & Schensul, 1999; Saldaña, 2014). Saldaña's (2014) strategy of "**theming the data**" is useful for differentiating between codes and themes; he suggests that researchers add "is" or "means" to a major code/concept and complete the phrase. For example, the code "DEFINITION OF COMMUNITY" by itself is not a theme, but the phrase "Definition of community is informed by sense of involvement in community" makes a thematic point about how definitions of community are constructed.

As part of second-cycle coding methods, researchers might also recode data and employ more refined and interpretive codes to make sense of data. A **pattern code** is a "meta-code" that can be used to identify relationships between codes (Saldaña, 2014). Researchers might read again through similarly coded data, or related codes, to identify a pattern. Once a pattern is determined, it can be used as a new code, and it can be applied to other instances within the data. For example, researchers conducting a study on youth civic engagement might be interested in connections between definitions of community and youth involvement in community projects. Therefore, they examine data coded as DEFINITIONS OF COMMUNITY and COMMUNITY PROJECTS and discover that youths' definitions of community and involvement in community projects are informed by their roles and identities; they then create a pattern code that captures this relationship, titled IDENTITY INFORMS COMMUNITY. These initial patterns can provide researchers with directions for further exploration, which can lead to the strengthening and expansion of the pattern and the development of assertions related to a particular pattern.

**Focused coding** builds on initial coding and provides categories for data based on thematic or conceptual similarity, thus, allowing researchers to make connections within the data set (Charmaz, 2014). It involves identifying the most salient and frequently occurring codes to "sift, sort, synthesize, and analyze large amounts of data"

(Charmaz, 2014, p. 138). After first-cycle coding, researchers might identify several particularly robust codes and review these to make comparisons between and across instances within the data, and they might identify commonalities, differences, and variation. This process can help researchers develop subthemes and subcodes, further refining the characteristics and properties of coding categories. Drawn from grounded theory designs (Glaser & Strauss, 1967), **axial coding** can be a useful approach for community-based qualitative researchers interested in identifying and describing processes within the data. Axial coding can help researchers identify a coding category's properties and dimensions and determine if, when, and why something happens (Saldaña, 2014). Researchers can select dominant codes from initial coding, which becomes the axis, and describe the conditions, causes, and consequences of processes related to particular codes, which serve as spokes. For example, researchers trying to understand better youth involvement in their communities might examine data coded as COMMUNITY INVOLVEMENT to ascertain specific conditions that motivate youth to become involved in particular community projects and activities, as well as document the skills and knowledge that youth gain from this involvement.

**Domain coding** (Spradley, 1979) can help community-based qualitative researchers identify, differentiate, classify, and detail classes of items, such as objects, things, ideas, or events, within a particular setting. Used often in ethnographic research intent on depicting the experiences and daily life of particular cultural groups, domain coding can be employed by community-based qualitative researchers to discover and describe the knowledge and practices that individuals in a community setting use to organize behavior and interpret their experiences. Domains are large units of cultural knowledge, which are composed of symbols. For example, researchers conducting a study on health education and programs within a community classified as a food desert and grappling with various health issues might be interested in domains of health knowledge and practices, such as nutrition, exercise, and other lifestyle practices, to

---

**FIGURE 7.2 ● Second-Cycle Coding Strategies**

**Theming the data:** Use to develop themes from codes by adding "is" or "means" to a major code/concept and completing the phrase.

**Domain analysis:** Identify, differentiate, classify, and detail classes of items, such as objects, things, ideas, or events, within a particular setting.

**Pattern coding:** Develop "meta-code" that can be used to identify relationships between codes.

**Focused coding:** Build on initial coding and provide categories for data based on thematic or conceptual similarity.

**Axial coding:** Identify a coding category's properties and dimensions, and determine if, when, and why something happens.

understand better what sorts of issues are being addressed by community initiatives. Researchers examining youth civic engagement might use domain analysis to identify types of civic engagement activities mentioned in the data, such as COMMUNITY PROJECTS, ACTIVISM, and ELECTORAL POLITICS, and might aim to identify the multiple tasks and elements that are part of each of these domains. As part of domain analysis, researchers establish boundaries for what is included in each domain and develop semantic relationships within and among items.

## Memoing

Within the analysis process, in addition to organizing and coding data, researchers might use various types of memos to make sense of the data. **Memos** are brief writings that can serve reflective and/or analytical purposes and often help researchers address methodological and ethical issues within study. They serve as journal or diary entries that document researchers' thinking throughout the project. Memos can be written at any point in the study and be of varying lengths; some might be short commentaries that help researchers focus and reflect on particular aspects of study, whereas others could be longer, more formalized analytical pieces that move research forward and become part of final write-up.

As the name suggests, **reflective memos** provide the opportunity for researchers to reflect on aspects of the research process. Within a reflective memo, researchers can discuss how they relate to participants and examine commonalities or areas of divergence between themselves and participants. These memos could be written at the beginning of a study to record the initial impressions of a community. Throughout the study, memos can assist researchers in exploring any personal or ethical dilemmas with the study (Saldaña, 2014). For example, researchers might reflect on how they are building rapport with community members, or they might discuss tensions that arise within a particular interview. Researchers might use a memo to make connections between issues raised in the study and aspects of their background and biographies; for instance, a researcher might examine his or her educational experiences as a way of better understanding educational contexts within the community, or a researcher might reflect on his or her health issues as way of connecting with participants in a community health initiative. Researchers could use a memo to process new experiences or unsettling information or to explore any problems with the study. **Methodological memos** might be employed to work through obstacles encountered in data collection or to critique aspects of the data collection process. For novice interviewers, completing reflective methodological memos after listening to an interview can help call a researcher's attention to any leading questions, evaluative responses, or points where a follow-up question could have been asked. Researchers might write memos after a particularly successful, or challenging, observation. Members of a CBQR team might use memos to discuss communication issues or to reflect on group research processes.

An **analytical memo** is a "think piece" that focuses on analysis, both as part of ongoing analysis and during the more formalized coding process. Analytical memos provide researchers with the opportunity to "step back" from the research "to identify, develop, and modify broader analytic themes and arguments" (Emerson, Fretz, & Shaw, 2011, p. 188). Analytical memos can be written during data collection to assist researchers in exploring working hypotheses and hunches or to record a connection made across settings and/or participants. During coding, an analytical memo can help researchers reflect on and refine codes, make important coding decisions, and establish directions for second-cycle coding. At this stage, memos would include direct evidence and excerpts from the data corpus, either interview transcripts, field notes, and/or documents. As researchers are identifying patterns and developing assertions, memos can serve to narrow and focus themes within a study and make thematic and analytical connections across participants, settings, and types of data. Analytical memos can be employed to delve into a particular code, as well as to discuss coding more broadly. Saldaña (2014) has suggested that researchers write "meta-memos," which draw together information from memos produced throughout the study, and "tactically summarize, integrate, and revise what has been observed and developed to date" (p. 48).

Many researchers recommend that memos be completed at regular points within the study. For example, Annette Lareau (1989/1997) advised that every third visit to the field involve "some kind of effort to push the question forward," which could include a conversation with a colleague or a "long memo" that would be shared with and critiqued by others (p. 215). Researchers might also consider maintaining a researcher log with weekly entries to document the changing role and thinking of researchers throughout the course of the study. This can be especially important for community-based qualitative researchers as the emphasis within community-based studies is on

---

**FIGURE 7.3 ● Memos**

**Reflective**

Record initial impressions of community.

Reflect on common and divergent experiences relative to community members.

Explore ethical dilemmas.

**Methodological**

Reflect on strengths and weaknesses of a particular interview.

Examine challenges and tensions from an observation.

Work through obstacles in data collection.

**Analytical**

During data collection, explore working hypotheses and hunches.

During coding, delve into a particular code.

After coding, explore a pattern.

building collaborative relationships with community members, authentic participation in community settings, and the transformation of researchers' perspectives and viewpoints related to issues at the heart of the study.

## More on Coding and Analysis: Handling Different Forms of Data

Within a CBQR study, researchers can be faced with a great amount of data to analyze, which can prove an overwhelming task. Although many of the approaches described earlier can be used across data types, there are particular strategies that are most optimal for analyzing specific types of data. For example, open coding is appropriate for analyzing rich textual data, as fine-grained, line-by-line analysis is better suited for the identification of emergent themes than prescriptive or narrow means of analysis. Documents and textual artifacts can require more focused forms of data analysis as the goal in reviewing such documents is often to identify definitions and instantiations of particular, predetermined concepts. For example, researchers conducting a study on youth civic engagement at an alternative school might analyze the school's website for how it defines community, how many times the word *community* is used, or the different terms used to describe civic and community engagement, and for what purpose. A project examining the issue of teen motherhood might review local social service organizations' websites and materials for terminology and phrases used to describe young mothers. Methods such as **content analysis**, which involves the counting of certain terms and keywords, can be useful in identifying the use and resonance of particular terms. Although this approach entails quantifying qualitative data, and is not the sort of rich and emergent data analysis associated with most qualitative research, it can be a helpful strategy, in particular, when documents are being used as a secondary, rather than as a primary, source of data.

Photographs and other visual data often require different sorts of data analysis strategies than do textual forms of data. Many of the aforementioned approaches focus on categorizing and describing participants' terminology and on identifying and labeling elements of language and discourse. However, some of these coding techniques can also be applied to images. For example, photographs might contain images of objects that are significant or meaningful to community members; photographs of events and activities can depict certain community practices and routines and indicate community members' roles, positions, and relationships. The mechanics of coding visual data can be tricky; researchers might paste prints of images to paper and manually circle and label elements. This can also be done electronically by using qualitative data analysis software, such as NVivo, Atlas.TI, or MAXQDA, or a computer's clipart tools.

Although the emphasis in CBQR is obviously on the collection and analysis of qualitative data, numeric data can play a role in these studies. For example, demographic data can function within CBQR projects to provide a context for the study, offering insight into community characteristics and issues. Information on educational attainment and literacy rates can be useful for researchers examining educational and learning issues within a community; statistics on childhood obesity and diabetes can assist researchers conducting a study on community health initiatives.

Data from sources such as the U.S. Census can give researchers a sense of changing community demographics, patterns, and trends; data and statistics from organizational program materials and reports can help researchers better understand how services are being used and by whom. These sorts of quantitative data should not be used as a primary source of data, but they can be analyzed alongside qualitative data and be used to support and elucidate findings from other forms of data.

### Developing Assertions

A goal of analysis and coding is to construct primary and subassertions related to the topic and issues under study. An **assertion** is "a summative and data-supported statement about the particulars of a research study" (Saldaña, 2014, p. 252) that explicates "patterns of generalization within the case at hand" (Erickson, 1986, p. 184). Although some CBQR studies might aim to develop broader theories from their research, most projects have the goal of better understanding the particulars of a specific community setting and sets of experiences, beliefs, and practices. These particulars can certainly be useful to others working in similar settings and addressing similar issues, but the primary purpose of CBQR studies is not to generalize findings to other settings.

As researchers elaborate patterns and develop key assertions, it is important that they seek out different types of evidence, across incidences, settings, and participants. The process of using multiple forms of data and various examples to support assertions is often referred to as **triangulation**; it enhances the strength and credibility of assertions because it provides multiple and intersecting data points to substantiate a claim. For example, a perspective or practice described in an interview might be observed during a community meeting or event; values articulated within an organization's mission statement and program materials could be shared and discussed within a focus group. Although analysis within CBQR studies is interpretive, assertions and claims need to be supported by data from the study and researchers need to make plausible arguments, what Erickson (1986) has referred to as the "demonstration of plausibility" (p. 149).

## Collaboration Within the Analysis Process

As discussed in previous chapters, CBQR studies involve collaboration with community members, and they might entail collaborative work with members of a research team. Whether a community-based research project is being conducted by a sole academic researcher in concert with a community organization, a larger research team including multiple academic researchers and various community stakeholders, or a group of graduate students conducting research with a community program as part of a community-based research class, several approaches can be employed within the analysis process to facilitate collaborative analysis. Too often, projects that purport to be community based or participatory use reciprocal approaches during the data collection stage only, excluding community partners and members as they review and analyze the data. This oversight is unfortunate, since community members' insights and perspectives are perhaps even more needed within the analysis process, as their distinct knowledge and awareness of the community can help the research team make sense of complex issues, experiences, and viewpoints.

Most often within qualitative research, participants' perspectives have been included within analysis as part of "member-checking" activities, which involves sharing initial findings with participants to gain feedback. Lois Weis and Michelle Fine (2000) have exhorted researchers to share their analysis with participants, providing them with opportunities to interpret and challenge findings, as well as to engage in conversations that can result in "texts in which multiple interpretations flourish" (p. 64). They recommend that these "negotiated interpretations" take place as part of follow-up focus groups or interviews with participants. Although these types of mutual data analysis activities are significant in the way that they depart from more traditional research approaches, as well as acknowledge the important role that participants can play in analytical processes, for the most part, they are conducted after data have first been analyzed by academic researchers, rather than as part of ongoing collaborative and reciprocal data analysis among academic researchers and community partners.

In CBQR studies, researchers should aim to be as inclusive and reciprocal as possible within the analysis process. In her research with lesbian, gay, bisexual, transgender, and queer (LGBTQ) youth, Mollie Blackburn (2014) has articulated the notion of "humanizing analysis," which entails addressing and overcoming "discrepant positionalities" between the researcher and participants (p. 53). She suggests that researchers do this by immersing themselves in literature and scholarship relevant to the individuals and communities they are studying. Filling in these knowledge gaps can help researchers see issues and experiences from other points of view: "To compensate for our limitations, researchers must assume responsibility for learning as much as they can about experiences beyond their own so that they better understand the people represented in their data" (Blackburn, 2014, p. 53). This sort of humanizing analysis can be integrated into CBQR projects through constant analytic discussion and the raising of "dialogic consciousness" (Paris & Winn, 2014) among and across research team members and community members. As part of this process, researchers should connect emergent findings to particular experiences articulated within relevant literature and scholarship.

Reciprocal and collaborative ethnography, with their emphases on collaboration and reciprocity throughout the research process, provide some useful approaches for collaborative analysis (Lassiter, 2005; Lawless, 1991, 1993). Within reciprocal ethnography, researchers review interview transcripts with participants as part of dialogue groups where participants and the researchers discuss the content and structure of life stories and engage in reciprocal discussion, and knowledge is "shared/examined/reexamined" (Lawless, 1991, p. 38). In collaborative ethnography, researchers engage in a process of co-interpretation through the reviewing of ethnographic texts within focus groups with "principal consultants"—Luke Lassiter (2015), drawing on earlier ethnographic work, defines these consultants as "co-intellectuals" (pp. 23–24). Researchers acknowledge the difficulty of incorporating such approaches as they require the reconciliation of "differing visions, agendas, and expectations" (Lassiter, 2005, p. 137).

Some other ways that research team members might engage in collaborative analysis can occur as part of formal coding. One such process is one that I refer to as **collective coding**. Members of the research team and community partners can individually code the same transcript and then come together to share and discuss codes by using this initial coding process to develop a common list of codes that would comprise a working list to code subsequent data sources. After the initial list has been approved, group members would each be assigned a data source to code and could add codes to the list as they emerge from data, checking with others to achieve consensus. As part of this collective coding process, one or two group members might create a **codebook** that would include lists and descriptions of codes, as well as examples of when each code should be applied; this codebook would help research group members apply codes appropriately. Meetings could be used to discuss and refine codes, as well as offer opportunities for the provision of training and support to research team members and community partners new to the process of qualitative coding.

When reviewing strategies that can be used for group coding, Saldaña (2014) emphasizes the importance of reaching "interpretive convergence" (p. 35), which refers to the amount of agreement among research group members regarding codes and coding. Other researchers have sought interrater reliability among group members regarding codes and coding, which involves systematically measuring the amount of agreement with the goal of achieving a certain percentage of agreement. Many have questioned this sort of rigidity related to coding in qualitative research and have deemed it inappropriate because of qualitative research's acknowledgment of the multiple frames and lenses of interpretation at play within the research process. Seeking this sort of agreement is especially out of place in CBQR studies, which recognize the existence of, and aim to document, multiple and divergent experiences, not just within the community but also among research group members. Within CBQR studies, tensions and disagreements should be debated and explored rather than glossed over or discarded in the interests of achieving consensus. The danger in trying to obtain agreement among research group members is that it may silence individual and dissenting voices and flatten out analysis in favor of the perspective of the majority.

However, it may be helpful to institute some protocols or strategies to expedite analysis; some researchers have pointed out how frustrating and cumbersome it can be to "code by committee" and, thus, have suggested limiting the number of group members taking part in these processes of consensus building (Saldaña, 2014, p. 35). Community-based qualitative researchers working as part of a large team may want to consider breaking into smaller coding groups, or establishing a working group, composed of academic researchers and community partners, to initiate coding and to share coding schemes with the larger group later on, eliciting additional feedback and making revisions as needed. Researchers may want to pair up academic researchers and community partners to work as teams of two on pieces of data, which would ensure the integration of different perspectives, grounding analysis in community perspectives and academic scholarship; such a pairing could also generate productive discussions between research team members as they grapple with their differing positions and experiences related to particular knowledge, practices, and behaviors.

Throughout the analysis process, research group members should check in with one another to assure that all voices are being included and that multiple perspectives are informing interpretations. Academic researchers should not merely seek approval or a rubber stamp from community members for their findings, but they should engage community partners in authentic and genuine dialogue aimed at moving analyses forward. Some of the analysis discussions might also be recorded and documented, as well as integrated into the final write-up. As a result, the ways that research team members wrestled with various perspectives and positionalities within the research would be demonstrated and depicted. Furthermore, this approach would show how researchers' viewpoints might be challenged and transformed within the research process as they are faced with, and better understand, others' experiences and how these are shaped by differing contexts and conditions.

## Chapter Summary

This chapter reviewed and discussed approaches for analyzing and coding data within CBQR studies. We learned how researchers can engage in ongoing analytical processes throughout a project and as part of formal coding and analysis activities conducted toward the end of the project. Alongside various first- and second-level coding processes, writing reflective and analytical memos can help researchers identify patterns and themes and construct assertions. Although CBQR studies use many of the same analytic strategies that are employed within other qualitative designs, there is an emphasis within community-based studies on collaborative processes of analysis. Thus, researchers should integrate opportunities for collective coding and reciprocal dialogue and analysis among academic researchers and community members.

## Key Terms

| | | |
|---|---|---|
| Analytical memos  127 | Content analysis  129 | Methodological memos  127 |
| Assertion  130 | Deductive  122 | Pattern code  125 |
| Axial code  126 | Domain coding  126 | Pattern level  121 |
| Code  123 | Inductive  122 | Reflective memos  127 |
| Codebook  132 | In vivo coding  123 | Structural level  121 |
| Coding  123 | Item level  121 | Theming the data  125 |
| Collective coding  132 | Memos  127 | Triangulation  130 |

## ● Activities for Reflection and Discussion

1) Examine research questions for a particular community-based study. What codes might be generated from these questions? Given the type of data collected for the study, what sorts of coding approaches make sense?

2) In pairs or small groups, code a similar piece of data. After coding, discuss how you approached the coding process. What sorts of knowledge did you draw on to code data? What does a particular way that each group member coded data indicate about members' frames of interpretation and analytical lenses? What questions do you have of data? What more do you want to know about?

3) After coding the piece in #2, compile a list of codes generated by pairs/group members. What are the similarities/differences among the codes? Engage in coding cleanup: What codes can be merged, renamed, or discarded? Try to organize codes into three to five overarching categories.

# HANDOUT 5
## Sample Coding Worksheet

Code (first level): _____

Data coded as:

What patterns do you identify? Metaphors? Insider terms?

Ideas for second-level coding? Other codes you want to look at? What questions do you have?

**FIGURE 7.4  ●  Sample List of Codes**

**Community**

Community projects/programs

Interactions with community leaders

Views of community

Community apathy

Gentrification

Community issues

Description of community

Community identification

Description of community events

Community involvement

Active community members

"Food desert"

Views of outsiders of community

Gang violence

Youth involvement in community

**Education/Teaching**

Views of education

"Reinventing education"

"Community as classroom"

Lack of support in school

Descriptions of educational experiences/schooling

**Family/Life/Identity**

Descriptions of life

Life transitions

Relationships w/parents

Developing identities

Ethnicity

Share community work with family and friends

After school activities

Youth issues

*Source:* Adapted from research by Rosario-Ramos and Johnson (2015).

# Next Steps:
# From Research
# to Action

# Write-Up, Dissemination, and Transformation

## Building Partnerships, Developing Reciprocal Research Relationships, and Enacting Change

## Introduction

This chapter explores ways that students, researchers, and community partners conducting CBQR can share and disseminate their research findings with community members and with university faculty and other constituencies and audiences. In addition to discussing ways that research findings can be reported in journals, policy reports, and local and national conferences, this chapter examines how CBQR can be used to promote university–community partnerships and initiatives and to strengthen existing community programs, or even to develop new community projects. Most of the dissemination ideas described in this chapter can be undertaken by a sole community-based researcher collaborating with community partners and participants, as well as by larger research teams composed of multiple academic researchers and community partners and members.

## Learning Goals

After reading this chapter, students will be able to:

1. Identify ways that community-based qualitative research (CBQR) teams can share findings with various local stakeholders through written reports and documents.

2. Discuss how community-based qualitative researchers can disseminate findings to broader local, national, and global audiences.

3. Detail strategies and approaches for using findings from CBQR studies to develop community programs and enhance services.

4. Explain how CBQR projects can be employed toward the development and preparation of a variety of materials and resources, including journal articles, policy documents, public service announcements, and program curricula.

# Reporting Findings From Community-Based Qualitative Research

Once community-based qualitative research (CBQR) teams have analyzed data and generated findings from the study, they should consider how they want to present or report findings, and to whom. Research findings can be disseminated in a multitude of ways, ranging from those associated with traditional academia, such as journal articles and conferences, to more innovative and engaging means that bear the potential to engage wider audiences. The type of write-up or presentation will depend on the purpose and audience, and projects should use several dissemination formats to share and broadcast research findings. For example, if trying to use research to increase participation in certain community programs, researchers might want to plan a community forum to discuss recommendations and/or create a social media campaign based on findings. If wanting to contribute to academic scholarship in a particular area, researchers can prepare a manuscript for submission to a peer-reviewed journal or present at a local or a national academic conference. Since CBQR studies are intended to engage community members related to the issues that are at the heart of the study, and often aim to address certain community problems or concerns, dissemination efforts are usually more action oriented than is common in traditional qualitative research studies.

Although qualitative research yields findings that cannot be generalized to other populations and contexts, researchers have highlighted how qualitative research findings can be useful to others working on similar issues, in similar settings, and with similar populations. They are interested in identifying concrete universals, a process that has been referred to as **particularizability** (Erickson, 1986), CBQR maintains an extreme focus on local conditions and circumstances, yet that does not mean that findings from these studies are only relevant to local stakeholders. The issues and topics of concern to many CBQR studies—be they youth community engagement, educational attainment, homelessness, police brutality, or community health outcomes—are related to factors and conditions beyond the community, and they can be connected to what is taking place in other communities and contexts. This section discusses the various approaches for sharing findings from CBQR studies and explore how research teams can use research to participate in and contribute to a variety of academic, community, and public venues.

## Reporting Back to the Community: The Culminating Event

A central way that researchers might share findings from CBQR studies is through the hosting of a **culminating event**, which would include a brief presentation by members of the research team, as well as opportunities for dialogue and discussion among various stakeholders and constituencies. These events are significant in their potential to inform and engage multiple audiences and to articulate new ideas related to the study's topic.

Participants in a culminating event would, of course, include an individual researcher or members of the research team and community partners, but the event might also be open to other community leaders and members, such as local politicians, participants in certain community programs, and recipients of specific community services related to the issues at the heart of the study. Those who participated in interviews and played central roles in data collection efforts should also play a role in the final activity, through sharing their experiences participating in the study and/or providing feedback on the findings and implications of the study. Academic researchers might invite other faculty and/or administrators from their educational institution as a way of building university–community partnerships. For community-based research classes I have instructed, graduate students have invited family members to participate in the culminating event, which has generated interesting discussions as family members have often represented a variety of backgrounds and professional roles.

The presentation should start off with a brief introduction to the study and the research team, and it should include a description of the project's design and methods and information on the community context, especially as related to the key issues of the study. The researchers should provide a summary of key assertions and central themes and patterns revealed in the study by using data and evidence from the study to substantiate assertions and enliven the presentation. Researchers might also connect findings to other research and scholarship, but they should keep in mind the backgrounds of the audience. This does not mean that researchers should "dumb down" their presentation or not include any related theoretical or empirical literature but that the research should be presented in ways that are accessible to a broad audience and connected to conditions and factors within the community. The event should end with implications from the study, which could include recommendations

Poster advertising youth-led research conference.

for the organization, ideas for new services and initiatives, or a demonstration of some sort of outcome or product of the study, such as a public service announcement or website. Time should also be allotted for a discussion of issues and ideas raised in the presentation and opportunities for dialogue across audience members.

To ensure the success of the culminating event, care should be taken to advance planning of the event. Attention to logistical issues, such as location, scheduling, and publicity, are often integral to guaranteeing adequate participation from a wide variety of participants in the event. Whenever possible, events should be held within the community in a space that can accommodate a large group. Hosting events within the community helps showcase the community setting and community organizations that participated in the study, as well as increases the likelihood that community members can attend the event. Researchers should collaborate with community partners to plan the event, identifying a day and time that would be most convenient for the constituencies targeted for the event. Other issues to be considered include the provision of transportation, child care, and refreshments for the event. The event can be publicized by using a variety of means and materials: organizational websites, social media, electronic mailing lists, and leaflets.

All research group members should play a role in the planning and implementation of the event, although specific group members might take on responsibility for particular aspects of the event. For example, one group member might take charge of procuring the location, whereas another might coordinate the preparation of the formal presentation; other group members could oversee event setup and cleanup or serve as facilitators during the discussion period of the event. Whatever roles group members take on, the research team should take a shared approach and involve community partners in the planning and implementation of the event. For events I have hosted as part of my summer research course, I have asked the executive director of the partnering organization to speak; research team members might also invite local youth poets and cultural groups to perform.

The discussion and dialogue portion of the culminating event can offer important feedback to the research group regarding the usefulness and applicability of findings and possibly push the research in new directions. Research group members might pose questions to the audience, provide opportunities for small group discussion of issues raised in the research, or allow for unstructured discussion, although this discussion should be facilitated by a research group member. Although the discussion period can furnish new insights for the project and elicit additional perspectives on the project's findings, there are challenges posed by sharing findings in a more open, dialogic format. Particularly if the project addresses controversial topics, or if the issues or concerns at the heart of the study have been a source of dissension among community members and institutions, the culminating event could end up revealing significant and long-standing tensions and disputes. Organizations and leaders within the community might have competing visions or ideas regarding how to solve community problems and use the event to air grievances. Researchers should not shy away from heated debate within the culminating event, but they should be prepared for any disagreements and ensure that the discussion and feedback is constructive and respectful. Researchers should welcome multiple opinions and perspectives, and they should be open to critiques of the research project. The event should not be viewed as merely an occasion to obtain a "rubber stamp" for research findings, but it should be seen as an opportunity to continue the collaborative efforts undertaken throughout the project. I find that projects that have engaged in authentic collaboration and shared research processes with community partners and various stakeholders throughout the project are less likely to be "surprised" by negative feedback at the end. However, especially if researchers invite individuals and parties from outside of the community, or include those who are less familiar with the research study, opposing viewpoints could be raised. Researchers should be careful not to be defensive in the face of feedback, but if a group of youth researchers are presenting, organizers should make sure that invited guests offer feedback in supportive ways so that youth researchers do not feel they are under attack.

## Journal Articles and Book Chapters

Publishing articles in academic journals is a common way that researchers disseminate research findings and is a requisite for most university faculty trying to obtain tenure. Because of the more traditional reporting structure of most peer-reviewed academic journals, they may not seem like a good fit for CBQR studies, which as we have learned, do not often follow a traditional research model in their design, implementation, and dissemination. However, several journals are specifically dedicated to community-based and service learning research and could serve as an appropriate venue for sharing findings with an academic audience. Many of these journals are focused on a particular field, such as public health or community informatics, or anchored in a particular discipline, such as anthropology or sociology. Other potential venues for publication include journals devoted to a discussion of certain methods within qualitative education. Articles in these journals might provide insight into particular aspects of conducting CBQR or offer discussions of processes of building relationships with community members. Some notable journals are listed in Handout 9.

Many journals also have "tales from the field" sections or include community reflection pieces. These sorts of writings would be shorter and more informal than traditional journal articles, but they could provide for the sharing of in-process research projects and offer the opportunity to privilege community voices and perspectives. Researchers might also consider online-only journals for publishing articles; within the field of community informatics, virtual and electronic journals are more prevalent and a suitable outlet for publication.

Although the publication of journal articles can be part of efforts to "get the word out" regarding CBQR studies, there are drawbacks to this form of publication. First off, academic journals are often geared toward a limited and narrow audience as they are expensive and therefore usually only accessible through university libraries. Smaller journals may be even harder to get and, thus, not ideal for reaching a broad community audience. Furthermore, the format and style of many journal article manuscripts can be constraining, and the highly collaborative and participatory nature of community-based projects may not be accommodated by the rigid structure and writing expectations imposed by many journals. Another impediment involves the lengthy time for review by many journals: An initial submission can often be "under review" for months, and additional revisions are often required before the article is finally accepted for publication. Even after years of submitting revisions, the manuscript can be rejected, which can be frustrating for CBQR teams eager to share their research findings with an academic audience.

Preparing book chapters for edited volumes on CBQR projects is another way to circulate research findings. Researchers can be on the lookout for calls for chapters or reach out to others conducting CBQR to inquire about upcoming book projects. Participating in organizations and networks associated with community-based and participatory research and/or service learning can be a great way to keep apprised of calls for chapter submissions. Books sometimes maintain a quicker publication timeline than do journals, although some of the earlier concerns, regarding the narrowness of the audience, also apply to book chapters. Academic books can be expensive and often cannot be accessed through digital libraries and databases.

In preparing and writing journal articles and book chapters, research team members should be mindful of the various roles that members will play in the writing and publication process. Academic researchers who are part of the research team likely possess more knowledge and expertise related to scholarly publication and may oversee the writing process, but they should not be the only authors. These sorts of writing endeavors offer a great opportunity for further collaboration among research group members, and they should be viewed as an occasion to continue the reciprocal teaching and learning instituted within the design and implementation stages of the project. Community partners, especially youth researchers, can gain invaluable skills from the scholarly writing process.

## Conference Presentations and Proceedings

Academic conferences offer a variety of outlets for CBQR teams to present research accomplishments; many conferences provide multiple formats for researchers to share and discuss the research process and findings, such as interactive workshops, panels, roundtables, and poster sessions. Conferences can have a variety of target audiences—including youth, practitioners, teachers, students, activists, researchers, administrators, and/or policy makers—and occur at a local, regional, national, or international level. Researchers should make decisions regarding the appropriate format, audience, and scope for their presentation to assist them in the design of the conference proposal and implementation of the presentation.

The various presentation formats available offer different levels of formality and engagement with the audience. The most common format at many conferences is the paper presentation, which usually occurs as part of a panel of papers on a similar topic. The session might have a chair who is responsible for introducing the session and maintaining time limits and a discussant who provides some concluding remarks that tie together themes and findings from the papers; time for questions and discussion is often allotted. Paper sessions usually run 90 to 120 minutes and could include three or four papers, which often allows for about 20 minutes per paper presentation. Researchers might also consider proposing a symposium to highlight their research efforts, which would allow them an entire session; this could be used to present numerous papers on various aspects of study and/or provide the opportunity for youth and community members to share perspectives and reflect on experiences. Some conferences also offer interactive workshops as a potential format, which enables researchers to engage with attendees around specific issues and provides for more in-depth discussion than is possible in a paper panel. Such workshops might include a more direct presentation, along with small group activities, reflective exercises, and discussion. Another popular format for conference presentations are roundtables, which are more informal than paper sessions and workshops; as part of a roundtable, researchers investigating similar topics are grouped together at a table and interested individuals can "drop by" to find out more about the research and ask questions. This format is useful for in-process studies, although it can pose challenges for larger research teams and does not allow for much direct presentation. Poster sessions are also more informal than panels and workshops, and they entail the preparation of a professional poster, which often includes details about the research design, methods, implementation, findings, and implications. Posters are displayed in a large room or hall, and attendees can mill about and ask questions of researchers regarding the study. This format is ideal for novice researchers and presenters as they are often less formal and more accessible than previously mentioned formats.

Most conferences require that potential presenters submit a proposal for review before being accepted to present. Sometimes this proposal involves preparing an abstract or summary of a paper, whereas other conferences ask for the entire paper to be submitted for review; many conferences also have specific guidelines for proposals. Research teams should seek out conferences focused on community-based and participatory research approaches, university–community partnerships, and/or service-learning initiatives. For large conferences and organizations, researchers might consider participating in or applying to a specific group or division. For example, the American Educational Research Association (AERA) has numerous special interest groups, referred to as SIGs, that would be appropriate for CBQR projects, such as Critical Educators for Social Justice; Action Research, Grassroots Community & Youth Organizing for Education Reform; and Service Learning & Experiential Education.

Research teams might also consider being part of an invited session at a conference, which would require contacting conference organizers to arrange a session. This sort of format would be appropriate if researchers wanted to include a youth performance as part of a presentation or highlight the community and the work and accomplishments of particular organizations. Researchers might also help organize tours of the community for interested conference attendees. These are great opportunities for promoting awareness of community issues and programs, fostering dialogue across academic and scholarly settings, and building community–university partnerships.

Although conferences can be great venues for dissemination of CBQR, and often occur at a quicker pace than via publication in journals and books, they are not without disadvantages. Some of the aforementioned concerns related to narrowness of the audience for journals also apply to conference presentations, which may even reach a smaller audience. Although there can be tens of thousands of attendees at large conferences, if a session is not adequately publicized, there could be only a few audience members, which could be especially demoralizing for community partners and members who have never presented at an academic conference and have devoted time to preparing a presentation to share with an academic audience. Thus, the research team should take measures to ensure that the session is well publicized and use various professional networks to broadcast the presentation and mobilize audience members. For invited sessions, research teams should work with conference leadership to advertise the event and make sure that the event/session is valued and prioritized.

## Policy Reports and Presentations

Researchers might also want to use findings from CBQR studies to impact local and national policy related to the topic under study. This can be done through the preparation of policy reports and the creation and publication of editorial writings, as well as by making direct presentations to elected officials and legislators. Some research projects might include an explicit policy agenda as part of their project at the outset of their research, whereas other studies might develop an interest in policy during the data collection and analysis phases. CBQR studies are often aligned with current policy issues and debates because they tackle authentic issues in real-life settings.

When making decisions regarding how a research team could participate in policy debates, it is important to frame the problem and find a "hook" or direction for a policy message and then establish a target audience (Hess, 1999). Projects might reveal multiple findings related to the topic but select one particular finding to focus policy-oriented efforts. This is important because the recommendations for policy changes need to be clear and succinct. Although CBQR studies aim to examine the complexities of specific issues and experiences, a policy report or presentation that covers too many issues may be difficult for policy makers too grasp or seem too unwieldy. Therefore, researchers should initially identify issues that can be addressed by changes in policy and make sure that their message is in line with the interests and priorities of the target audience. For example, researchers studying youth civic engagement in collaboration with a community-based alternative high school elaborated a host of findings related to the youth's definitions of the community and community projects that engaged youth and facilitated their involvement in the community and on behalf of particular issues of importance to them; however, they focused their policy recommendations on the need for structured mentorship opportunities for youth at local organizations. A CBQR team investigating issues related to young parents within school settings used findings to develop policy proposals calling for the expansion of education for school personnel on the educational rights of young parents, as well as increasing support for Title IX policies and programming.

Researchers can employ findings from their studies in numerous ways to inform, and possibly shape, policy. Researchers might prepare an editorial piece or write a letter to the editor dedicated to a particular issue or concern, especially if it is one that is receiving increased attention in public media. For example, researchers conducting a study with a community organization working on immigrant issues might write a letter to the editor of the local paper advocating for undocumented immigrant families in response to recent protests against undocumented immigrants and denial of services to immigrant families. If funding for local youth afterschool programming is about to be cut, researchers might prepare an editorial piece that shares findings from their research with community-based organizations that design and implement youth after-school programs as a way of making a case for the maintenance of funding. These letters generally need to be short (often less than 300 words); thus, researchers need to maintain a tight focus on their message.

Researchers might also consider working with policy-oriented organizations to prepare policy briefs or reports that can be distributed to local and national legislators. Research team members might participate in local, state, and national advocacy and lobbying efforts by making formal presentations at a city council meeting or legislative session. Some organizations host advocacy days, which provide the opportunity for leaders, activists, practitioners, youth, and researchers to meet directly with legislators and discuss pertinent issues. Sometimes these events are focused on particular issues, such as funding for AIDS/HIV programs or legislation impacting undocumented immigrant college students, whereas other advocacy days might be broader in scope and include a variety of groups doing work in areas such as education, poverty, and health care.

### Websites and Blogs

Another outlet for broadcasting findings from CBQR studies involves the creation of websites and blogs, which can highlight key findings, as well as provide a space for spotlighting community perspectives and accomplishments. Because these sorts of dissemination platforms are dynamic and can be regularly updated in real time, they are useful for tracking the development and progress of studies throughout the course of the project and/or sharing findings from ongoing studies and projects. They are also unique in that they can engage a variety of audiences in ways not possible via journal articles and conference presentations. Although one needs to have access to the Internet to view websites and blogs, many locales and sites, such as libraries and community centers, offer free Internet access, which makes research shared on websites more readily available than that published in an academic journal or presented at a conference.

Websites offer researchers the opportunity to share information related to the study in a variety of forms. A website might include background on the community, photos of the community, and information on local events and activities. Findings from the study could be presented in several ways, from traditional write-up formats to more innovative approaches that might include photos, timelines, or maps. Extensive reflections and responses from participants and community members could be featured in ways not possible in journals and presentations. Researchers could also include links to related research and resources and connect research findings to current events and news articles. Enabling postings and comments by users allows research team members to engage in an ongoing conversation with the public related to certain issues and topics, although offering this sort of feature requires that researchers appoint moderators to monitor comments.

A website that serves as an exemplar for community-based qualitative researchers is one created by the Black Youth Project (blackyouthproject.com). Although not focused on a specific community setting, the site is notable in the ways that it spotlights research conducted by and for youth as part of a space "where black youth can speak for themselves about the issues that concern them" (blackyouthproject .com). The site includes a section that details research conducted by youth researchers "about the ideas, attitudes, decision making, and lived experiences of black youth, especially as it relates to their political and civic engagement" (blackyouthproject .com). The project sprung from the work of Dr. Cathy Cohen at The University of Chicago, and as part of the project, researchers tackle a host of issues, such as police brutality, same-sex marriage, voting reform, and the Affordable Care Act. In addition to brief reports of research findings, the site includes perspectives of Black youth from across the country, commentaries on current topics, and calls to action and links to other resources.

# From Research to Action: Using Findings to Develop Programs, Initiatives, and Campaigns

What sets community-based and participatory models of research apart from traditional research paradigms and approaches is their emphasis on action and change as essential components of the research process. Unlike research that is solely focused on identifying and describing a problem, or even that seeking to understand better an issue and possibly make recommendations for research and practice, a major aim of CBQR projects is to engage critically and actively with settings that are the focus of the study by using findings to push for change and transformation of conditions and resources. Findings from CBQR projects can be employed to support and expand existing services and programs within a community setting, as well as lead to the creation of new programs and initiatives. Researchers might use research to participate in grassroots campaigns or get involved in national efforts around a specific issue. These more active means of disseminating research are appealing to those who critique academic research as overly theoretical and lacking in practical implications and wish to "do something" with their research, lamenting that work published in scholarly journals just "sits on a shelf" or is read by too few people to make any sort of meaningful impact. This section discusses methods for using findings from CBQR studies to participate actively in initiatives and efforts aimed at improving conditions and expanding services and resources related to issues undertaken by the project.

## Supporting Community Efforts and Programs

In many cases, community-based qualitative researchers are conducting research to help identify and describe work that community-based organizations have been engaged in for years, but have not been able to document themselves, because of lack of time and adequate resources. Individuals from these organizations might have been approached by researchers regarding potential projects and who expressed interest in learning more about a specific program or service. Researchers can work with community partners to design a study that can gather the perspectives of participants on the program and provide evidence of programmatic successes and challenges. These findings can be included in a report to funders and thus help sustain funding for the program; furthermore, evidence from the study might be shared with the board of directors as part of a year-end report to provide a rationale for the continuance of the program.

Researchers could also use study findings to help community partners strengthen and refine services. For example, feedback from young mothers regarding the usefulness of certain elements of a mentoring program could assist program staff as they enhance and expand services that participants found most beneficial. Similarly, aspects that participants found the least helpful could be scrapped, or retooled, to meet community needs better. The various community perspectives offered on

A planting project aimed at providing fresh food for the community.

particular community issues could help establish new directions for community organizations and programs. In addition to incorporating data and findings from CBQR studies into program and grant reports, researchers could include findings on program websites, and in program brochures and materials, as a way of highlighting program accomplishments. Such information can also be employed to recruit new participants to programs and services. Researchers might also use evidence from studies to develop workshops, training, and other professional development for program staff, aimed at improvement of services.

## Creating New Programs and Projects

Findings from CBQR studies can also be used as a foundation and as leverage for the development of new programs and initiatives. Within the research project, researchers might identify an unmet need within the community and gain insight into how the organization might address this need. Some research projects might be designed to examine an issue or a problem, such as LGBTQ youth homelessness or childhood obesity, that one or more organizations have determined is important and want to tackle through the creation of new projects and services. For example, leaders, educators, and students in a community designated as a food desert and battling a host of health issues worked with researchers to undertake an effort to understand health better in their community. Findings from their research were used to create a rooftop greenhouse at the local alternative high school and to establish more community gardens. A new health initiative was developed that sought to improve the access of individuals with diabetes to individualized health interventions and engaged in preventive health efforts, which were aligned with community beliefs and practices.

To establish such new programs and initiatives adequately, it is often necessary to acquire additional funding sources. Many community-based organizations are run on extremely tight budgets and are limited in terms of how monies might be allocated. Research teams might thus decide that the preparation and submission of grant proposals are integral elements of the dissemination process and work with community partners to identify appropriate funding agencies and calls for proposals. Evidence from the study can be included in the proposal to establish the need for additional programs and services. Potential funding sources could include federal, state, and local public entities and private foundations. Most funding agents have established priorities, and research team members should familiarize themselves with the agenda and interests of relevant organizations.

In addition to more traditional means of acquiring funds for programs, researchers might use crowdfunding as a means of raising monies. This might involve using a website platform and social media to solicit small donations from a large number of individuals. Information from the CBQR study could be featured as part of the funding plea. These crowdfunding efforts could be particularly useful for the creation of new projects or initiatives of existing programs as they might require smaller amounts of money, although a carefully crafted and widely disseminated crowdfunding campaign can yield large sums.

## Developing University Initiatives

A major goal of many CBQR projects is to build new university–community partnerships or to strengthen and expand existing relationships. Research teams might use findings from studies to help garner institutional support for the development of a community-based research initiative or to contribute toward the establishment of university centers or academic programs dedicated to community-based research. Data from studies could be included in a report to university administrators or integrated into a presentation conducted by research team members and various community partners for university stakeholders. Researchers might prepare proposals or white papers to obtain seed funding for a university research center or collaborate with others across the university conducting community-based research to coordinate efforts.

University researchers might use lessons learned from conducting a CBQR study to establish a community-based research course, or they might create a new program of study focused on community research. This could help formalize community-based research endeavors across disciplines, providing structured opportunities for this sort of research and stimulating community-based research university-wide. If creating a program of study is not possible, many institutions offer specialized certificates or concentrations for students; researchers could compile a list of courses that include community-based research components as a way of directing students toward courses where they could engage in this sort of research.

## Building Grassroots Movements and Campaigns

Many community-based qualitative researchers hope to not just create or develop local initiatives but also use their findings to participate in broader campaigns related to their topic. For example, researchers might apply findings from studies to plan a direct action campaign or organize a demonstration focused on an issue related to the topic of the study. Youth researchers might employ their research on youth civic engagement to plan a demonstration or rally calling for an expansion of afterschool programs. Researchers could collaborate with other organizations to plan and publicize the event; local leaders, activists, and research team members could speak to attendees, sharing their experiences and purveying relevant information, as well as making recommendations for policy and/or programming and directing attendees to specific ways that they can become involved. Press releases could provide details

Young mothers promoting positive images of teen parents at a community parade.

about the event and tout findings from the research study. Researchers could also organize community teach-ins and workshops designed to educate others about the topic and plan next steps for the campaign. Such activities can help expand a movement and get others involved, and they might lead to the development of new research projects.

Researchers might also consider launching a media campaign as part of their dissemination efforts. This could include designing print advertisements related to the topic that can be displayed in local businesses and organizations, as well as that can be shared more broadly via other print media and social media. For example, youth enrolled in a community afterschool program conducted research on underage drinking in the community. They shared key findings on large colorful posters and postcards that they designed as a way of educating others in the community about underage drinking. They also hosted a series of youth-led events to share and discuss some of their research findings. Increasingly, individuals bring awareness to various causes and participate in broader activist movements through the use of hashtags. These can be used as part of social media postings on platforms such as Facebook and Twitter to reference a particular current issue or event. Community-based qualitative researchers might use a Facebook page or Twitter account to disseminate research findings and post calls to action; they can also direct others to index relevant posts with a specific hashtag. In addition, these posts can enable researchers to connect with others working on similar issues and concerns. Researchers might create a hashtag for their project and/or employ a hashtag developed as part of a larger campaign, such as #blacklivesmatter to connect research on youth experiences with police and law enforcement in a particular community to protests and activism occurring nationwide or #noteenshame to reference others working to challenge stereotypes about teen mothers.

## Chapter Summary

This chapter discussed various ways that community-based qualitative researchers might disseminate findings from their studies. These could include more traditional venues for scholarly work, such as publications in academic journals and presentations at conferences, along with more innovative approaches, such as community events, websites, and media campaigns. The purpose of dissemination might be to share work and research findings with the local community or a wider audience. Research teams might also use findings to effect changes in public policy through the preparation of policy reports and involvement in advocacy efforts. Evidence from CBQR studies could also help inform the expansion or redesign of existing programs or the creation of new initiatives or services.

Often, CBQR teams employ findings from studies to build, or contribute to, activist movements and grassroots campaigns. Since these sorts of studies are focused on not just identifying or describing a problem or issue but also aim to change certain structural conditions and local access to resources related to a particular issue, they usually include action-oriented approaches as part of the dissemination plan. Projects usually include more than one method of disseminating findings from research studies as a way of reaching a variety of audiences. Regardless of the approaches selected to share information from the study, members of the research team should make sure that all members are involved in dissemination efforts and that community partners and residents are engaged in various dissemination activities and processes.

## Key Terms

Culminating event   140          Particularizability   139

## ● Activities for Reflection and Reflection

1) For a CBQR study, generate a list of the different ways that you might disseminate research findings. What is the audience for each approach? What materials and resources are required? How would various research teams be involved? What roles would they take on? How would community partners and members be involved in each dissemination effort? What are the advantages of each approach? What are the drawbacks or challenges?

2) For a CBQR study, identify some grants and funding sources that you might use to support and expand programs or initiatives. What are the requirements for funding? What information would you need to prepare and complete the proposal? How would research group members and community partners be involved in preparing the proposal?

3) In small groups, discuss ways that you might use research findings to develop university–community partnerships. What university resources are available and needed? What community resources are available and needed? What activities should be planned to help initiate and build partnership?

# HANDOUT 6
# Journals Publishing Community-Based Qualitative Research

*Anthropology & Education Quarterly*

http://onlinelibrary.wiley.com/journal/10.1111/(ISSN)1548-1492

**Journal description:** *Anthropology & Education Quarterly* is a peer-reviewed journal published by the American Anthropological Association on behalf of the Council on Anthropology and Education that draws on anthropological theories and methods to examine educational processes in and out of schools in U.S. and international contexts. Articles rely primarily on ethnographic research to address immediate problems of practice as well as broad theoretical questions. (Text adapted from the journal website.)

*Ethnography & Education*

http://www.tandfonline.com/toc/reae20/current#.VfmVOhFVhBc

**Journal description:** *Ethnography and Education* is an international, peer-reviewed journal publishing articles that illuminate educational practices through empirical methodologies, which prioritize the experiences and perspectives of those involved. The journal is open to a wide range of ethnographic research that emanates from the perspectives of sociology, linguistics, history, psychology and general educational studies as well as anthropology. The journal's priority is to support ethnographic research that involves long-term engagement with those studied to understand their cultures, uses multiple methods of generating data, and recognizes the centrality of the researcher in the research process. (Text adapted from the journal website.)

*International Quarterly of Community Health Education*

https://us.sagepub.com/en-us/nam/international-quarterly-of-community-health-education/journal202401

**Journal description:** *The International Quarterly of Community Health Education* is committed to publishing applied research, policy, and case studies dealing with community health education and its relationship to social change. Since 1981, this peer-reviewed journal has stressed systematic application of social science and health education theory and methodology to public health problems and consumer-directed approaches to control of preventive and curative health services. Environmental and structural changes are emphasized and victim-blaming approaches are closely examined. (Text adapted from the journal website.)

*Journal of Community Engagement and Scholarship*

http://jces.ua.edu/

**Journal description:** *The Journal of Community Engagement and Scholarship* (*JCES*) is a peer-reviewed international journal which integrates teaching, research, and community engagement in all disciplines, addressing critical problems identified through a community-participatory process. The journal aims to reach not only professional scholars but also undergraduate students, community partners, and the general public. (Text adapted from the journal website.)

### Michigan Journal of Community Service Learning

https://ginsberg.umich.edu/mjcsl/

**Journal description:** The *Michigan Journal of Community Service Learning* (*MJCSL*) is a national, peer-reviewed journal for college and university faculty and administrators with an editorial board of faculty from many academic disciplines and professional fields at the University of Michigan and other U.S. higher education institutions. *MJCSL* goals include growing the community and deepening the practice of service-learning educators, campus-community partnership practitioners, and community-engaged scholars; sustaining and developing the intellectual vigor of those in this community; encouraging scholarship related to community-engagement; and contributing to the academic/scholarly legitimacy of this work. (Text adapted from the journal website.)

### Partnerships: A Journal of Service-Learning and Civic Engagement

http://libjournal.uncg.edu/prt

**Journal description:** *Partnerships* recognizes that successful, engaged learning depends on effective partnerships among students, faculty, community agencies, administrators, disciplines, and more. The articles in this peer-reviewed journal focus on how theories and practices can inform and improve such partnerships, connections, and collaborations. Studies co-authored by faculty, students, and/or community partners; examining practices across disciplines or campuses; or exploring international networks are all encouraged. (Text adapted from the journal website.)

### Progress in Community Health
### Partnerships: Research, Education, and Action

https://www.press.jhu.edu/journals/progress_in_community_health_partnerships/

**Journal description:** *Progress in Community Health Partnerships* (*PCHP*) is a national, peer-reviewed journal whose mission is to identify and publicize model programs that use community partnerships to improve public health, promote progress in the methods of research and education involving community health partnerships, and stimulate action that will improve the health of people and communities. It is the first scholarly journal dedicated to Community-Based Participatory Research (CBPR). (Text adapted from the journal website.)

*(Continued)*

(Continued)

---

### Qualitative Inquiry

http://qix.sagepub.com/

**Journal description:** *Qualitative Inquiry* (*QIX*) provides an interdisciplinary forum for qualitative methodology and related issues in the human sciences. The journal publishes open peer-reviewed research articles that experiment with manuscript form and content and that focus on method-ological issues raised by qualitative research rather than the content or results of the research. *QI* also addresses advances in specific methodological strategies or techniques. (Text adapted from the journal website.)

### The International Journal of Research on Service-Learning and Community Engagement

http://journals.sfu.ca/iarslce/index.php/journal/index

**Journal description:** *The International Journal of Research on Service-Learning and Community Engagement* (*IJRSLCE*) is a peer-reviewed online journal dedicated to the publication of high-quality research focused on service learning, campus–community engagement, and the promotion of active and effective citizenship through education. (Text adapted from the journal website.)

### The Journal of Community Engagement and Higher Education

https://discovery.indstate.edu/jcehe/index.php/joce

**Journal description:** *The Journal of Community Engagement and Higher Education* is an online, ref-ereed journal concerned with exploring community engagement and community-based learning perspective, research, and practice. *The Journal of Community Engagement and Higher Education* publishes accounts of a range of research focusing on practical and theoretical insights and under-standing in higher education and across the disciplines and professions. There is a focus on case studies emphasizing community engagement and engaged learning practices, methodology, and pedagogy. (Text adapted from the journal website.)

### The Journal of Community Informatics

http://ci-journal.net/index.php/ciej

**Journal description:** *The Journal of Community Informatics* provides an opportunity for community informatics researchers and others to share their work with the larger community. Through peer review, knowledge and awareness concerning the community use of information and communi-cations technology (ICT) is being brought to a wider professional audience. In addition, the journal makes available key documents, "points of view," notes from the field, and other materials that will be of wider interest within the community of those working in community informatics. (Text adapted from the journal website.)

# Case Studies in Community-Based Qualitative Research

## Introduction

This chapter includes case study examples of a few ongoing CBQR studies as a way of providing insight into the design and implementation of specific projects, as well as to share some of the successes and challenges entailed in conducting these sorts of projects. Examples include a small-scale project undertaken by a single faculty member in collaboration with an alternative high school, focused on intergenerational mentoring for young mothers in the Humboldt Park community of Chicago; a broad University initiative that provides research funding and supports projects for women and girls in Charlotte, North Carolina; and an innovative research program that explores and facilitates ethnic minority immigrant youth in their roles as technological intermediaries. Within each case study, certain aspects of the project that illustrate key elements of CBQR—collaborative, critical, transformative—are highlighted to provide more specific examples of how researchers integrate these elements into a project.

PROYECTO ATABEY INTERGENERATIONAL
MENTORSHIP PROGRAM FOR YOUNG MOTHERS,
DR. PEDRO ALBIZU CAMPOS HIGH SCHOOL/LOLITA LEBRÓN
FAMILY LEARNING CENTER, CHICAGO, IL

**Description of community setting and partners:** Dr. Pedro Albizu Campos High School was created in 1972 in a church basement as an alternative educational space for students whose educational, social, and cultural needs were not being met by the local public school. The school's mission is to "provide a quality educational experience needed to empower students to engage in critical thinking and social transformation, from the classroom to the Puerto Rican community, based on the philosophical foundation of self-determination, a methodology of self-actualization and an ethics of self-reliance" (from the school website: www.pedroalbizucamposhs.org). The school has been nationally and locally recognized for its excellence and its ability to work with, and promote success among, students who have not been successful in mainstream settings. The school serves students (the student body is about 180 students) who have been "pushed out" of the public school system, as well as those who are seeking a community-based, culturally focused alternative. The high school is part of Chicago's Alternative Schools Network and the Youth Connection Charter School and offers courses that take a project-based learning approach to meeting the Illinois State Learning Standards.

This community-based qualitative research (CBQR) project was carried out at The Lolita Lebrón Family Learning Center (FLC), an educational program serving the needs of Puerto Rican/Latina and African American mothers in Humboldt Park, Chicago, a community located about four miles northwest of the downtown loop that has long been associated with the city's Puerto Rican community. The FLC was founded in 1993 through an Even Start Family Literacy grant. Initially, the program provided intergenerational literacy and support services to female-headed families with children younger than the age of seven. Around 2000, the program became an embedded program of PACHS and began to serve mothers aged 16-21 only. Services offered include high-school classes, women's studies classes, health and nutrition workshops, life skills workshops, childcare, parenting courses, parent and child activities, and support services to help participants address obstacles that hinder consistent participation. On-site childcare for infants, toddlers, and preschoolers is also available. Thus, alongside classes that will help parents earn their high-school diploma, they are also receiving information and support to assist them in their roles as parents. In addition, their interactions and relationships with other parents help them develop important networks of support. The school's website describes the mission of the program: "The FLC confronts the problems of limited education in the community by providing an opportunity for students to engage in a quality educational experience based in critical thought and social transformation from the classroom to their homes. The program strives to make learning relevant, utilizing the rich and varied experiences of the participants as the basis for instruction" (www.pedroalbizucamposhs.org).

*(Continued)*

(Continued)

The larger community within which PACHS is located is Humboldt Park, an area situated about 3 miles northwest of downtown Chicago. In the 1880s and 1890s, the area was home to Germans and Scandinavians, and later Polish and Italians residents also settled the area. Puerto Ricans began arriving in the area in the 1950s and 1960s, and many more moved to Humboldt Park in the 1970s and 1980s, often displaced from gentrifying Lincoln Park to the east. The main business district in the community is referred to as *Paseo Boricua* (or Puerto Rican way), and it is clearly demarcated on each end by large (each one 56 feet tall and weighing 45 tons), steel Puerto Rican flag gateways erected in 1995 as part of an economic development project meant to improve conditions, strengthen the local Puerto Rican community, and stave off encroaching gentrification. Paseo Boricua is home to many Puerto Rican–owned businesses, such as cafes, restaurants, and barber shops. Every June, the community holds nothing back in preparation for the Puerto Rican People's Parade and *Fiestas Puertorriqueñas,* which features a carnival and musical acts from the island. Other community events include a Three Kings Celebration in January that annually distributes toys and gifts to area children and *Fiesta Boricua,* or *"Bandera a Bandera"* (Flag to Flag), an arts and culture street festival held Labor Day weekend. Major community institutions include the Puerto Rican Cultural Center, which co-sponsors many of the aforementioned activities and oversees a bilingual childcare center, an HIV/STI program, and a housing and support program for homeless lesbian, gay, bisexual, transgender, and queer (LGBTQ) youth; the National Museum of Puerto Rican Arts and Culture; Association House, which offers a variety of educational and mental health services; Casa Central; and 72 Block, an organization that provides individualized and group health interventions and services aimed at addressing obesity and diabetes.

Although the community has achieved many successes over the years, many residents still struggle with issues such as low educational attainment rates, unemployment, domestic violence, gang violence, poor housing conditions, and various health ailments. For example, although graduation rates have increased at the local public high school, scores on standardized tests remain low, in the bottom 15% nationally (Chicago Public Schools, 2014). Furthermore, gentrification has been pushing up housing costs and displacing many longtime residents. Limited support services are available to young parents, such as homebound services and childcare, to help them remain in school. Although the high-school diploma attainment rates for all teen mothers is lower than their nonparenting peers, among adolescent mothers, Latinas are the least likely of any racial/ethnic group to obtain their diploma or GED by age 22 (Perper, Peterson, & Manlove, 2003).

**Description of project:** This CBQR project was borne out of a long-standing relationship between the lead researcher, Dr. Laura Ruth Johnson, and the FLC. Laura had previously been the director of the program, from 1993 to 1998, and had conducted ethnographic research for her dissertation research at the program, from 2002 to 2004. She had also served as a volunteer for many community activities and had worked with PACHS and the FLC to develop instruction and programming and provide support for students. In her role as a professor at a nearby university, she had worked to build some partnerships with the community, offering a summer research course, involving graduate students in community events, and organizing presentations by teachers and youth from the school at the university. In 2012, she began to work more closely and collaboratively with FLC staff to design several research projects that focused on promoting mentorship and advocacy among generations of young mothers.

Over the course of a school year, Laura and the director of the program, Danette Sokacich, co-taught a course for young parents at the school, which involved the development of research projects addressing issues associated with young parenthood. By using a Youth Participatory Action Research (YPAR) model, students created projects exploring fathers' rights, stereotypes about teen parents, and time management for young parents. In addition to these projects, program graduates were recruited to provide presentations to current students, which detailed some of the challenges they have faced as young mothers, as well as to discuss how they have overcome these challenges and achieved educational, professional, personal, and/or economic success. Alongside coordinating and overseeing YPAR projects, Laura and Danette worked together to develop an interview guide for conducting interviews with young mothers, which they hoped would provide insight into the needs of enrolled mothers, and offer feedback on strengths and areas of improvement for the program. They also convened several focus groups, which furnished an opportunity for students to share thoughts on presentations by program graduates and discuss mentorship needs. Danette and Laura video recorded and/or audio recorded class sessions, focus groups, and presentations, and they collaboratively analyzed transcripts and video data. Findings from this analysis were used to design presentations for dissemination at numerous local and national conferences.

**Collaborative**

A major refrain within the data sprang from young mothers' need for authentic mentoring experiences with mentors who have had similar experiences. Many young mothers expressed a desire for mentors who were themselves young mothers and could, thus, relate to their lives. One student praised a staff member who had previously worked at a school and identified what made her a particularly good mentor: "Cause she's been through a lot of what we have." Within focus groups, students were wary of presenters or staff from organizations who claimed to understand their situations but did not have children or who had fairly stable lives. They stressed the need to recruit mentors who had achieved success in certain areas of their lives but who had faced similar challenges and obstacles. These findings related to mentorship needs were employed to apply for grants to expand the mentoring program, which led to the creation of *Proyecto Atabey* (Project Atabey). Atabey refers to the Taíno (indigenous people of the Caribbean) goddess of fertility. With a grant for $25,000, the program was able to recruit program graduates and other women who had been young mothers to serve as mentors for current students; mentors were

*(Continued)*

(Continued)

provided with training and stipends to work individually with students 4 to 8 hours a month. During these mentorship sessions, mentors helped students complete college applications, hosted mentees at their workplaces or educational sites, helped mentees identify goals and develop plans for achieving those goals, and participated in family activities. Mentors continued to present their experiences to classes of parents, and they met regularly as a group to discuss work with mentees and provide feedback and support to one another. Funding was able to support several family activities and visits to local colleges customized for student parents (including tours of childcare facilities and discussion panels with student parent groups).

A primary goal of *Proyecto Atabey* is to help young parents acquire skills and knowledge to help them finish high school, become more independent, and achieve personal, academic, and professional goals. The project also aims to furnish mentors with important skills and promote relationships among generations of mothers. Members of the research team, which also includes a few graduate students and an undergraduate intern, are collecting data on the program, by conducting in-depth interviews with mentors and mentees and analyzing program resources and materials and social media posts. This ongoing research is being used to strengthen program elements, as well as to contribute to scholarship and practice regarding mentorship and other approaches for supporting young parents.

**Resources/support:** This project was the result of a continuous collaborative relationship between an academic researcher and the leadership and staff of a community-based organization and program. This ongoing relationship allowed for the sharing of knowledge and information across settings and the creation of mutual goals and purposes. Both Laura and Danette maintained a strong commitment to the project, which was integral to ensuring its success, particularly before the project received funding. The project was also facilitated by regular planning and communication between Laura and Danette in the form of weekly meetings and email communication.

The project was also made possible because both the university and the community-based organization had committed resources to the partnership and project, mostly in terms of allowing for personnel to devote time to the project and providing in-kind resources such as space and materials. Although the university did not provide monetary support for Proyecto Atabey, they had previously furnished funding to support Dr. Johnson's work with the school, such as helping to pay for a trip for staff and students to present at a national conference in San Francisco, California; Laura's department also supported her delivery of a research course within the community and allowed for a graduate student to complete research at Proyecto Atabey as part of the requirements for her thesis. This institutional support, from both the university and the community organizations, was a vital component to the project.

**Key successes/accomplishments:** A major success of this CBQR project was the awarding of initial funding to expand and formalize program activities. Proyecto Atabey helped build and promote strong intergenerational relationships between mentors and mentees and facilitated productive discussions and work related to mentee's educational, professional, and personal goals. The program's capacity to build a community of women among mentors and mentees is also considered a major success. Participants in the program purveyed support across generations to one another, sharing experiences and providing insight and feedback on how to confront various challenges. The project also helped the research team develop an intergenerational mentorship model that they hope to disseminate through publications and conference presentations. Program staff, mentors, and students were recognized for their accomplishments through an award conferred by Division G of the American Educational Research Association (AERA) and an invited session at AERA's annual meeting in Chicago in 2015.

**Transformative**

The project also helped foster advocacy skills among parents at the school. Through the YPAR projects, students were able to share their experiences of stigma and discrimination, as well as further develop their critical awareness of the role of media in the portrayal and stigmatization of specific populations. Students designed and produced public service announcements, which focused on challenging the stereotypes of young parents and disseminating positive images as part of a broader media campaign; they also shared their positive messages as part of a contingent at the annual Puerto Rican parade, proudly displaying signs with the hashtag #noteenshame. The project created a Facebook page, which allowed research team members, staff, mentors, and mentees to share activities and accomplishments—such as photos from when mentors hosted mentees at their workplace—as well as to connect with other organizations and individuals engaged in similar work.

**Critical**

**Challenges:** Although members of the research team have been able to maintain consistent communication throughout the project, the demands of overseeing and implementing a mentorship program without dedicated staff have been onerous at times, making planning and continued fundraising difficult. Both Danette and Laura were completing tasks associated with *Proyecto Atabey* in addition to numerous other work and research activities. Furthermore, communication with mentors and mentees posed a challenge throughout the project. The program scheduled regular meetings with mentors, with mentees, and with mentors/mentees together, to facilitate communication, but in some cases, additional follow-up was needed. Mentors and mentees had extremely busy schedules as they were juggling the multiple roles of mother, worker, and student; thus, scheduling meetings that accommodated everyone's schedules was a challenge.

Fundraising to support the project continues to be a challenge. Proyecto Atabey services were initially provided in 2012 with no funding and then expanded through a $25,000 grant from Grinnell College's Wall Alumni Service Award in 2014. Research team members have been working to identify grants and other funding sources, particularly to fund mentor stipends, but they have been frustrated in many their efforts and have only received small grants; funding for a part-time staff member to manage and implement the program would greatly facilitate the delivery of program activities and allow for the expansion.

*(Continued)*

(Continued)

Staff and students rehearse PSAs promoting positive images of teen parents.

## Contact Iinformation

Proyecto Atabey/Lolita Lebrón Family Learning Center

Dr. Pedro Albizu Campos High School

2739 W. Division Street

Chicago, IL 60622

https://www.facebook.com/Proyecto-Atabey-902963249730304/

# WOMEN + GIRLS RESEARCH ALLIANCE, UNIVERSITY OF NORTH CAROLINA—CHARLOTTE

**Description of community setting and partners:** In 2006, a group of four women met to discuss the status of women in the Charlotte-Mecklenburg area. After the initial meeting, a community-based Steering Committee formed task forces to collect and analyze data in the areas of women's health, poverty, political engagement, work, and violence. In 2008, the findings of the task forces were presented at the Women's Summit Conference. Known thereafter by the name associated with its premier event, the Charlotte-Mecklenburg Women's Summit operated as a community-based, volunteer-driven organization until July 2010 when it merged into the Metropolitan Studies and Extended Academic Programs unit at University of North Carolina at Charlotte. As an integrated unit of the university, the Women's Summit gained access to additional opportunities for research funding and support.

In 2013, the Summit began an extensive strategic planning process and changed its name to the Women + Girls Research Alliance (W+GRA). The new name stemmed from a desire to recenter the work of the organization on applied social science research, as well as from a belief that working in alliance with members of the community, business, local and state government, agencies, and service providers will lead to a better world for women and girls.

In fall 2014, the organization took the next step and hired its first full-time executive director, Dr. Heather Brown. Dr. Brown is also the first academic researcher to lead the organization; her research focuses on the connections between weight and learning in girls and women. Dr. Brown has more than a decade of experience in nonprofit and higher education administration and management, eight years of experience in faculty development (focusing on junior faculty research development), and more than six years of experience in student development (focusing on underserved and stigmatized populations). Under Dr. Brown's leadership, W+GRA is working to foster increased collaborations between community members and UNC Charlotte; increase both faculty and student research that addresses issues affecting women and girls; and develop efficient and effective ways to help the community use research as a catalyst for positive community change.

Charlotte is the largest city in North Carolina and the third fastest growing major city in the United States. It is the second-largest banking center in the United States and is home to eight Fortune 500 companies. In the most recent U.S. Census, 45% of residents were White, 35% were Black, 13% were Hispanic or Latino, and 5% were Asian. Nearly 11% of the population lives below the poverty line; Charlotte is ranked as the worst city for economic mobility in the nation. UNC Charlotte is North Carolina's urban research university.

**Description of project:** All the work W+GRA does is grounded in the community. First and foremost, it is overseen by an advisory council that is made up of individuals from the community representing service organizations, local government, and

**Collaborative**

*(Continued)*

(Continued)

corporations. This council plays a significant role in determining with whom the program partners on both research and educational programs as well as where to direct seed grants.

Second, the project uses a proactive approach to determine community needs. Working in partnership with a graduate-level research methods class, the program holds regular focus group sessions with community thought leaders, service providers, and government officials. Dr. Brown facilitates the focus groups, while the students take notes, analyze the data, and then present a report to W+GRA that not only provides guidance on the research needs of the community but also on how W+GRA can be a better partner to the community.

Third, all of the funded research projects must be driven by a community need or guided by the community itself. Although the project works with large data sets, much of the work involves finding ways to make the data more accessible to the community, so that the community—organizations, elected officials, etc.—can use data to make better decisions around policies and programs. In addition, most of the seed grants fund research that is done in partnership with the community, either addressing a need at a specific community partner organization or using participatory action research to allow communities to drive their own change.

Fourth, instead of hiring a graduate student to conduct research, program staff elected to hire a graduate student as a research communications coordinator. The graduate assistant works with faculty and staff to help translate their research into formats that work better for community partners, such as blog posts, infographics, etc. This also helps the program work more closely with the researchers at UNC Charlotte who are already doing incredible research in relevant areas of interest but who are directing their work to peer-review journals; this project helps them reach new audiences for their work.

Finally, the W+GRA pursues research funding for projects in partnership with community partners. Community organizations that serve girls and women often struggle to support their work, and additional funds—even for badly needed research—can be difficult to secure. By working together to secure funding, the alliance can relieve community partners of this burden while providing them with a highly valued and needed service.

**Transformative**

**Resources/support:** UNC Charlotte is the perfect home from which to operate a research organization that is dedicated to working in partnership with the community; the university has as one of its primary goals the creation of "meaningful collaborations among university, business, and community leaders to address issues and opportunities of the region." In other words, the work of the university is tied specifically to supporting the community. Metropolitan Studies and Extended Academic Programs, which houses W+GRA, has as its core mission "to provide community-based research services to local, regional, and state-level clients." Related projects in the unit include other community-focused groups such as the Institute for Social Capital, which is designed to facilitate data sharing, outcomes measurement, and evaluation among local agencies, while advancing university research, and the Charlotte Action Research Project, which works in marginalized communities in Charlotte.

**Key successes/accomplishments:** W+GRA is a relatively young organization and, until recently, has focused primarily on hosting the biennial Summit. However, since its strategic planning process led to a refocusing on research, W+GRA has (a) formed three formal community partnerships that are undertaking research projects; (b) provided seed grants to four community-based research projects; (c) launched the Research Affiliate Program to facilitate connections between UNC Charlotte researchers and community organizations; (d) implemented the Summer Learning Lab, which pairs graduate and undergraduate students to conduct research for W+GRA; and (e) begun work on a newly designed Women's Summit that will place the organization's research in conversation with community thought leaders.

**Critical**

**Challenges:** The greatest challenge of the W+GRA is that it possesses huge dreams and goals but has an incredibly small staff and budget. The organization is staffed by one full-time staff member and one part-time graduate assistant. The program's aspiration is to be the primary source for research on issues affecting women and girls in the Charlotte-Mecklenburg area. Having such a small staff and budget is forcing the program to be incredibly creative in marshalling resources, which is actually leading to the implementation of several innovative new processes and programs. However, the lack of staff and budget dramatically curtails the amount of work the program can accomplish.

**Reflections from participants:** The community-centered approach employed by the program has been beneficial for both researcher and community. For example, one faculty member the project works with studies employment outcomes with the goal of informing future policy and providing valuable information to local service providers who help unemployed individuals find work. She applied for and received a W+GRA grant at the end of her second year at UNC Charlotte. The grant gave her a "unique opportunity as an early career researcher to reach out into the community." As a result of the work she undertook with W+GRA support, she feels that she has a strong base for future research that not only benefits the community of Charlotte but also her academic career.

**Transformative**

**Contact Information**

Women + Girls Research Alliance

UNC Charlotte

9201 University City Blvd.

Charlotte, NC 28223-0001

http://womengirlsalliance.uncc.edu

*Source:* © Heather Brown.

# INFOME, UNIVERSITY OF WASHINGTON, SEATTLE

**Description of community setting and partners**: In the United States, almost one in nine people is foreign born. Nearly one in four children in the United States younger than the age of eight has immigrant parents. The percentage of foreign-born residents has increased from 11% in 1980 to 20% in 2010; people come from more than 70 countries, speaking more than 90 languages. Immigrant children and teens typically acquire English fluency, cultural understanding, and technology competency more quickly than their elders. Thus, the youth often take on mediary and helping roles within their families and ethno-linguistic communities. In Seattle's public school system, about 25% of students speak a language other than English at home. Seattle is known as a progressive, high-tech, youth-friendly, relatively safe, metropolitan area, rich in natural beauty and with residents from a broad socioeconomic spectrum. Surrounding a compact city core are residential neighborhoods that mix small apartment buildings and single-family dwellings, each with unique identities and small commercial hubs.

**Collaborative**

The primary project partners include the Seattle Public Library System, which serves a population of 600,000 people, 20% of whom are foreign born, and the King County Library System, which serves a population of 1.2 million. Administrators, teen librarians, and diversity staff are providing project guidance, assisting with recruiting youth, participating in interviews about their ethnic minority patrons, and hosting InfoMe Teen Design Days and InfoMe training workshops for community youth leaders. The project also works closely with local nonprofit community organizations that serve immigrant and refugee families. The Northwest Communities of Burma builds community by providing opportunities to come together, enjoy friendly activities, and become more familiar with those who come from different ethnicities, faiths, and backgrounds. Horn of Africa Services offers individual and family counseling and referral services. The staff at both organizations has helped recruit immigrant youth, host InfoMe's Teen Design Days, participate in interviews, and provide feedback on outreach strategies, program design, and other activities.

**Description of Project:** The InfoMe research program draws youth participants (primarily aged 14–18) from the Seattle/King County area in Washington, which includes a multitude of immigrant and refugee communities. InfoMe explores the ways in which ethnic minority immigrant and refugee youth help their friends, families, and communities with information and technology. The project aims to understand and support the information mediary activities of immigrant and refugee youth, while contributing to their development and encouraging public library and community agency innovation.

The project generates data with youth in 2- to 5-day workshops called "Teen Design Days" that operate during school vacations and weekends. With an interactive series of design tasks that move from identifying common needs to the creation of several iterations of prototypes to meet those needs, researchers learn how and why teens surface information needs; the ways in which they find, assess, remix, share, and curate information in everyday life situations; the ways in which digital technologies are involved in their efforts to help others; and the influences of cultural, gender, and social factors. Working collaboratively around design allows researchers to focus on youth assets and provide enjoyable and capacity-building experiences for youth.

Participants in each Teen Design Days workshop include about 20 to 25 teens (both young women and men, and clustering around one cultural group); 4 to 6 adult facilitators who are InfoMe project staff (female and male university professors and graduate students who represent several countries of origin); 1 to 2 adult facilitators whose backgrounds are similar to those of the teens and who already know at least some of the youth; and several adults from the university and community who engage with the youth around special topics of interest to them, such as local employment for teens, university admissions, computer programming, digital media production, professional and amateur design, and simply how to follow your dreams in the United States. The project has conducted Teen Design Days in a church, a public library, and community centers located in the neighborhoods where the participating teens live. Youth participants have come from East Africa, Nepal, Viet Nam, Myanmar, and Latin and South America.

**Critical**

The various elements of Teen Design Days are built around principles and practice related to youth development, community building, design thinking, and standard social science qualitative and quantitative research. The elements included in Teen Design Days, in roughly this order, are as follows: small- and whole-group discussion to illuminate concepts and share ideas and experiences related to basic study phenomena (e.g., What is information? Who makes up your social circle? What is your favorite app?); games and physical activity that tie in with project aims; creative expression around the teens' everyday information mediary behavior (i.e., stories, drawing, and skits drawn from personal experience); low-tech prototype design (using simple arts and crafts supplies like paper, pipe cleaners, and popsicle sticks) of gadgets and services that would make it easier for teens to get and share information; ample food breaks; and a culminating community showcase in which teens share what they've learned, created, and accomplished with their families, friends, and community leaders.

Throughout the Teen Design Days workshop, researchers use a variety of means for gathering data from youth, including collecting data on demographics and basic technology use through a 2-page written questionnaire and conducting a 3-minute oral and written evaluation at the end of each day (asking what went well, what didn't go well, and how can we make things better tomorrow). Researchers observe and create field notes throughout. Primary data are the drawings and written stories youth create to illustrate their information behavior and the skits and design prototypes they create, which are documented through photography and video-recording.

In addition to the Teen Design Days, researchers have developed a comprehensive questionnaire for about 500 students on information and technology mediary behavior. The survey will be implemented in high-school classrooms in the Seattle area.

*(Continued)*

(Continued)

**Resources/support:** InfoMe is funded by the U.S. Institute of Museum and Library Services. Additional financial support has come from Microsoft Research and Microsoft Global Community Affairs. InfoMe's Principal Investigator is Dr. Karen Fisher, a Professor at the University of Washington Information School in Seattle, which has also contributed financial, material, and human resources. The project has also relied on the professional expertise of the University of Washington's Institutional Review Board and Survey Design Research Group. The LEGO Foundation provided LEGO bricks and kits to use in prototype design. The Center for Digital Inclusion at the University of Illinois and Google have provided funding for follow-on research.

Community resources are also fundamental to our work: Library systems contributed their knowledge related to teen immigrant needs, as well as sites for Teen Design Days. Seattle Public Schools provide access to students and classrooms to conduct the InfoMe survey and helped recruit youth. Community nonprofit staff provided expertise regarding immigrant experiences, served as go-betweens in recruiting teens and communication with parents, identified and provided appropriate community sites for Teen Design Days, and participated as Teen Design Days facilitators.

**Collaborative**

**Key successes/accomplishments:** Researchers have analyzed the hundreds of stories, pictures, and design artifacts created by immigrant and refugee youth to produce a series of conference papers and presentations that shed light on their information mediary behavior, as well as on their capacity to serve as design partners. Youth seem largely unaware of their info mediary behavior, but they articulate it easily in multiple ways once it "clicks." Examples teens provide include explaining telephone bills to a parent; searching the Internet to find medical information for family members; helping people find their way around town; sharing religious and cultural information; giving tips to friends about sports and how to avoid fights; helping friends with homework; and translating for relatives. Tool prototypes designed by the youth include a wristwatch cell phone; a multimedia information kiosk at bus stops; a free van for the elderly equipped with "comfy seats" and information monitors that would take the seniors from their homes to various information and educational hubs (including museums and classes) in the city and home again; teen "safety glasses" equipped with digital information access, maps, and an alarm system; and a "helper robot" equipped with tools for cleaning, gardening, and shopping, as well as digital how-to information in pictorial form, music, stories, and robot pets.

**Transformative**

Researchers have found the teen design methodology helpful in developing an organic and holistic understanding of the needs, goals, capabilities, and strengths of immigrant and refugee youth. Many youth struggle under the obligations of helping not only friends and families; they are also called on to offer extensive support to their school systems as cultural and language mediaries.

In addition to gathering data from teens, researchers have created, based on their experiences, training workshops and short courses for others who wish to learn about and implement youth design projects. These have been attended by professionals who serve youth in Seattle, as well as by attendees at international conferences devoted to literacy, information science, and design. Also, most importantly, community partners have expressed interest in building on the relationships created in the InfoMe project.

With Teen Design Days, the project strives to create positive research experiences for youth, to build their capacity, and to scaffold positive impacts for them, their families, and their community. This is done by establishing a research process in accordance with the seven principles of youth development: physical activity; competence/achievement; self-definition; creative expression; positive social interaction; structure/clear limits; and meaningful participation. Small mindful ways for developing positive experiences include playing music the teens select during the workshop and over-catering so the youth can bring extras home. Youth are shown respect by giving them the authority to set behavior guidelines and make activity choices in the workshops, paying them meaningful stipends, and explicitly drawing attention to, and showing appreciation for, the important knowledge they hold and the critical help they give others. The overwhelming majority of teens participate actively in and, according to evaluation surveys, say they enjoy and have learned something valuable from Teen Design Days. Participating youth mentors have noted that the teens gain social skills and confidence and form new friendships that are especially important for newly arrived immigrants and refugees. In sharing experiences about finding and conveying information, teens gain pointers from each other that may help them in the future. The project also supports teens' participation in national conferences to build their communication skills, give them a sense of accomplishment and self-confidence, and provide them with a chance to travel and experience professional work activities that would otherwise likely be beyond their means and imagination.

The project works toward institutional innovation by conducting Train-the-Trainer Workshops with public library and community organization staff on how to use the Teen Design Day method with their youth clientele so that staff beyond the InfoMe project team learn how to collaborate with teens in designing products and services for ethnic minority youth.

**Challenges:** Recruiting immigrant youth for Teen Design Days has sometimes been hard even though a participant stipend of $100 to $200 is offered. The most successful activity occurred when the project was able to piggyback on a job fair at one high school with a large number of African youth. Another successful strategy was to first identify a youth advocate who worked for a nonprofit serving immigrant youth—it was easy for that person to explain the project to families and teens he already knew and facilitate their participation. Another issue faced was the attitude of some of the adult facilitators for Teen Design Days. It was difficult for educators, researchers, and graduate students whose backgrounds relied on more traditional, top-down, and deficit models of teen behavior and learning to be comfortable with the asset-based, participatory model of youth engagement and to let the youth take the lead in Teen Design Day activities. To help adult

*(Continued)*

**Transformative**

(Continued)

facilitators, the amount of preparation time was increased, they were given a few key readings on community-based participatory research, and more time was allotted for discussion around the theory and practice for youth engagement. Finally, the funder was asked for an extension because of the drastic underestimation of the amount of time it would take—over 1 year—to work through human subjects' review procedures to conduct the written survey on teen information behavior in public school classrooms.

**Contact information**

InfoMe

The Information School

Box 352840

Mary Gates Hall, Suite 370

Seattle, WA 98195-2840

http://infome.uw.edu/contact-us/

*Source:* © Ann Peterson-Kemp.

# • Glossary •

**Allies:** Individuals from outside of a community who offer support for community work and life by frequenting local businesses, attending and volunteering at community events, or providing monetary support for particular initiatives.

**Analytical memos:** Written "think pieces" that focus on analysis as part of both ongoing analysis and during the more formalized coding process. These memos can help researchers explore working hypotheses and themes, reflect on and refine codes, and establish new directions for analysis.

**A priori:** The act of devising or deciding upon a framework or hypothesis before entering a research setting.

**Assertion:** Substantive statement or claim, substantiated by data, that elaborates and explicates patterns and makes important thematic and analytical points related to the central phenomenon or topic of study.

**Axial code:** Coding process, usually used during second-cycle coding, that identifies a coding category's properties and dimensions and helps determine if, when, and why something happens.

**Central phenomenon:** Key issue or topic at the focus of a qualitative study.

**Checking privilege:** Process that requires that researchers working with communities be conscious of their privileges, imparted by characteristics such as race, class, educational background, sexual orientation, and gender. Such privileges need to be constantly revisited throughout the project.

**Code:** Label, term, or short phrase that assigns an attribute to a section of data, such as a single word or phrase, a sentence, a paragraph, or an entire page of an interview transcript, a field note, or a textual document; codes can also be used to label and categorize visual images.

**Codebook:** Guide that includes lists and descriptions of codes, as well as examples of when each code should be applied.

**Coding:** Process of applying codes to data, which usually involves a close, line-by-line reading of data. Closed coding involves determining codes before reviewing data, while open coding entails allowing codes to be generated from data.

**Collective coding:** Collaborative coding process that involves research team members individually coding the same transcript and then coming together to share and discuss codes. This initial coding process can help the team develop a common list of codes to be used as a working and dynamic list to code subsequent data sources.

**Community ambassadors:** Individuals from outside of a community who disseminate information about the community in a variety of other external contexts, such as workplaces, college courses, and civic organizations, as well as spread the word about community efforts and successes.

**Content analysis:** Type of analysis, usually used with documents, which involves the counting of certain terms and keywords. It can be useful in identifying the use and resonance of particular terms.

**Culminating event:** Event organized at the end of a research project, which would include a brief presentation by members of the research team, and opportunities for dialogue and discussion among various stakeholders and constituencies.

**Cultural competence:** Characteristics, skills, and knowledge that help individuals work respectfully with others from various and diverse cultural backgrounds.

**Deductive:** "Top-down" process of analysis, which involves applying and testing theories and hypotheses *a priori* within research.

**Descriptive field notes:** Notes taken as part of participant observation that provide in-depth descriptions and depictions of particular settings and events, as well as the participants, objects, activities, behaviors, and interactions that make up these contexts.

**Documents:** Written material, including student journals, program brochures and policy statements, and meeting notes, that can provide insight into participant perspectives, reveal institutional values and priorities, and substantiate beliefs and practices observed elsewhere.

**Domain coding:** Coding process that helps researchers discover and describe the knowledge and practices that individuals in a community setting use to organize behavior and interpret their experiences. Domains are large units of cultural knowledge, composed of symbols.

**Elicitation devices:** Strategies used within individual interviews and focus groups that make use of vignettes, examples, or visual images to evoke responses from participants related to particular issues and experiences.

**Emic:** Perspectives of insiders who possess local knowledge and understandings of a setting and relevant issues.

**Etic:** Outsider perspectives or understandings.

**Experiential course-based model:** College courses that include research and fieldwork experiences that involve students in working with community organizations and partners as part of an additive course component.

**Formalized field notes:** Field notes prepared after an observation has occurred based on jotted notes written in the field. These notes create a fuller and more detailed rendering of activities and events than is possible with jotted notes.

**Freesorts (also called free pilesorts):** Elicitation device employed within interviews or focus groups involving the use of index cards on which are written various items or cultural domains that participants can group or sort into categories.

**Gatekeepers:** Individuals, such as school principals, executive directors, and community leaders, who control access to a program or site, and its material and human resources.

**Heterogeneous groups:** Groups that vary on a specific characteristic, such as age, gender, professional role, or membership in an organization. Used in focus groups to facilitate debate across groups and characteristics.

**Homogeneous groups:** Groups that share a common characteristic, such as age, gender, professional role, or membership in an organization. Used as a way of organizing focus groups that helps researchers tap into group norms and practices.

**Immersive course-based model:** These courses are held within community settings, thus, offering an immersive experience within a community and providing multiple opportunities for students to be engaged with community residents.

**Inductive:** A "bottom up" process of analysis that allows for the emergence of themes and analytical and theoretical categories from participants' beliefs and experiences and community understandings and practices.

**Informed consent:** The process whereby researchers obtain approval from individuals to participate in the study. Basic elements of informed consent include a statement of research purposes and goals, what participants will be expected to do, any potential risks and/or benefits to participants, and a disclosure that participation is voluntary and participants might withdraw at any time.

**Insiders:** Those that have a preexisting relationship with the community or institution in which they are conducting research or that share significant commonalities with research participants.

**Institutional review boards:** Groups at colleges, universities, and other institutions where research is conducted tasked with reviewing research protocols to ensure that they follow ethical research procedures, particularly as related to the treatment of human subjects.

**In vivo coding:** Coding process that uses the participants' words and phrases as codes to describe conceptual categories.

**Item level** (of analysis): Process of breaking down data into specific, and smaller, units through coding or labeling.

**Jotted field notes:** Notes taken in the field as part of participant observation, traditionally in a notebook but more increasingly using laptops and other technology such as tablets and phones.

**Mapping exercises:** Elicitation device used during interviews or focus groups, which asks participants to identify locations, resources, or sites on a map.

**Markers:** References made by a participant, during interviews or focus groups, to events that the interviewee deems as significant to his or her life but that might not be directly related to the study topic.

**Memos:** Brief writings that can serve reflective and/or analytical purposes and often help researchers address methodological and ethical issues within the study.

**Methodological memos:** Brief writings employed to help researchers work through obstacles encountered in data collection, or to critique aspects of the data collection process.

**Observer's comments:** Reflective comments made by a researcher within field notes that are bracketed and separated from descriptive notes.

**Open-ended questions:** Broad questions on interview and focus group guides that cannot be answered with a yes/no response and that elicit extended descriptions of particular experiences and perspectives, rather than one-word responses.

**Orienting experiences:** Initial experiences and activities planned within a community, such as tours of a community, that help members of a research team become familiar with community issues and concerns and provide important background information on the community and particular organizations.

**Otherizing:** Focusing solely on differences between oneself and a community/community members.

**Outsiders:** Individuals who are not familiar with a setting prior to research and have little in common with participants.

**Participant observation:** Data collection approach that involves either formal or informal observations of settings, activities, and/or events, such as classrooms/classes, meetings, performances, tutoring sessions, workshops, protests and demonstrations, daily rituals, and workplaces, with the goal of gaining insight into the practices, life routines, and culture of a particular group.

**Particularizability:** Notion that particular aspects or features of a phenomenon or issue, as identified through fine-grained observation and data collection within a specific setting or context, can be useful to others working on similar issues, in similar settings, and with similar populations.

**Pattern code:** Second-cycle coding methods that seek to develop a "meta-code" that can be used to identify relationships between codes and elaborate patterns within data.

**Pattern level** (of analysis): Process of identifying patterns and thematic categories within data through the examination of coded items and data.

**Positionality:** Notion that a researcher's background, perspectives, and experiences inform one's viewpoints, theoretical lenses, and relationships with community residents.

**Praxis:** One of the central activities, along with *theoria* and *poesis*, of human life (Aristotle, 2004) that refers to practical knowledge, with the end goal being action. Within education, the concept was elaborated on by Paulo Freire (1970), who viewed praxis as a liberatory act involving a combination of reflection and action upon the world "in order to transform it" (p. 36).

**Rapport:** Refers to building close relationships of mutual understanding with others and to developing understanding of others' beliefs and values, finding areas of commonality whenever possible.

**Reflexivity:** Process of examining one's perspectives, background, assumptions, and biases related to a topic/phenomenon, setting, and participants.

**Research purpose statement:** Broad statement that provides an overall direction for the study, which includes the identification of the central phenomenon or issue under study, as well as some general information about setting and participants.

**Research questions:** Questions that narrow the focus of a research study and help researchers develop data collection tools and instruments.

**Reflective field notes:** Notes completed during research, as part of fieldwork, that contain reflective commentary and that are often focused on the role or stances of the researcher in relation to the setting and participants or include discussions of methodological challenges or ethical dilemmas faced during fieldwork.

**Reflective memos:** Memos that provide the opportunity for researchers to reflect on aspects of the research process.

**Structural level** (of analysis): Process of identifying broader relationships among certain patterns with the goal of constructing and developing a theory that depicts or explains a particular phenomenon.

**Semistructured interviews:** Interviews that make use of a flexible interview guide composed of open-ended questions but that also allow for the interviewer to ask related follow-up questions not on the guide.

**Social media** (as a data source): Websites, Twitter feeds, and hashtags that can often provide a window into current perspectives and debates on relevant community issues and controversies.

**Stakeholders:** Those who have a vested interest in a particular community issue or concern, such as personnel and participants in key organizations and programs, and are critical to understanding the issue and how it impacts various groups.

**Structured interviews:** Type of interview used within quantitative studies and survey research that relies on a prescribed and standardized interview guide with closed questions and a fixed set of responses. Questions are all asked in the same order and manner, and there is no opportunity for interviewees to veer from the guide.

**Theming the data:** Second-cycle coding strategy useful for differentiating between codes and themes that involves the researcher in adding "is" or "means" to a major code/concept and completing the phrase with a statement that indicates the significance, meaning, or characteristics of the code/concept, as substantiated by data.

**Triangulation:** Use of different types of evidence, such as interview transcripts, field notes, documents, visual data, and artifacts—across incidences, settings, and participants—to support assertions.

**Unstructured interviews:** Interviews that do not make use of an interview guide and may only have areas or topics for discussion, such as "family life," "education," "community," or "work," as prompts. Questions are meant to emerge from experiences of interviewees and are developed and posed within the context of the interview.

**Verbatim transcripts:** Word-for-word printed renderings of interviews or focus groups for analysis.

**Visual data:** Images and visual documents, such as photographs of community settings and activities and posters and advertisements for services and events, that can document community activities and highlight significant community issues.

**Websites:** Community portals and program websites that can offer information on initiatives, services, and events.

**White skin privilege:** Conditions and factors that purvey advantages to individuals, based on racial background, in their daily lives, such as being able to be sure that people of their race are represented positively in the media and that curricular materials reflect their race.

# • References •

Abu-Lughod, L. (1993). *Writing women's worlds: Bedouin stories*. Berkeley: University of California Press.

Aristotle. (2004). *The Nicomachean ethics*. London, England: Penguin.

Beck, S. (2007). Healthy Wednesdays in our hood: An exploration of an anthropological service-learning with premeds. In H. Rosing & N. G. Hoffman (Eds.), *Pedagogies of praxis: Course-based action research in the social sciences* (pp. 39–58). Boston, MA: Anker.

Behar, R. (1996). *The vulnerable observer: Anthropology that breaks your heart*. Boston, MA: Beacon Press.

Bernal, D. D. (2002). Critical race theory, Latino critical theory, and critical raced-gendered epistemologies: Recognizing students of colors as holders and creators of knowledge. *Qualitative Inquiry, 8*(10), 105–126.

Bishop, A. P., & Bruce, B. C. (2009). Community inquiry and collaborative practice: The iLabs of Paseo Boricua. *The Journal of Community Informatics, 5*(1). Retrieved from http://ci-journal.net/index.php/ciej/article/view/312/435

Bishop, A., & Molina, A. L. (2004, October). ¡Felicitaciones, Paseo Boricua! A community of librarians, activists, and students. *Voice of Youth Activists*, pp. 268–269.

Blackburn, M. V. (2014). Humanizing research with LGBTQ youth through dialogic communication, consciousness raising, and action. In D. Paris & M. T. Winn (Eds.), *Humanizing research: Decolonizing qualitative inquiry with youth and communities* (pp. 43–57). Thousand Oaks, CA: Sage.

Bogdan, R. C., & Biklen, S. K. (2006). *Qualitative research for education: An introduction to theory and methods* (5th ed.). Boston, MA: Allyn & Bacon.

Bonilla, Y., & Rosa, J. (2015). #Ferguson: Digital protest, hashtag ethnography, and the racial politics of social media in the United States. *American Ethnologist, 42*(1), 4–17.

Boser, S. (2007). Power, ethics, and the IRB: Dissonance over human participant review of participatory research. *Qualitative Inquiry, 13*(8), 1060–1074.

Bowen, S. (2005). Engaged learning: Are we all on the same page? *Peer Review, 7*(2), 4–7.

Brown, J. S., Collins, A., & Duguid, P. (1989). Situated cognition and the nature of learning. *Educational Researcher, 18*(1), 32–42.

Bruce, B. C., Bishop, A. P., & Budhathoki, N. R. (Eds.). (2014). *Youth community inquiry: New media for community and personal growth*. New York, NY: Peter Lang.

Cabrera, N. (2011, October 6). *State of Arizona versus ethnic studies program*. Paper presented at Northern Illinois University, DeKalb.

Cahill, C., Rios-Moore, I., & Threatts, T. (2008). Different eyes/open eyes: Community-based participatory action research. In J. Cammarota & M. Fine (Eds.), *Revolutionizing education: Youth participatory action research in motion* (pp. 89–124). New York, NY: Routledge.

Cammarota, J., & Fine, M. (2008). *Revolutionizing education: Youth participatory action research in motion*. New York, NY: Routledge.

Campbell, E., & Lassiter, L. E. (2010). From collaborative ethnography to collaborative pedagogy: Reflections on the other side of Middletown project and community-university research partnerships. *Anthropology & Education Quarterly, 41*(4), 370–385.

Charmaz, K. (2014). *Constructing grounded theory* (2nd ed.). Thousand Oaks, CA: Sage.

Chicago Public Schools. (2014). Search schools. Retrieved November 16, 2015, from http://cps.edu/Schools/Find_a_school/Pages/findaschool.aspx

Cochran-Smith, M., & Lytle, S. (1992). *Inside/outside: Teacher research and knowledge*. New York, NY: Teachers College Press.

"Community as intellectual space: Preliminary program [Symposium]." (2005, June 17–19). Chicago, IL. Retrieved November 3, 2015, from http://conferences.illinois.edu/cis/cis.program.draft7.pdf

Curran, W., Hague, E., & Gill, H. (2007). Practicing active learning: Introducing urban geography and engaging community in Pilsen, Chicago. In H. Rosing & N. G. Hoffman (Eds.), *Pedagogies of praxis: Course-based action research in the social sciences* (pp. 79–94). Boston, MA: Anker.

Dallimore, E., Rochefort, D. A., & Simonelli, K. (2010). Community-based learning and research.

*New Directions for Teaching and Learning, 124,* 15–22.

DeWalt, K. M., & DeWalt, B. R. (2011). *Participant observation: A guide for field workers.* Lanham, MD: Altamira Press.

Dewey, J. (1958). *Experience and nature.* New York, NY: Free Press.

Dewey, J. (2009). *Democracy and education: An introduction to the philosophy of education.* New York, NY: WLC Books. (Original work published 1916)

Dyrness, A. (2011). *Mothers United: An immigrant struggle for socially just education.* Minneapolis: University of Minnesota Press.

Duster, T., & Waters, A. (2006). The vertical integration of food for thought. *Liberal Education, 92*(2), 42–47.

Emerson, R. M., Fretz, R. I., & Shaw, L. L. (2011). *Writing ethnographic fieldnotes* (2nd ed.). Chicago, IL: University of Chicago Press.

Erickson, F. (1986). Qualitative methods in research on teaching. In M. C. Wittrock (Ed.), *Handbook of research on teaching* (pp. 119–161). Washington, DC: American Educational Research Association.

Fals Borda, O. (2006). Participatory (action) research in social theory: Origins and challenges. In P. Reason & H. Bradbury (Eds.), *Handbook of action research* (pp. 27–37). London, England: Sage.

Fernández, L. (2002). Telling stories about school: Using critical race and Latino critical theories to document Latina/Latino education and resistance. *Qualitative Inquiry, 8*(10), 45–65.

Fine, M. (1994). Working the hyphens: Reinventing self and other in qualitative research. In N. R. Denzin & Y. S. Lincoln (Eds.), *Handbook of qualitative research* (pp. 70–82). Thousand Oaks, CA: Sage.

Fine, M., Ayala, J., & Zaal, M. (2012). Public science and participatory policy development: Reclaiming policy as a democratic project. *Journal of Education Policy, 27*(5), 685–692.

Freire, P. (1970). *Pedagogy of the oppressed.* New York, NY: Continuum.

Gallagher, M. (2006). *Examining the impact of food deserts on public health in Chicago.* Retrieved October 28, 2015, from http://marigallagher .com/projects/

Gay, G. (2002). Preparing for culturally responsive teaching. *The Journal of Teacher Education, 53*(2), 106–116.

Geertz, C. (1973). *The interpretation of cultures.* New York, NY: Basic Books.

Geron, S. M. (2002). Cultural competency: How is it measured? Does it make a difference? *Generations, 26*(3), 39–45.

Ginwright, S., & Cammarota, J. (2007). Youth activism in the urban community: Learning critical civic praxis within community organizations. *International Journal of Qualitative Studies in Education, 20*(6), 693–710.

Glass, R. D. (2001). On Paulo Freire's philosophy of praxis and the foundations of liberation education. *Educational Researcher, 30*(2), 15–25.

Glaser, B. G., & Strauss, A. L. (1967). *The discovery of grounded theory: Strategies for qualitative research.* New Brunswick, NJ: Aldine.

González, N., Moll, L., & Amanti, C. (Eds.). (2005). *Funds of knowledge: Theorizing practices in households, communities, and classrooms.* Mahwah, NJ: Lawrence Erblaum.

González, N., Moll, L., Tenery, M. F., Rivera, A., Rendón, P., González, R., & Amanti, C. (2005). Funds of knowledge for teaching in Latino households. In N. González, L. Moll, & C. Amanti (Eds.), *Funds of knowledge: Theorizing practices in households, communities, and classrooms* (pp. 3, 89–111). Mahwah, NJ: Lawrence Erblaum.

Gramsci, A. (1971). *Selections from the prison notebooks.* New York, NY: International Publishers.

Hacker, K. (2013). *Community-based participatory research.* Thousand Oaks, CA: Sage.

Hacker, K., Chu, J., Leung, C., Marra, R., Pirie, A., Brahimi, M., English, M., Beckmann, J., Acevedo-Garcia, D., & Marlin, R. P. (2011). The impact of immigration and customs enforcement on immigrant health: Perceptions of immigrants in Everett, Massachusetts, USA. *Social Science & Medicine, 73*(4), 586–594.

Hall, B. L. (1992). From margins to center? The development and purpose of participatory research. *The American Sociologist, 23*(4), 15–28.

Haymes, S. (1995). *Race, culture, and the city: A pedagogy for Black urban struggle.* Albany: State University of New York Press.

Heath, S. B., & Street, B. V. (2008). *On ethnography: Approaches to language and literacy research.* New York, NY: Teachers College Press.

Hellawell, D. (2006). Inside-out: Analysis of the insider-outsider concept: A heuristic device to develop reflexivity in students doing qualitative research. *Teaching in Higher Education, 11*(4), 483–494.

Heller, J. (1972, July 26). Syphilis victims in U.S. study went untreated for 40 years; syphilis victims got no therapy. *New York Times*.

Hess, G. A., Jr. (1999). Using ethnography to influence public policy. In J. J. Schensul, M. D. LeCompte, G. A. Hess, Jr., B. K. Nastasi, M. J. Berg, L. Williamson, J. Brecher, & R. Glasser (Eds.), *Using ethnographic data: Interventions, public programming, and public policy* (pp. 57–113). Lanham, MD: Altamira Press.

Hessler, R. M., Donald-Watson, D. J., & Galliher, J. F. (2011). A case for limiting the reach of institutional review boards. *American Sociologist, 42*, 145–152.

Hofman, N. G. (2007). Checks and balances: The aftermath of course-based action research. In H. Rosing & N. G. Hofman (Eds.), *Pedagogies of praxis: Course-based action research in the social sciences* (pp. 153–173). Boston, MA: Anker.

hooks, bell. (1990). *YEARNING: Race, gender, and cultural politics*. Boston, MA: South End Press.

Horton, M., & Freire, P. (1990). *We make the road by walking: Conversations on education and social change*. Philadelphia, PA: Temple University Press.

Hsiung, P-C. (2008). Teaching reflexivity in qualitative interviewing. *Teaching Sociology, 36*(3), 211–226.

Hwang, S., & Roth, W. M. (2005). Ethics in research on learning: Dialectics of praxis and praxeology. *Forum: Qualitative Social Research, 6* (1), Art. 19.

Irizarry, J. G. (2011). *The Latinization of U.S. schools: Successful teaching and learning in shifting cultural contexts*. Boulder, CO: Paradigm Press.

Israel, B. A., Schulz, A. J., Parker, E. A., & Becker, A. B. (2001). Community-based participatory research: Policy recommendations for promoting a partnership approach in health research. *Education for Health, 14*(2), 182–197.

Johnson, L. R., & Rosario-Ramos, E. M. (2012). The role of educational institutions in the development of critical literacy and transformative action. *Theory Into Practice, 51*(1), 49–56.

Johnson, L. R. & Rosario-Ramos, E. M. (2015, April). "I just don't want to be quiet anymore": Youth developing skills, finding voice, and transforming their communities through community engagement and Participatory Project-based Learning. Paper presented at Annual Meeting of American Educational Research Association, Chicago, IL.

Johnson, L. R., Stribling, C., Almburg, A., & Vitale, G. (2015). "Turning the sugar": Adult learning and cultural repertoires of practice in a Puerto Rican community. *Adult Education Quarterly, 65*(1), 3–18.

Kelly, D. M. (2000). *Pregnant with meaning: Teen mothers and the politics of inclusive schooling*. New York, NY: Peter Lang.

Kolb, D. (1984). *Experiential learning: Experience as the source of learning and development*. Englewood, NJ: Prentice Hall.

Ladson-Billings, G., & Tate, W. F. (1995). Toward a critical race theory of education. *Teachers College Record, 97*(1), 47–68.

Lareau, A. (1997). *Home advantage: Social class and parental intervention in elementary education*. Philadelphia, PA: Falmer Press. (Original work published 1989)

Lassiter, L. E. (2005). Collaborative ethnography and public anthropology. *Current Anthropology, 46*(1), 83–106.

Lassiter, L. E. (2005). *The Chicago Guide to collaborative ethnography*. Chicago, IL: University of Chicago Press.

Lather, P. (1986). Research as praxis. *Harvard Educational Review, 56*(3), 257–277.

Lawless, E. (1991). Women's life stories and reciprocal ethnography as feminist and emergent. *Journal of Folklore Research, 28*(1), 35–60.

Lawless, E. (1993). *Holy women, wholly women: Sharing ministries of wholeness through life stories and reciprocal ethnography*. Philadelphia: University of Pennsylvania Press.

Lawless, E. (2000). "Reciprocal" ethnography: No one said it was easy. *Journal of Folklore Research, 37*(2/3), 197–205.

Lawrence-Lightfoot, S. (1997). Illumination: Searching for patterns. In S. Lawrence-Lightfoot & J. H. Davis (Eds.), *The art and science of portraiture* (pp. 185–214). San Francisco, CA: Jossey-Bass.

Lave, J., & Wenger, E. (1991). *Situated learning: Legitimate peripheral participation*. New York, NY: Cambridge University Press.

LeCompte, M. D., & Schensul, J. J. (1999). *Analyzing & interpreting ethnographic data* (Ethnographers Toolkit) Lanham, MD: Altamira Press.

LeCompte, M. D., Schensul, J. J., Weeks, M. R., & Singer, M. (1999). *Researcher roles & research relationships* (Ethnographers Toolkit) Lanham, MD: Altamira Press.

Lewin, K. (1951). *Field theory in social sciences.* New York, NY: Harper & Row.

Liamputtong, P. (2011). *Focus group methodology: Principles and practice.* Thousand Oaks, CA: Sage.

Malinowski, B. (1961). *Argonauts of the western Pacific.* New York, NY: Dutton. (Original work published 1922)

Mayo, P. (2007). Antonio Gramsci and his relevance for the education of adults. *Educational Philosophy and Theory, 40*(3), 418–435.

McIntosh, P. (1998). White privilege: Unpacking the invisible knapsack. In P. S. Rothenberg (Ed.), *Race, class, and gender in the United States: An integrated study* (pp. 177–182). New York, NY: Macmillan.

McIntyre, A. (2008). *Participatory action research* (Qualitative Research Methods Series, 52). Thousand Oaks, CA: Sage.

Meleis, A. I. (1996). Culturally competent scholarship: Substance and rigor. *Advances in Nursing Science, 19*(2), 1–16.

Mendias, E. P., & Guevara, E. P. (2001). Assessing culturally competent scholarship. *Journal of Professional Nursing, 17*(5), 256–266.

Morrell, E. (2004). *Becoming critical researchers: Literacy and empowerment for urban youth.* New York, NY: Peter Lang.

Morrell, E. (2006). *Critical participatory action research and the literacy achievement of ethnic minority youth* (55th Annual Yearbook of the National Reading Conference), *55,* 60–78.

Moynihan, D. P. (1965). *The negro family: The case for national action.* Washington, DC: Office of Policy Planning and Research, U.S. Department of Labor.

Nygreen, K. (2013). *These kids: Identity, agency, and social justice at a last chance high school.* Chicago, IL: University of Chicago Press.

O'Meara, K., Sandmann, L. R., Saltmarsh, J., & Giles, D. E., Jr. (2010). Studying the professional lives and work of faculty involved in community engagement. *Innovations in Higher Education, 36*(2), 83–96.

Paris, D., & Winn, M. T. (2014). *Humanizing research: Decolonizing qualitative inquiry with youth and communities.* Thousand Oaks, CA: Sage.

Perper, K., Peterson, K., & Manlove, J. (2003). *Diploma attainment among teen mothers.* Washington, DC: Childtrends.

Piaget, J. (1952). *The origin of intelligence in children.* New York, NY: International University Press.

Pritchard, I. A. (2002). Travellers and trolls: Practitioner research and institutional review boards. *Educational Researcher, 31*(3), 3–13.

Radhakrishnan, R. (1987). Ethnic identity and post-structuralist difference. *Cultural Critique, 6,* 199–220.

Rinaldo, R. (2002). Space of resistance: The Puerto Rican Cultural Center and Humboldt Park. *Cultural Critique, 50,* 135–174.

Rosaldo, R. (1993). *Culture and truth: The remaking of social analysis* (2nd ed.). Boston, MA: Beacon Press.

Rosing, H. (2007). Food for more than thought: Course-based action research on corner stores in Chicago. In H. Rosing & N. G. Hofman (Eds.), *Pedagogies of praxis: Course-based action research in the social sciences* (pp. 1–20). Boston, MA: Anker.

Rosing, H., & Hofman, N. G. (2007). Introduction. In H. Rosing & N. G. Hofman (Eds.), *Pedagogies of praxis: Course-based action research in the social sciences* (pp. vii–xx). Boston, MA: Anker.

Saldaña, J. (2014). *The coding manual for qualitative researchers* (2nd ed.). Thousand Oaks, CA: Sage.

Saltmarsh, J., Giles, D. E., Jr., Ward, E., & Buglione, S. M. (2009). Rewarding community-engaged scholarship. *New Directions for Higher Education, 147,* 25–35.

Santiago, R. (Ed.). (1995). *Boricuas: Influential Puerto Rican writings—an anthology.* New York, NY: One World Books.

Schensul, J. J. (1999). Focused group interviews In J. J. Schensul, M. D. LeCompte, B. K. Nastasi, & S. P. Borgatti (Eds.), *Enhanced ethnographic methods* (pp. 51–114). Lanham, MD: Altamira Press.

Schensul, J. J., & Schensul, S. L. (1992). Collaborative research: Methods of inquiry for social change. In M. D. LeCompte, W. L. Millroy, & J. Preissle (Eds.), *The handbook of qualitative research in education* (pp. 161–200). San Diego, CA: Academic Press.

Seidman, I. (2013). *Interviewing as qualitative research: A guide for the researchers in education and the social sciences.* New York, NY: Teachers College Press.

Solórzano, D. G., & Bernal, D. D. (2001). Examining transformational resistance through a Critical Race and LatCrit framework: Chicana and

Chicano students in an urban context. *Urban Education, 36*(3), 38–342.

Spradley, J. P. (1979). *The ethnographic interview.* Belmont, CA: Wadsworth.

Spradley, J. P. (1980). *Participant observation.* Belmont, CA: Wadsworth.

Stoeker, R. (2013). *Research methods for community-change: A project-based approach.* Thousand Oaks, CA: Sage.

Stovall, D. (2006). From hunger strike to high school: Youth development, social justice, and school formation. In S. Ginwright, P. Noguera, & J. Cammarota (Eds.), *Beyond resistance: Youth activism and community change* (pp. 97–109). New York, NY: Routledge.

Strand, K., Marullo, S., Cutworth, N., Stoeker, R., & Donohue, P. (2003). *Community-based research and higher education: Principles and practices.* San Francisco, CA: Jossey-Bass.

Tea, M. (Ed.). (2003). *Without a net: The female experience of growing up working class.* Emeryville, CA: Seal Press.

Tierney, W. G., & Corwin, Z. B. (2007). The tensions between academic freedom and institutional review boards. *Qualitative Inquiry, 13*(3), 388–398.

Torre, M., & Fine, M. (2006). Researching and resisting: Democratic policy research by and for youth. In S. Ginwright, P. Noguera, & J. Cammarota (Eds.), *Beyond resistance: Youth activism and community change* (pp. 269–285). New York, NY: Routledge.

Vélez-Ibáñez, C. (1983). *Border visions: Mexican cultures of the Southwest United States.* Tucson: University of Arizona Press.

Vogel, A. L., Seifer, S. D., & Gelmon, S. B. (2010, Fall). What influences the long term sustainability of service-learning? Lessons from early adopters. *Michigan Journal of Community Service Learning,* pp. 59–76.

Vygotsky, L. S. (1978). *Mind in society: The development of higher psychological processes.* Cambridge, MA: Harvard University Press.

Wallerstein, N. B., & Duran, B. (2010). Community-based participatory research contributions to intervention research: The intersection of science and practice to improve health equity. *American Journal of Public Health,* 100 (Suppl. 1), S40–S46.

Weis, L., & Fine, M. (2000). *Speed bumps: A student-friendly guide to qualitative research.* New York, NY: Teachers College Press.

Weiss, R. S. (1994). *Learning from strangers: The art and method of qualitative interview studies.* New York, NY: The Free Press.

Wenger, E. (1998). *Communities of practice: Learning, meaning, and identity.* New York, NY: Cambridge University Press.

Whitman, S., Williams, C., & Shah, A. M. (2004). *Sinai Health System's Improving Community Health Survey: Report I.* Chicago, IL: Sinai Health System.

Yosso, T. (2005). Whose culture has capital? A critical race theory discussion of community cultural wealth. *Race, Ethnicity and Education, 8*(1), 69–91.

Yosso, T., & García, D. G. (2007). "This is no slum!": A critical race theory analysis of community cultural wealth in Culture Clash's Chavez Ravine. *Aztlán: A Journal of Chicano Studies, 32*(1), 145–179.

Yosso, T., Smith, W. A., Ceja, M., & Solórzano, D. G. (2009). Critical race theory, racial microagressions, and campus racial climate for Latino/a undergraduates. *Harvard Educational Review, 79*(4), 659–690.

# • Index •